GARDEN VOICES

Garden Voices

Two Centuries of Canadian Garden Writing

Edited by

Edwinna von Baeyer and Pleasance Crawford

VINTAGE CANADA
A Division of Random House of Canada

Canadian Cataloguing in Publication Data

Main entry under title:

Garden voices: two centuries of Canadian garden writing

ISBN 0-679-30860-1

1. Gardening - Canada - History.   2. Gardens - Canada - History.
I. von Baeyer, Edwinna 1947–   . II. Crawford, Pleasance.

SB451.36.C3G37 1997   635'.0971   C96-932176-7

Cover photograph: "Alexandra Park Rose Garden circa 1918" courtesy of
the City of Toronto Archives, SC 244-1251, William James Collection.
Jacket and interior design: Sharon Foster Design

Printed and bound in the United States of America
10 9 8 7 6 5 4 3 2 1

To past, present and future gardeners,
and especially to Elizabeth Horn Kaufman

—ᏜᏟ—

Contents

—⚉—

Acknowledgements   [XI]

Introduction   [XIII]

Calling All Gardeners
    William Bond, 1801   [3]
    W. T. G., 1864   [5]
    D. W. Beadle, 1872   [8]
    Edith Stevenson Rutherford, 1919   [10]
    Henrietta Tuzo Wilson, 1933   [13]
    Jean McKinley, 1952   [17]
    H. F. Herbert, 1960   [20]
    Roscoe A. Fillmore, 1961   [25]
    Ray Guy, 1987   [28]

Breaking New Ground
    Elizabeth Simcoe, 1792   [35]
    Louisa A. Aylmer, 1831   [37]
    F. E. J. Lloyd, 1886   [39]
    Julia Bullock-Webster, 1894–1895   [41]
    J. T. Bealby, 1909   [43]
    Mary Irene Parlby, 1920   [45]
    H. B. Dunington-Grubb, 1935   [49]
    Holland Cox, 1940   [53]
    Frances Steinhoff Sanders, 1948   [56]

Laura Berton, 1954 [58]
Frank Leith Skinner, 1967 [60]
Carol Stairs, 1979 [63]
Percy Janes, 1980 [68]
Midge Ellis Keeble, 1988 [70]
Claudette Burton, 1990 [76]

Laying Out The Grounds

William Claus, 1806 [83]
Mary Gapper O'Brien, 1828–1830 [87]
Asa Parker, 1851 [90]
Linus Woolverton, 1889 [92]
W. T. Macoun, 1912 [96]
Frederick G. Todd, 1929 [100]
N. de Bertrand Lugrin, 1931 [103]
W. L. Mackenzie King, 1931 [109]
Lorrie A. Dunington-Grubb, 1938 [113]
Kerry Banks, 1980 [118]
Nancy Pollock-Ellwand, 1987 [122]
Des Kennedy, 1994 [127]

Gardening in Public

Editor of *The [Colonial] Pearl*, 1839 [133]
Editor of *The Canada Farmer*, 1868 [135]
H. A. Engelhardt, 1872 [139]
Agnes Scott, 1900 [141]
D. P. Penhallow, 1907 [143]
C. Ernest Woolverton, 1909 [146]
Cecil M. Simpson, 1915 [148]
Henrietta Wood, 1917 [150]
Dorothy Perkins, 1918 [152]
F. Leslie Sara, 1934 [156]

Collier Stevenson, 1943 [160]
H. Fred Dale, 1972 [163]
Carole Giangrande, 1987 [167]

NAMING FRIENDS AND FOES

Elizabeth Russell, 1806 [175]
A Canadian Farmer, 1859 [177]
A. M. Smith, 1873 [179]
Annie L. Jack, 1911 [183]
George Thompson, 1919 [185]
Ella M. Harcourt, 1930 [189]
F. Cleveland Morgan, 1936 [191]
Sister Mary Rosalinda, 1944 [193]
George H. Hamilton, 1953 [195]
W. R. Leslie, 1956 [197]
Bernard S. Jackson, 1977 [200]
Marjorie Pridie, 1980 [205]
Brian Fawcett, 1992 [210]
National Capital FreeNet, 1994 [213]
Marjorie Harris, 1994 [216]

PRAISING FAVOURITE PLANTS

Catharine Parr Traill, 1833 [221]
Juliana Horatia Ewing, 1869 [224]
A. Hood, 1879 [229]
Mrs. Symmes, 1879 [232]
Velma Peterson, 1939 [235]
Elsie Reford, 1944 [238]
Percy H. Wright, 1950 [243]
Isabella Preston, 1956 [246]
John H. Tobe, 1958 [249]
Lois Wilson, 1970 [253]

Helen Skinner, 1984   [256]

Jo Ann Gardner, 1989   [260]

Elspeth Bradbury, 1994   [265]

LOOKING BACK

Michael Gonder Scherck, 1905   [271]

L. M. Montgomery, 1910   [274]

Ada L. Potts, 1929   [280]

J. Russell Harper, 1955   [286]

William Douglas, 1959   [291]

Barry Broadfoot, 1977   [296]

Anne O'Neill, 1985   [298]

D. Wayne Moodie, 1987   [301]

Tim Ball, 1987   [306]

Catherine Hennessey and
    Edward MacDonald, 1990   [309]

Charles R. Saunders and
    many others, 1992   [314]

Asta Antoft, 1972   [316]

Sources and Permissions   [319]

Index   [327]

ACKNOWLEDGEMENTS

—⚹—

Many people helped us stroll down this particular garden path. Linda Marshall brought about our momentous meeting in 1981, from which a friendship formed that has continued despite both compilers' strongly voiced opinions during the making of this book. Richard Teleky gave valuable advice when we first proposed an anthology of Canadian garden writing. Sarah Davies, our editor at Random House, gave us the continuing reassurance of her enthusiasm for the project.

The supporters of the newly emerging electronic highways deserve our undying gratitude for providing access to the wonderful world of e-mail, where two authors, no matter how distant, can exchange ideas and written texts in the flash of an electron.

We each thank the friends and colleagues who have provided help and shared information for this and many other garden–history projects, especially: Susan Buggey, John Burtniak, Sue Donaldson, Robert Hunter, Ann Milovosoroff, Stephen Otto, Ina Vrugtman, and Florence Watts.

We are heartened by the goodwill of the copyright holders who freely granted us permission to use their materials in our anthology.

We are immensely grateful for the help and information we received—either in answer to our general queries or to our specific questions—from many people, including Carrie Adam, David Bain, Roland Barnsley, Francis Bolger, Margaret Cantwell, Janet Cobban, Gabrielle Earnshaw, Edith Firth, Jeanne Hopkins, Dorothy Jackson, Fred Janson, Clive Justice, Margaret McMillan, John Omohundro, Cuyler Page, Brian Pickell, James Pringle, Alexander Reford, Sandra Reford, Deborah Rink, Neil Rosenberg, Thelma Rosner, Rosemary

Sadlier, Gunter Schoch, John Sommer, Rod Staples, Betty Ward, and Susan Wilson.

We could not have done without the ever-helpful archivists at the National Archives of Canada, the Archives of Ontario, and the City of Toronto Archives; or the equally helpful librarians at the National Library of Canada, the Ottawa Public Library, the Agriculture Canada library, and the Metropolitan Toronto Reference Library.

We also salute the librarians who answered our long-distance questions promptly and in detail: Shelley Barkley, Jennifer Bobrovitz, Linda Brownlee, Debera Earle, Lindsay Moir, and Marjorie Kevlahan.

Most important of all, our families were wonderful supporters. On the von Baeyer side, Vera Clappe did a prodigious amount of typing. Jakob kept his mother laughing when deadlines crept ever closer. Eliza did mounds of photocopying and, when away at university, continued a long-distance interest in the project. Cornelius, as always, was a great advisor and more important, as the deadline approached, kept coming home when he never knew who would be behind the door—the lady or the tiger.

On the Crawford side, Elizabeth Kaufman was our queen of serendipity. Brenda Blake was our ingenious contract advisor, and Arleigh Crawford our intrepid intercity courier. Liz Crawford understood the enormity of the undertaking, and Ted Hunter spent hours retrieving 10,000 words from a damaged disk. Chuck Crawford was magnificent, not only as skilled resident computer scientist and electronic-election official, but also as patient holder-together of house and garden.

We take credit for our mistakes, and we welcome readers who call them gently to our attention.

INTRODUCTION

—⚏—

Countless voices have animated the Canadian garden—at times sorrowful, joyful, nostalgic, inventive, humorous, even cranky. Whenever we pick up a trowel or dream of next year's garden, these voices resonate faintly around us. They are a vital part of our horticultural heritage. This anthology of Canadian garden writing brings nearly ninety of these voices together for the first time.

Gardening in this country began thousands of years ago, when aboriginal people first broke the soil to plant vegetable seeds, or gathered wild rice to sow at the lake edge. While we pay homage to these original gardeners, we highlight in this book the voices in our recorded history. Through the pens, typewriters, and computers of these writers, we visit the humble flower patches of the pioneer period, the gardenesque landscapes of the post-Confederation years, the showplace country-estate gardens of the 1920s and 1930s, and the small, eclectic urban gardens of the late twentieth century.

We celebrate the legions of intrepid gardeners, from every decade since the 1790s and from every province and territory, who have created a link between past and present gardens, and who have continually extended the possibilities of Canadian horticulture. We celebrate those who, in print, reaffirmed our connections with the natural world, helped our gardens bloom and bear fruit, and beautified our rural and urban environments.

The voices are arranged in seven sections. In "Calling All Gardeners," we hear the ringing call to garden, which has been a common theme throughout our garden literature. Some voices beckon us into the garden with humour or an appeal to our sheer love of growing things, while others call on our sense of civic duty or self-preservation.

In "Breaking New Ground," we watch the pioneering efforts of settlers across the country as they cleared land and planted orchards and gardens. We witness the surprise of some at the harshness of the climate. We see others breaking into new professions and new types of gardening.

In "Laying Out the Grounds," we hear nineteenth-century gardeners talking about expanding gardens beyond their original boundaries, to accommodate flowers, trees, and shrubs arranged for pleasure, ornament, and display. We hear twentieth-century gardeners wrestling with the usual problems of where to place a choice plant or garden element, and we hear two very different stories of landscape restoration.

In "Gardening in Public," we listen to voices from beyond the garden gate. We witness pre-World War I horticultural reformers and city beautifiers joining civic-improvement societies and promoting public parks and plantings. We witness writers urging people to produce food on any available land during both world wars. As well, we watch the parade of vacant lot gardens.

In "Naming Friends and Foes," we listen to gardeners warbling happy tunes over the latest horticultural fads and fancies, or wailing a familiar litany over the ravages of two-legged, four-legged, and six-legged pests. We hear of their trials by sun, rain, frost, and snow, and learn of their pleasure in having other gardeners as neighbours.

In "Praising Favourite Plants," we share the ageless enjoyment in a new discovery or a cherished old favourite. Some voices sing the praises of one particular genus or species, while others are equally enthusiastic about whole groups of plants.

In "Looking Back," we hear the voices of historians investigating the evolution of the Canadian cultural landscape. We hear, too, the recollections of people with very personal memories of past gardens. Together, these writers suggest the depth and richness of our horticultural heritage.

This book is not a history of Canadian gardening—for that book has yet to be written. Everywhere, in fact, the thorough study of landscape and garden history is a twentieth-century discipline. Not surprisingly, the horticulturally minded English seem to have been particularly active in this fertile field, but others—including North Americans—are now equally involved.

Interest in landscape and garden history has expanded greatly during the past quarter century. In addition to landscape historians and history-minded gardeners, the list of enthusiasts has grown to include archaeologists, cultural geographers, historical botanists and horticulturists, landscape and restoration architects, literary scholars, local historians, museums staff, rare-book collectors, and many others. Keen researchers can now join speciality organizations and read their journals; can access the Catalog of Landscape Records in the United States, maintained at Wave Hill in Bronx, New York; and can consult the Pioneers of American Landscape Design data base of the U.S. National Parks Service. Anyone, when in London, England, can visit the first-ever Museum of Garden History, which held its inaugural exhibition in 1981.

In Canada, since the 1970s, the Royal Botanical Gardens in Hamilton, Ontario, has housed a growing collection of Canadian garden documents in its Centre for Canadian Historical Horticultural Studies, and the Canadian Centre for Architecture in Montreal has been actively collecting records of the built landscape. Other libraries and archives house specialized collections, such as papers of prominent landscape architects, nursery owners, and plant breeders.

The selections in this sampler come from both published and unpublished sources, and from both professional and dedicated amateur writers and gardeners. The range of material may surprise anyone who believes that Canada has no garden history and few interesting gardens. If you choose to journey further into the history, Edwinna von Baeyer's *A Selected Bibliography for Garden History in Canada*, Revised Edition (Ottawa: Parks Canada, 1994), will guide you. If you wish to visit interesting contemporary gardens, Nicole Eaton and Hilary Weston's *In a Canadian Garden* (1989), Marjorie Harris's *The Canadian Gardener* (1990), and *David Tarrant's Canadian Gardens* (1994) will give you an armchair tour.

Creating this anthology involved a lot of hard decisions. To limit possible choices, we decided to include only items originally written in English. The absence of French voices is especially unfortunate because a tremendous body of landscape description and garden writing in that language exists. We look forward to seeing an anthology of French-Canadian garden writing. As well, we decided not to include obvious fiction—although some may argue that we all fictionalize a little when writing about our own gardens.

When the two of us embarked on this great anthologizing adventure, we were each armed with knowledge gained from working in Canadian landscape and garden history since 1980, and with massive files of material collected along the way. But we also sent more than sixty queries to colleagues and to various newsletters, magazines, and journals, asking for additional suggestions. As we revisited favourite pieces and explored newfound sources, we recognized gaps in our preliminary selections: underrepresented decades, geographic regions, groups, and subject areas. Following a further search, we assembled a short list of 350 published and unpublished writings.

Let us say here that this book owes a lot of its life to e-mail. We argued, we suggested, we selected, through cyberspace. In fact, we held an electronic vote to reduce the 350 possibilities to the selections that appear here. In doing so, we tried to remain as representative as possible, and we apologize to readers whose favourite piece, passage, or writer we have left out because of space constraints. (We are convinced that enough good material exists for another anthology.)

One of the unexpected pleasures of compiling this anthology was preparing the notes that accompany the selections. For some writers we found the needed information at our fingertips, but for others we had to begin digging. With a deadline looming, we uncovered more information about some than others, but in every case we gained new respect for each of the individuals whose voices had called to us in the first place.

Because we wanted the original voices, we edited our selections as little as possible. We tried to transcribe them accurately—retaining spellings, however quirky, and inserting only the occasional comma. (It was particularly interesting to observe the changing conventions in the naming of plants and the comings and goings of British and American spellings.) Where space constraints made trimming necessary, we used our pruning shears carefully.

Feel free to sample the offerings in any order—the book does not have to be read from beginning to end to be enjoyed. Discover, as we have through the years, the charms of our Canadian garden-writing tradition. Enjoy eavesdropping on our fellow gardeners as they putter and experiment. Take heart, when comparing your own efforts with theirs, that even in the Canadian garden, there is nothing new under the sun. Finally, let this collection inspire you to carry on in the perennially hardy spirit of Canadian gardening and garden writing.

Edwinna von Baeyer, Ottawa
Pleasance Crawford, Toronto

DECEMBER 1994

CALLING ALL GARDENERS

—᠁—

WILLIAM BOND
1801

"To be given away" advertisement in *Upper Canada Gazette or American Oracle* (York)

—∿—

illiam Bond was a native of England, and a gentleman. In 1794, after petitioning that he wished "to become an inhabitant of this Province," he was granted 600 acres on Yonge Street, at what became known as Bond's Lake. In 1796, he was granted an additional one-acre lot in the Town of York (later Toronto).

The Upper Canada Gazette *was issued by authority of the Crown. Although existing mainly for official pronouncements, it also published "Not official" notices such as Bond's eye-catching offer to give away the town lot he had so recently acquired.*

Prospective buyers apparently found his actual price of 6,000 shillings (£300) rather high for a lot east of the centre of town. Again in 1803–04 he advertised the property—which by then contained "ten to twelve thousand fruit trees." Finally, in August 1804, he auctioned it off, along with its burgeoning nursery.

Bond retained an entrepreneurial interest in agriculture nonetheless. He travelled to England on behalf of the Agricultural and Commercial Society of Upper Canada; and upon his return, explored land around the north branch of the Thames River, in the southwestern part of the province, but sent word to the government in 1810 that the area seemed unfit for the cultivation of hemp.

—∿—

To be given away, That beautifully situated Lot No. 1, fronting on Ontario and Duchess Streets; the buildings thereon, a small two and half story House, with a Gallery in front, which commands a view of the Lake and Bay; in the Cellar a never failing spring of fine Water, and a stream of fine Water running through one corner of the Lot; there is a good kitchen in rear of the House, and a Stable sufficient for two Cows and two Horses, and the lot is in good Fence.

The conditions are, with the person or persons who accepts of the above present, that he, she, or they purchase, not less than two thousand Apple Trees at three shillings N.Y.C. each; after which will be added as a further present, about one hundred Apple, thirty Peach, and fourteen Cherry Trees, besides wild Plumbs, wild Cherries, English Goose-berries, white and red Currants, &c. &c.— There are forty of the above Apple Trees, as also the Peach and Cherry Trees, planted regular as an Orchard, several of which appeared in blossom last spring, and must be considered as very valuable, also as a kitchen Garden, will sufficiently recommend itself to those who may please to view it.—

The above are well calculated for a professional or independent Gentleman, being somewhat retired—about half way from the Lake to the late Attorney General's and opposite the town farm of the Honble. D. W. Smith.

Payment will be made easy—a good deed—and possession given any time from the first of Nov. to the first of May next. For further particulars enquire of the subscriber on the premises,

WILLIAM BOND.

York, Sept. 4, 1801.

W. T. G.
1864

"Gardening in Canada," in *The Canada Farmer*

—ༀ—

*I*n this rousing piece, W. T. G. revealed only that he had seen London and the Thames, that he was now settled in Canada, and that he could write an eloquent—if somewhat biased—call to gardeners. Have the basic ingredients for an effective letter to the editor really changed since 1864?

W. T. G. was addressing W. F. Clarke, the editor of the second journal to be called The Canada Farmer. The first had existed in 1847; and the second began publication in Toronto in January 1864, under the energetic proprietorship of George Brown of The Globe, and with the horticultural department conducted by D. W. Beadle.

W. T. G.'s letter is just one of the many corners into which present-day landscape historians look for period-garden details. For pre-Confederation Ontario, his comments provide partial answers to two of the most frequently asked questions about gardens anywhere, of any period: What filled the beds, and what covered the walks?

—ༀ—

To the Editor of The Canada Farmer.

Sir, —All must confess, that in our gardening, we in Canada are far behind the age. Seldom do we see a really handsome, or well regulated, lawn or garden, even in the oldest towns and cities. The age is truly utilitarian, and the great and engrossing strife for wealth seems to absorb the minds of the majority. This passion is a great mistake, and the neglect of all that is true and beautiful in nature will be regretted in after years. The mind as well as the body needs relaxation; and where can leisure hours be more delightfully or profitably spent than in the garden? Would that the aim of all was not to accumulate wealth, but to dispense to the profit of themselves and their fellow men the means placed at their disposal.

It is a singular fact, that those brought up and living in populous towns are persons who exhibit most taste for and love of gardening. They feel the refreshing influence produced by the sight of a few flowers, amid the monotony of brick and mortar. I have seen a most charming collection on the deck of a coal barge on the Thames; and in the poorest and most-densely populated parts of London, florists' flowers are grown to great perfection.

On the other hand, with the denizens of the country, where pure air abounds, and where nature luxuriates, the love of gardening and a taste for flowers does not seem to exist, or at all events is not developed.

How much more attractive might many homesteads be made by the addition of a few well-kept flower beds and a neatly-gravelled walk; or the rough ground nicely levelled and graded, and converted into a snug little lawn, with a few ornamental trees and shrubs here and there. Instead of this, we see places either utterly neglected, or perhaps cabbages or potatoes grown by way of adornment, where the fragrant Heliotrope or the flaunting Geranium should flourish; or perhaps a few ragged Hollyhocks and a matted and tangled rose-bush exhibit the taste and culture of the proprietor. One of the most infallible indications of the want of refinement is the neglect of the garden. The absence of it betokens a certain amount of idleness. Those most busy either in the field or in the counting-house, will be those whose gardens are most flourishing, where weeds do not grow, and where neatness and order reign supreme. Thus, it is the home of the wealthy gentleman or farmer which proves generally most attractive. Not because the owners can better afford it than their poorer neighbours, but the industry and natural talent, which lie at the root of their prosperity, beget in them the love of *improvement*, and the garden affords the widest scope for it. The poor man's establishment may be small, but it will be well filled, and the pleasure he derives from it will, perhaps, be keener than that felt by the proprietor of a large and handsome place. It is also a stepping stone to something better, for no *true* horticulturist allows himself to fall back. "Onward" will be his motto, and for this reason the day of small things must not be despised.

Let us hope that the end of the present year will show a marked improvement, and that the taste for gardening will be extended and developed throughout the country. Let horticultural exhibitions be encouraged, and an honest rivalry maintained. Dig up your old, neglected flower beds, and re-plant and re-arrange them. Plant more trees and shrubs, and take better care of those already out. Clean and trim up the neglected paths and walks. Keep your spades and rakes busy enough to wear the rust off them; and "last but not least," extend as much as possible the circulation of THE CANADA FARMER.

W. T. G.

D. W. BEADLE
1872

"Conclusion," in *Canadian Fruit, Flower, and Kitchen Gardener*

—⚏—

*D*elos White Beadle (1823–1905) was the best-known Canadian garden writer of the post-Confederation period. But as a young man he had studied law at King's College (Toronto) and Harvard Law School and had practised law for six years in New York City before returning in 1854 to his native St. Catharines, in the Niagara Peninsula of Ontario, and entering his father's well-established nursery business.

Although Beadle remained a nurseryman until his retirement in 1887, he also worked hard to promote fruit growing. In 1859 he, with A. M. Smith and sixteen others, founded the Fruit Growers' Association of Upper Canada (later Ontario). Two years later, he became its secretary—a position he held until 1886.

His simultaneous career as a garden journalist began when George Brown established The Canada Farmer in 1864. Beadle conducted its horticultural department for about ten years. Then, in 1878, he became editor of The Canadian Horticulturist, the Fruit Growers' new monthly "for the promotion of Horticulture in this Canada of ours."

Beadle's magnum opus was the Canadian Fruit, Flower, and Kitchen Gardener. Into this first thoroughly Canadian volume on all branches of horticulture, he poured nearly thirty years of experience.

—⚏—

There may be "no royal road to learning," but there is a royal road to success in the cultivation of fruits, vegetables and flowers in Canada. It is a road that none but those who have royal blood in their veins may travel. It is for those who, though they boast not their descent from regal sires, are nature's noblemen; men of earnest purpose, who, with head and heart devoted to the culture of the garden, have learned "to labor and to wait."

"Knowledge is power," as truly in the cultivation of the soil as in anything else. It was quaintly replied by a successful cultivator, when asked what fertilizer he used to obtain such splendid results: "Brains, sir, brains; I manure my grounds with brains!"

Use, then, your brains. Study your business. Bring all the activities of your mind to bear upon your gardening. Enlarge your powers of thought and observation by studying the opinions and doings of others; follow nothing blindly, but bring all to the test of your own common sense. Keep your eyes open to the operations of nature, and let the experience of each year teach you how to remedy the defects of the past, and place you on vantage ground for the operations of the future.

In the hope that the hints contained in these pages, drawn mainly from the writer's own experience and observation, may contribute something to the reader's progress, and stimulate to increased thoughtfulness and zeal in the cultivation of the garden, we bid you

> "Study culture, and with artful toil,
> Meliorate and tame the stubborn soil."

EDITH STEVENSON RUTHERFORD
1919

From "Peace, Springtime and a Garden," in
The Canadian Horticulturist

—⚹—

*E*dith Stevenson Rutherford (1872–1937)—who was born in Ontario, but moved with her husband to Nelson, British Columbia, in 1897—was a popular writer in the pages of The Canadian Horticulturist *in the early twentieth century. There, for more than eleven years, she wrote a gardening column, "Spirit of the Garden," and numerous articles. As well, she wrote a column for the* Nelson Daily News *called "Gossip from a Mountain Garden."*

Rutherford was the creator of a famous garden, "Peep o'Day," in the mountains near Nelson. It was described as "a garden of great beauty, along unstudied natural lines . . . containing flowering trees and shrubs, creepers, rock plants, mosses, water plants and many varieties of all the standard species known to the gardener." She also loved native wild plants, and had a large collection of them. She evidently ran the garden in later years as a commercial venture, and sold seeds from her garden through her husband's Mann-Rutherford Drug Company.

In this article she called her contemporaries away from the worries and tragedies of World War I, and back into a sunnier garden, to celebrate the rebirth of peace in the Western world.

—⚹—

Peace, springtime and a garden! What a heavenly combination! Surely everyone who has a garden this spring of 1919 must be happy to a superlative degree, and here's hoping we can make our gardens worthy of this first wonderful year of peace. Seems to me we should all plant some long-lived tree or flower to commemorate the passing of the shadow that even in our gardens these last terrible years almost shut out the sun. How fine it would be if every gardener should plant a maple tree this spring to be called the Peace Tree; and be to our children's children a token of the honor and glory won by our gallant boys in the great war. Maple leaves must always be a sacred symbol to Canadians, and I for one mean to plant a maple tree even if I have to sacrifice a fruit tree to make room for it.

Yesterday I returned to my dear garden after an absence of three months and you can imagine my delight at finding little colonies of snowdrops pushing their fragile stems right through the snow to nod a welcome to me. Surely a happy omen. It is the seventeenth of March, and being Irish, of course, I have a pot of shamrock on my desk, but I also have a tiny basket of snowdrops tucked in with the green moss, and I'm thinking they should be sacred to St. Patrick, too, because they usually appear on his natal day, and the three inner petals each carry a miniature heart of rich emerald green.

Isn't it difficult to decide what to do first of all in the garden in spring? So many things are calling out for attention . . . .

A delightful way to spend one of these glorious spring mornings is tidying up the bulbs. Out here our winters are so mild that protection is rarely necessary, but where the beds have been mulched one needs to keep a sharp eye on them lest the tulips or daffodils begin to push up through the mulching materials, after which it is almost impossible to remove it without injury . . . .

Every hour gained on spring work these days is just so much to the good, and it is a fine plan to get everything possible done before the ground is fit to work so you may have the decks cleared for action and turn all your forces to getting the soil prepared and seeds planted . . . .

Last year one of my perennial borders was very poor so I know the plants need dividing and that is one of the many things that should be done first. Isn't it terrible how everything in the garden seems to demand that "first" attention. However, I am looking forward to a very happy time shifting and altering this border and—let me whisper it—at the same time enlarging my garden a little. This border, which has been untouched for more years than I care to count, has a background of three cherry trees, and by getting a little nearer the trees I can add quite a space to my garden proper and have a better chance to get the ground in good shape. The succession of bloom is arranged something like this: There is an edging of June Pinks and beneath their foliage I have Emperor Narcissi planted so they lead off in early spring followed by groups of Darwin tulips in May, then Oriental Poppies, June Marguerites and the white pinks keep one end of the border ablaze, and Iris, Columbines and Persian daisies hold sway at the other end. These are quickly followed by tall Larkspurs and Foxgloves, and later by hardy phlox in white and pink, and the season closes with a big display of Michaelmas daisies and Golden Glow. My heart almost fails me when I think of digging out all these things, but it must be done . . . .

There is a song sparrow in the plum tree outside my window with his little head thrown back and his throat swelling as he proclaims in delicious trills that "spring is coming." Indeed it is already here and all things conspire to fill one's heart with dreams of happy days among the flowers. It is the busiest time of all the year to every true gardener, and I sometimes wonder if we do not forget to take time just to realize and enjoy the miracle of spring. Why not take a half hour off once in awhile just to sit on your doorstep in the sun and look at the soft spring skies, the little new green leaves and the birds flitting through the orchard, and let the peace and healing of the springtime fill your soul?

Henrietta Tuzo Wilson
1933

"Women and Gardening," in *Report of the Horticultural Societies of Ontario for 1933*

—⚬—

*H*enrietta Loetitia Wilson, née Tuzo, (1873–1955) was an exceptional woman. She was an active member of many different local and national public-service organizations. For a long time, she was the only woman on the Ottawa Horticultural Society's board of directors. She was also president of both the National Council of Women and the Red Cross Society, while still finding the time to write articles in such magazines as the Canadian Geographic Journal *and to maintain a much-praised garden. In 1935 Wilson was awarded the King's Jubilee Medal, and two years later the Coronation Medal.*

Although born in Victoria, British Columbia, where her father was a pioneer doctor, Wilson grew up in England, but returned to Canada as young woman. She began mountain climbing in Europe in 1896, pursued it enthusiastically at Banff, and became a founding member of the Alpine Club of Canada in 1906. That same year, in perhaps her most notable climb, she and her guide made the first ascent of Peak Seven of the Ten Peaks in the Rockies near Moraine Lake. In her honour, the peak was named Mount Tuzo.

—⚬—

Many Horticultural Societies have women directors. All should have them as they are trained in many Societies to conduct business meetings, and realize the needs of the small gardener, have good taste in the choice of plants, are economical purchasers, and moreover, have time to devote to Society affairs.

There are many mistresses of large gardens, who employ men to do the work, but supply most of the ideas and knowledge of plants and who are quick to take up new fashions. Not long ago, gentlewomen led quiet lives, and were keen to have gardens of popular mode. At Royal Horticultural Society Shows in England, the keenest visitors are ladies, often of high degree, marking new varieties and comparing notes. Here we have had distinguished gardeners at Government House, for Lady Grey, Lady Willingdon, and Lady Byng, all gardened. Lady Byng laid out the fine rockery at Government House, collected Canadian wild flowers and originated several Iris. She was the friend of all botanical and flower folk.

Many useful books on the subject have been written by women and several of the authors are specialists whose works are unique.

With women, there is a desire to have a garden, and a love of country life. A woman may induce her family to go back to the land, and, in this time of hardship, it is well to consider the merits of a home outside the town with a vegetable plot and additional wholesome food. Even a small garden, wisely stocked, will provide a great deal of good food through the summer and some surplus for winter. It is the Mother of the family who will provide the enthusiasm for such a change, which requires much courage and thought.

There is tremendous scope for women's work in the various types of garden, and women who are busy in other ways can give their leisure to the study of some section of the work.

Perhaps the charm for rock work has caught her fancy, and indeed it is a great field for feminine enthusiasts. A great deal of interesting and valuable work lies ready to be done, in the study of native flora, here it would be great to specialize in, perhaps the ferns of the country, or in any of the species.

Besides the many lovely bulbous plants from other countries that can be grown on rockeries, there are a number of native bulbous plants which could be brought into the market. The lovely fritillaries of the Okanagan Valley, or the erithronium grandiflora. Many of our native lilies are already much used in gardens, but by no means all of them, while there are plants all over Canada, which are local in their habitat, and could be made popular throughout the country.

There are many possibilities in such a collection; the fair owner should take up painting and photography and from her sketches or photographs, start a series of post cards and Christmas cards, while many could be used for designs for wall papers and fabrics. Accurate portraits of her treasures are valuable, botanically, and might well be turned to financial advantage.

Then there is the collection of seeds of rare garden or of wild plants and one Canadian woman, at any rate, collected these, sent out a small catalogue and had a thriving business in the sale of British Columbia wild flower seeds.

Most women will want flowers to pick, and it is very desirable to allow some space for cutting flowers, besides those that can be taken from the perennial border. If space allows, gardens for some variety alone are very attractive, tulips in the spring, iris and paeonies during the summer, and asters in the fall.

Now, it so happens, that many women have to keep house, and therefore a well-stocked kitchen garden appeals to them, and there is a lot of beauty in such a garden. This garden provides the table, and tender young vegetables for bottling purposes. Start an asparagus bed as soon as possible, for it takes a couple of years before any cutting can be done. Grow hubbard squash to hide ugly spots and don't forget the charms of scarlet runner beans with their lovely flowers and delicious pods.

Trees, shrubs and fruit all come into garden work and the generality of small gardens could stand more variety in foundation shrubs. As to fruit, it is worth noting that such crops as raspberries, in small gardens, are often more paying than vegetables, and the children like preserves, and jam, in the winter as well as fruit in the summer.

There is a great field for women in more scientific garden work, hybridizing and plant pathology. Hybridizing needs the neat fingers and patience of women, it calls for taste and perception of colours. We have in Canada a woman, Miss Isabella Preston, who has done remarkable work with lilies. Her example is an inspiration to gardeners, for so many exquisite lilies have resulted from crossing varieties. Cross fertilization is clearly explained in Miss Preston's book.

The pollenization of lilies is not so difficult, the problem is in know-ing which species to cross, and this must be learned by experience. Moreover, it is tedious work, for in thousands of seedlings, perhaps only one is an improvement on its parents.

Gardening is a remunerative pursuit and presents opportunities for women's work and is a great educator, teaching patience, gen-erosity and self-discipline.

Jean McKinley
1952

"What Makes the Canadian Garden Canadian?" in
Canadian Homes and Gardens

—·—

From the mid-1940s to the mid-1950s, Jean McKinley worked her way up the editorial ladder at Canadian Homes and Gardens. *She began as an assistant editor in 1943, and by the time she wrote this article, she was editor-in-chief. When she retired from the magazine in 1955, the new editor remarked that McKinley "had much to do with the tremendous growth of the magazine in recent years."*

McKinley, in this selection, tries to pin down the elusive Canadian-ness of our gardens and ends up focussing on climate as the critical factor. To help define one of our national pastimes, she certainly contacted some of the most active Canadian garden writers and horticulturists of the early 1950s. For example, Thelma Boucher of Kingston, Ontario, wrote a gardening column under McKinley, and a chatty 143-page book called One Gardener to Another *(Toronto: Ryerson Press, 1956). Boucher also helped plan the gardens of the St. Lawrence Parks Commission's Upper Canada Village at Morrisburg, Ontario.*

—·—

Gardening is a hobby people enjoy the world over. In Japan, you'll find a native exerting meticulous care over the tilt of a rock. In England, you'll see little clipped formal gardens, enjoyed through a long season. In the United States, you find horticulture ranges from near tropic lushness to desert growth and a hardy type much like our own. In this country you find that our Canadian garden is as individual as our Canadian spirit—and shaped by many of the same forces that have influenced our national character.

Climate plays the biggest part. To survive in Canada, a garden must be tough. Thelma Boucher, who writes "My Garden Scrapbook," says: "Hardiness is most desirable; we need plants to take any Canadian winter: cedars, maples, hawthorns, native flowers; hepatica, trilliums. Magnolias and laurels are not for us; instead, we have the rosybloom crabapple, the hardy rose, the lily."

We talked to the seedman, the nurseryman. From Bob Keith (of CBC's "Ontario Gardener"), came the same answer: "The great Canadian plant characteristic—is hardiness; will it survive?" Norman (Down to Earth) Scott elaborates: "The first requirement of any Canadian plant is its ability to withstand lower temperatures, alternate freezing and thawing, drying wind and excessive moisture—all within one year."

Since our climate entails a white winter or a long grey cold season, the Canadian scene can take abundant color. Over large areas we enjoy the spectacular shades of the red and sugar maples; in smaller gardens the Ginnala maple, the spindle tree and other species of Euonymus. Yellow tamaracks spark the richness of dark spruces and the duller crimsons of viburnum foliage and scarlet berries of mountain ash brush color into the scene.

Our typical small lot poses its own problems of gardening. R. W. Oliver, Division of Horticulture, Canadian Central Experimental Farm, tells Canadians to practice restraint in their planting of the small city lot, rather than work with contrast. He suggests that we can make the front lawn seem larger by keeping our plants to the boundaries and leaving the centre. He reminds us to avoid the large shrubs with coarse foliage. These make space shrink. The smaller, fine blue-grey foliaged shrubs retreat in our views and make a small backyard seem larger.

Hedges are part of our Canadian scene, as they are a part of the English tradition. In our country, however, Mr. Oliver points out, we clip them to a different shape. If we keep them broad at the base, curving to a narrow point—in a Gothic kind of shape—they will not break down as easily under the weight of our winter snow and ice.

The Canadian personality itself is reflected in our gardens. We find in our gardening, as in our culture, the influences of forefathers from the older countries. In the Canadian garden you see traces, says

Mr. Oliver, of the English love for profuse bloom. You see evidence of the French love for detail. You recognize the Scottish traditional love for restraint and simplicity. The Canadian homeowner is apt to combine these traits in his garden. He wants as much effect as possible in return, for the time, energy and money he can afford to spend.

There is one characteristic of the Canadian garden most garden consultants failed to mention. The Canadian small garden is a delight and almost a fetish to its owner. He does not employ hired help; nor does he spend a great deal of money. His garden is more a hobby than a task; more relaxation than a chore.

Across Canada we have our own seedmen and nurserymen who work to improve the strains of growing material suitable for Canadian gardens. Horticultural experimental stations exist across the country where specialists seek to improve hardiness; to test varieties; study soil and the vagaries of our climate.

As our own gardening tradition develops we find a need for greater communication between enthusiasts—professional and amateur alike—from one area to another.

Lois Wilson of The Garden Club of Ontario, puts it this way: "In the East, we already have a tradition of head-high walls of sweet peas; we have drifts of flowering dogwood in the West; brilliant lichen and alpine flowers in the North-West. These plants are all part of the Canadian tradition and all Canadians should be familiar with them, even if they cannot grow them."

Present-day gardeners, as Leslie Laking [director of the Royal Botanical Gardens from 1954 to 1981] points out, get more help in this regard than did their predecessors who gardened in Canada. The experimental aspects lie less now with the individual. Canadians can benefit now from the information available through Government Experimental Stations, Agricultural Colleges, the better nurseries and recently at Botanical Gardens.

H. F. HERBERT
1960

"Why Does Your Garden Grow?: Warnings by our
anguished indoor man," in *Canadian Commentator*

—⁂—

*F. Herbert was the slightly disguised pseudonym of
Harold Francis Herbert (1917–1987), a chartered
accountant—first in Ottawa and later in Victoria,
British Columbia—who had been in Lord Strathcona's Horse and
the RCAF; whose association with the Department of National
Revenue began in the midforties; and who, by 1964, had become
director of its Planning and Development Branch in Ottawa. His
article on "Computers in the Tax Collecting Process," in the January
1964 issue of* The Canadian Chartered Accountant, *was an insider's
view of the start of a new age.*

Moonlighting as a humorist, he wrote seventeen pieces for
Canadian Commentator *between 1958 and 1963. Most—such as "Fun
in the Commons," "Our Emblem Drear," "O Canada! O Enterprise!"
and "Last Week, This Week, Any Week on Parliament Hill"—poked
fun, in the time-honoured tradition, at national politics.*

*He occasionally looked beyond the political scene. "Those Culi-
nary Columnists" questioned the motivations of some unnamed but
recognizable food writers. "Say Cheese" examined the social dynam-
ics of group photography. "Why Does Your Garden Grow?", reprinted here, echoed the frustrations of neophyte gardeners in any age.*

—⁂—

The writers of gardening rubrics are tyrants, dedicated to the introduction of the backache into every home. Bull whip in hand, they
exhort their readers like galley masters. "Now that the month of
March is here," they begin, "it is time to get into your garden and

dig. Don't wait until the ordinary day-to-day tasks of summer crowd in on you—start now." If this sounds a bit ominous to the new home-owner on Apple Jam Lane, with his silly fat head full of idle thoughts of hammocks and long cool drinks, he is right to feel disturbed; he is about to surrender himself to an inexorable and never-ending servitude to his garden, and to the high priests who council him on his duties. After he has dug, planted, tilled, reaped, mowed, weeded, hoed, ploughed, raked, weeded, transplanted, thinned out, pruned and weeded, he has no time for contemplation.

Writing about gardening has only begun to pay in recent times. In the agrarian society of our past, to write knowingly of growing things could hardly have occupied many people; a writer of gardening lore needs as a reader the untutored husbandman of an urban society, someone who will get breathless with enthusiasm over liquid cow manure. Moreover, for a gardening writer to sustain such interest, he must address himself to a special type of urban society—with its suburban girdle giving a deceptive appearance of pastoral living.

Although we live in an age in which the vine-covered cottage has given way to the vine-choked living room, all who own a house with ground around it become involved in gardening. If the modern Canadian who lives in the suburbs neglects his acres, he is soon bullied into action by neighbours concerned with the maintenance of property values. As a result, he is driven for advice into the arms of the gardening experts who lie in wait in the columns of every newspaper and magazine. What he reads there soon reduces the beginner to the status of a peon;—a slave to the few square yards of verdure which surround his split-level heaven.

Now, I want to make it clear that I am no hard-pavement Harry, looking down my smog-filled nose at pastoral delights. I am as fond as the next man of a jaunt in the bosky glades with a pretty companion, and nothing pleases me more than an invitation to a country hideaway for a summer weekend. What I object to in the current outpouring of articles on gardening is the sneaky way the authors inveigle the innocent into their clutches. What the new homeowner isn't told, of course, is that there are various levels of initiation associated with suburban gardening.

In the beginning, the writer of "gardening hints" seems content if his greenhorn reader merely "sets out some bulbs" and "sends for some shrubs." This, of course, is merely baiting the hook. These innocent items are made readily available, in advertisements located strategically near the gardening column. The neophyte sees little harm in spending a few minutes popping plants into the dirt under his windows, and sends away for "an introductory offer." I am one who has had bitter experience in this regard. Mesmerized by a five colour spread showing a gracious home smothered in the luxury of dark green pine and blue spruce, I posted off a week's pay for a collection which, I was assured, would "add dignity and charm to your dream house." I was awakened abruptly from my dream when I received in return a shoe-box full of dusty twigs, each with two dried roots and a label.

If I were to have gracious dignity from these, I realized, I would have to live in my dream house until my grandchildren started shaving. Fate, however, intervened. I planted them as directed. In the long grass near the house they were invisible, and I promptly eliminated them a week later while mowing. Ever since then I have been leery of articles that begin "Now You Too can have Wonderful Luck with Japanese Crab."

Your more experienced gardener is not of course deceived by these blandishments. As an advanced member of this esoteric band, he has long since had his green thumb pinched in such traps. Under the watchful eye of his favourite gardening columnist, to whom he is now completely in fee, he is working out his destiny in the "hidden kitchen garden where one can conceal the Kohlrabi from one's "U" friends." He has reached the stage where he has a monthly bulletin sent to him by his master, complete with a personalized time and motion study to ensure that he wastes no moment of his available time.

As the greenhorn works his way towards such mysteries, he will be able to understand articles such as the one I read recently, written by a woman and entitled, "My Wonderful summer with Stephanandra Nicisa [sic]." At first glance this seems to be the confessions of a Roman courtesan and this impression is not immediately dispelled in the text which begins, "Deutzia Gracilis is dwarf and compact, while Stephanandra is small and racy. I cultivated them both with great care in partial shade and achieved splendid results." It isn't until you get well into this article that you realize that you have wasted your blushes, to say nothing of your sweaty palms. This woman is writing about her flowering shrubs, not her boyfriends.

Once you've started delving around in the detritus left by the builder around your new living quarters,—once the sachems of the gardening world have enthralled you,—there is no turning back. At the end of your day of work, after your hour-long drive to your home, your day has just begun. Step out of your grey flannel suiting, helot, pop into your sweat-stained old battledress (a reminder of happier times) and get down to it. Like Diocletian, your Empire is now your truck garden.

Somewhere between your second and third year of training, you will be introduced to the insect world. You will be persuaded to buy an array of expensive potions, which, if the rites on the label are followed meticulously may well result in the death of numerous bugs, while with luck sparing your offspring. But no sooner have you acquired a portable spraying machine as advocated by your favourite garden expert, than the treacherous rogue advises you to beware of upsetting the balance of nature. There are, it seems, good insects and bad insects. Since the little brutes don't wear cowboy hats, how can a simple homeowner tell the good guys from the bad guys? Your glib adviser is always silent on this important point.

Another trap awaiting the unwary involves geography. Much of the writing on gardening is syndicated and may originate anywhere; when your authority says North he may mean Memphis, Tennessee. A recent springtime exhortation ran as follows: "If snow arrives, and you have not fed your lawn, apply a light sprinkling of complete fertilizer on the snow." My snow arrived all right, last November, and in March it was four feet deep. I wonder just how long I'd be permitted to sprinkle fertilizer on my snow, before a distant siren, growing louder as the paddy wagon from the booby hatch approached my house, would announce to me there had been an urgent summons from pessimistic neighbours.

Someday you will graduate to the advanced, or stained knee class of harried harrower. With your proud new role of abigail to innumerable beds of ragwort, scabiosa and gilliflower, to name but a few of the choicer varieties available, you will be able firmly to withstand such blandishments as the illustrated ad which reads "My, John, aren't you glad we got our very own soil test kit?" When that day comes, your favourite garden columnist will introduce you to that Ultima Thule of gardeners, the compost heap. Your preceptor in the local press spends more time in loving description of compost heaps than on any other aspect of horticulture. "You too can turn your garden rubbish into rich manure in six weeks" is the clarion call to action. But, friends beware! The presence of a compost heap will add nothing to that strawberry festival your wife is planning for the next warm sunny day. The compost heap is the gadget that really separates the men from the boys in the gardening fraternity. It has also cured many a suburbanite and driven him back to town, where, as a civilized man, he belongs.

ROSCOE A. FILLMORE
1961

From "Introduction," in *The Perennial Border and
Rock Garden*

—⁂—

*F*rom an early age, Roscoe A. Fillmore (1887–1968) was
involved in horticulture; when he was not, he said, he
was like "a fish out of water." He worked in nurseries all
over Canada—except for 1923, which he spent as head gardener on
a state farm in Siberia. In addition to being an ardent horticulturist,
Fillmore was an equally ardent socialist, who throughout his life
championed the working class.

In 1924, he established the Valley Nurseries in the Annapolis
Valley of Nova Scotia, and in 1938 became the head gardener of the
Dominion Atlantic Railways (a line between Yarmouth and Halifax).
This job included supervision of the DAR's Grand Pré Memorial Park
near Wolfville, which under Fillmore's care became a widely known
tourist attraction.

Fillmore wrote in many horticultural magazines, but did not publish his first book—Green Thumbs: The Canadian Gardening Book—
until 1953. Although he was to publish three more over the next
eight years, he once lamented that the Canadian public did not enthusiastically embrace, as it did the others, his favourite book, Roses
for Canadian Gardens.

In this passage from his final book, Fillmore urged readers to take
gardening easy. Surely he was not one of the tyrants against whom
H. F. Herbert had railed.

—⁂—

Canada is a fast-growing country. In the lifetime of a man it has
grown and changed beyond recognition. A few of our larger cities

have become congested ant-hills, as have all the world's great cities. The inevitable result has been what we call, for lack of a better word, Suburbanism, and among the commuters, I have recently read, there has appeared an alarming incidence of such psychosomatic troubles as ulcers. Many find that long and harassing drive to and from the city so nerve-wracking that their health is shattered.

As a humble worker with the soil I am going to prescribe that these suburban dwellers get their hands into the mud and never mind rubber gloves. And please do not do this just to keep up with the Jones's. And avoid aping each other. Try to develop a touch of originality even though this may mean thoroughly unconventional treatment of your lawn and garden. Refuse to be so solidly bound by convention that all the homes and gardens in a community look alike. Perhaps in working out some plans for yourself and with your own hands and minds you can quiet jittery nerves and begin the cure of those ulcers or head them off altogether. Perhaps after a quiet hour in the garden you can tackle that drive to the job in the morning without sweating blood.

You'll not be able to do this however if you jump into the garden as though the devil were after you. You must take it easily and calmly. If you have undertaken a programme that will keep you on the jump all your spare time, better cut that programme drastically or you are only hastening the growth of the ulcers. Gardening must not be a treadmill but fun for the gardener. Otherwise it has no healing or soothing value at all. Millions of our young people are on the treadmill of mechanized industry. Their jangling nerves require quiet and rest and peace of mind. This is much better taken from the soil of a small garden than from a bottle or the hectic scenes of battle, murder and sudden death on TV.

I have never believed that the be-all and end-all of our existence should be the production of the maximum tons of coal, ounces of gold, bushels of wheat, yards of textiles, barrels of oil or millions of kilowatt hours. However, welfare and happiness should be our collective objective. Jittery nerves, mental breakdowns and ulcers are the inevitable results of the urge and greed for more and greater production at any cost, coupled with an instinctive rejection of the treadmill that modern industry has become.

I well recognize the need for greater production in a world in which hundreds of millions go to bed hungry every night. But there is an old saying about the "cure being worse than the disease." And if such an urge for production develops merely for the purpose of rivalling somebody else in turning out obsolete or earth destroying weapons and rather useless gadgets, we find ourselves engaged in a rat race from which there is no escape.

I therefore humbly toss my suggestion into the pool of ideas for an easement of the strain to which modern industry and rivalries subject the frail human body and mind. So, my friends, make a garden by all means but do not tackle it frenziedly, do not try to do it all in one season and do not make it just to beat the Jones family. This may feed your ego but also worsen the ulcer.

It is my theory that even many of those who look upon the garden with a jaundiced eye may become interested by reading a little and by watching the results the neighbours are getting. Perhaps most important, their minds must be disabused of the idea that gardening skill is inherited, that a green thumb is necessary, that there are great mysteries to be solved.

RAY GUY
1987

"Plunge into Pineapple Plantation, Maude," in
Ray Guy's Best

—⚶—

ay Guy, a Newfoundland journalist, novelist, satirist, and essayist, wrote a regular column covering the proceedings of the Newfoundland House of Assembly that transformed him into "the most talked-about columnist" in the province's history. Guy's writing has also appeared in This Week, Saturday Night, *and a series of CBC radio monologues.*

He applies his irreverent humour to everyday situations that he then turns inside out, as well as to the perennially rich material of political satire. Guy has won a number of awards for his writing, including the Leacock Medal for Humour for That Far Greater Bay.

Here, underlying his humour, is the serious cry of the Canadian gardener: Throw off that inferiority complex bred from reading too many full-colour-illustrated British gardening books, and push back the frontiers of horticulture. Pineapples in Newfoundland? Why not!

—⚶—

Somewhere east of Eden the Lord God planted a garden, but the inhabitants of Newfoundland and Labrador have long been assured that theirs is the land He gave to Cain.

Paradise is too good for the likes of us. For instance, there used to be two Paradises in Placentia Bay—Great Paradise and Little Paradise—but the Smallwood administration resettled the inhabitants and sent a federal agent with a flaming sword to bar their return. And there's a town of Paradise within 16 km of St. John's, but it is classified as a Local Improvement District, so it's a safe bet that the chap with the tail has already clued those folk in on the knowledge of good and evil.

Yet horticulturalists here, while they may sometimes falter, never despair. The official line is that they are harmless lunatics in a class with NDP organizers or tourists to Moncton. Soil, they are told, doesn't exist because the last glaciers pushed it all into the ocean to form the Grand Banks, except for 127 bushels remaining in the Codroy Valley.

But we gardeners soldier on though the plot be rocky and the imported expertise confusing. For example, English gardening books advise setting out your peas in February (when we still have four feet of snow), and American texts warn that lupins languish on this side of the ocean (yet they grow like weeds by Newfoundland highways).

One of the few encouragements we get from the greater world is a thing called the "Canadian Plant Hardiness Zone Map," which divides the nation into swirling, coloured bands numbered from zero to nine. Nine occurs only in tiny pockets on the B.C. coast. It has only light frost and jolly little of it. The best Newfoundland can do is a narrow band of six. But that is far better than we'd been led to believe. Quebec and New Brunswick don't rise above a five. Ontario has got a small bit of six between Toronto and Windsor, Nova Scotia has got some and so does P.E.I. That's all the six there is in Canada until you get to British Columbia.

Newfoundland may never become the watermelon capital of North America, but neither are we the howling tundra. Hardiness zones aren't everything, of course. Soil, shelter, sun and protective snow cover also mean a lot. I recall my surprise outside a hotel in Grand Falls (zone four) when I found myself up to the hips in lavender. An unwholesome awe of English gardening texts and a certain local inferiority complex had said it wasn't possible.

Now, it would be grapes of the sourest kind to say that Victoria, B.C., doesn't have a slight horticultural edge on the Atlantic provinces. But it isn't Paradise. Bald rock sticks up everywhere in that city, and except in spots of constant irrigation, her lawns in high summer are the color of a camelhair coat. Our grass, in the middle of August, stays a blazing green and is as juicy as rhubarb stalks. But no one place has everything. Let us keen amateur horticulturalists be guided by Lord Aberconway. Who he? An old port-and-cigars personage, I fancy, without whose Forewords precious few English garden books slip by to the printers. And what says the great Lord Aberconway to the neophyte who has crept humbly to his knee to hear distilled in plain words the essence of what the greatest gardening nation in the world has to pass on? "Find out what you can grow well and grow lots of it, don't y'know! Harrump!" A lesson to us all, me lord. As in so many other areas, that cursed Newfoundland inferiority complex still has a filthy grip. There are scattered examples of what can be grown here and they are constantly before our eyes, but there's no general rush to proceed past potatoes and petunias. There's that lavender hedge in Grand Falls, for instance, and 15-foot rhododendrons in Bowring Park, and holly bushes to the eaves of a few houses around St. John's, or the 12-foot hollyhocks in Corner Brook or the apple, pear, cherry, plum and apricot orchard in Notre Dame Bay (zone four!). There's heather and lupins and foxgloves growing wild. Spring is late and you can't risk much in the ground outside before Empire Day, but the simple cure is a few sticks and a piece of plastic sheet, and we may smile at the Niagara Peninsula. On the other hand, winter is also tardy, and one rare year I and many others brought acceptable bunches of roses from the garden to the Christmas dining table.

We are constantly selling our little acre short. I was surprised to learn that 25% of P.E.I.'s agricultural produce is accounted for by— tobacco! If there, then surely here.

And if tobacco then surely barley-corn, and so provisioned we may smack our posteriors at those bloodsucking parasites at Revenue Canada and their Sintax. Magic mushrooms are another thing. Magic mushrooms, as you may recall, came into the news a few years ago when the younger set became uncommonly frisky in the meadows of Vancouver Island. Typical of Lotus Land, we sniffed, where anything'll grow and where anything that grows will be tried once.

Last summer, the constables at Grand Falls, the lavender capital of Newfoundland, raised the alarm that maggotty-headed young layabouts there had discovered that we had magic mushrooms, too, and were rapidly turning themselves into depraved, anti-social, drug-crazed gas-bar attendants.

A sad day for society but a glorious one for horticulture. Pine-apples in Pooch Cove next? Sugar cane in Seldom Come By? Frangipani in Fortune? And we thought turnips were the most we could manage here on the Arctic rim. By the way, the lotus, or your Nelumbo nucifera, can be brought along quite nicely in many parts of Newfoundland if the roots are brought into a cellar for winter, and I have had calla lilies overwinter outside for four years now here in St. John's.

This, need it be said, is all novelty and experimentation, but it is a tremendously stimulating exercise, amusing and not without its virtue. For how dull would be the gardens of England herself had not those remarkable Victorians brought back the plants of the world to her shores, where they were tested in a buoyant spirit of almost child-like curiosity. They rode their hobby horses up to glorious peaks.

I doubt that St. John's corn will ever equal Fredericton's or that Avondale will ever challenge the Annapolis Valley or that the Great Northern Peninsula will ever support a first class viticulture. The point is that we are not a bald rock whose soil was swept away 15,000 years ago to feed the fishes. We are a temperate place with many advantages but populated by timid gardeners.

So plunge into the garden, Maude, bring that mould to good tilth, dung well each steaming plot, "go bind thou up yon dangling apricocks," find out what we can grow well and let's grow lots of it.

Me? Well, actually, at this time of year I find that my back goes out and that, according to the best medical advice, I'm better off indoors on the couch with a glass of California plonk watching *Three's Company* reruns. To you, I pass, with failing back, the torch.

BREAKING
NEW GROUND

—⁓—

ELIZABETH SIMCOE
1792

From Elizabeth Simcoe's Diaries

—⚏—

*E*lizabeth Posthuma Simcoe, née Gwillim, (1766–1850) was a talented landscape artist and map maker, an adaptable traveller, and a prolific writer of diaries and letters. She spent five years in Canada (from late 1791 through late 1796), accompanying her husband, John Graves Simcoe, who was Upper Canada's first lieutenant-governor.

She wrote her enthusiastic descriptions of daily life and frequent excursions mainly for family and friends in England. Her diaries were rich with details of geography, climate, and natural life; with comments on settlements, social patterns, and individuals; and with assessments of the picturesqueness of various Canadian scenes. They contained numerous mentions of plants gathered in the wild, and of those grown in gardens.

Of the gardens themselves, she revealed only small bits of information: Orchards covered "nearly all the top of the mountain" at Montreal. "30 large May Duke Cherry Trees . . . & 3 standard Peach trees" grew behind government house at Niagara. John Green grew "quantities of Melons" and "800 pumpkins" at Forty-Mile Creek. The Ursuline "Superieure" sent her "a basket of Plumbs from their Garden" in Quebec.

In this entry for Friday, July 13, 1792, written at Kingston, Upper Canada, she described a process that would continue throughout the nineteenth century wherever new settlement occurred.

—⚏—

F. 13th

The way of clearing land in this Country is cutting down all the small wood, pile it & set it on fire. The Heavier Timber is cut thro' the bark 5 feet above the ground. This kills the trees which in time the wind blows down. The stumps decay in the ground in the course of years but appear very ugly for a long time tho the very large leafless white Trees have a singular & sometimes a picturesque effect among the living trees. The settler first builds a log hut covered with bark, & after two or three years raises a neat House by the side of it. The progress of Industry is pleasant to observe.

LOUISA A. AYLMER
1831

From "Some Notes on Architecture, Interiors, and Gardens
in Quebec 1831," in *APT Bulletin*

—⁂—

*L*ouisa Anne Aylmer (Lady Aylmer), née Call, lived in
Canada from October 1830 to August 1835 while her
husband, Matthew, (1775–1850), the fifth Baron Aylmer,
was colonial administrator and then governor of Lower Canada.
(Aylmer, Quebec—the home of two of our other garden voices, Asa
Parker and Mrs. Symmes—was named after him.) Depending on the
sessions of government and the seasons of the year, the couple moved
back and forth along the St. Lawrence River, among two houses and
a summer cottage at Sorel near Quebec City.

In a letter written from Sorel on August 4, 1831 (her wedding
anniversary), Aylmer described the cottage itself, and her efforts to
decorate it. Then—as excerpted here—she turned to the grounds and
her efforts to improve them.

—⁂—

[A] Verandah runs the length of the sitting rooms, in the front and
back of the Cottage, and the Treillage is Cover'd with Wild Vines
and Virginian Creepers, and nearly Excludes the sun. The River
Sorel, or Richelieu runs at the bottom of our little Lawn and at the
end of a large field at the back of the house, we have the finest natural Woods of Magnificent Firs, of the Red Cedar and other kinds,
mixed with the broad leaved oak, Sumacks (which in this Country is
a very ornamental Tree) and which with the Accacia rose and White,
forms the chief beauty of our Shrubberries. We have also at this
Cottage, the Siberian, and Virginian Crab Tree which, with its luxuriant bunches of cherry like looking fruit, I think quite ornamental

even on a Lawn. But to return to the Woods, we have the most lovely
drives through them, on a Grass road; the charm of this country is
in the drives and Walks and our amusement has been, in clearing and
Widening them for a carriage to pass through the close shade of
these pretty Woods . . . . All our offices and servants rooms are in
Wings, attached to the cottage, and there are Ice houses, dairy, and
very good Stabling, Kitchen, Garden &c, &c. I have been making a
flower Garden, and have sunk about 200 Geraniums and other
Green house plants, Dahlias, Balsams &c, &c, in plots basketted
round with Golden rods, or Willows which look very pretty. I have
also made Walks, and this Evening have been busy, transplanting
young Firs placed in Groupes where I propose other Trees should be
placed in the Autumn so that the whole is now nearly completed for
this year, and the next I trust, we shall have plenty of flowers and
very good turf, two necessary ingredients towards a pretty Cottage
pleasure ground, and which in England is so perfectly understood.
Here I have to contend with the worst of soil, I must toss-dress [sic]
the Ground and have compost for the shrubs and Plants before I can
hope to see any thing as thriving as I should wish to see my young
plantations.

F. E. J. Lloyd
1886

From *Two Years in the Region of Icebergs and
What I Saw There*

—⚹—

*T*he Reverend Frederic Ebenezer John Lloyd (1859–1933)
was born in England and ordained in the Church of
England. In 1882, ten years before Dr. Wilfred Grenfell's
arrival in the area, the Society for the Propagation of the Gospel sent
Lloyd to the Strait of Belle Isle mission. He was to minister to people
living in a huge section of the northern peninsula and part of the east
coast of Newfoundland, as well as along sixty-four kilometres of the
Labrador coast. He spent two years in the region, before moving to
Quebec and then writing his memoirs of his time in Newfoundland
and Labrador.

The harsh climate and short growing season must have been a
shock for the English-born Lloyd, for he sounded positively amazed
that the inhabitants of Newfoundland and Labrador could grow
anything in such conditions. Lloyd needed to talk to someone like
Ray Guy.

—⚹—

Gardens are to be found everywhere, and in some parts of the island
are cultivated with satisfactory results. Potatoes, cabbage, and other
familiar vegetables are produced all over the island in larger or
smaller quantities. In the North, the season is far too short to admit
of any great success being obtained in horticulture. The frost is never
out of the ground until April or May anywhere in the island; and in
the North no gardening can be done before the end of May at the
earliest. And, even after plants have shot their green leaves above the
ground, they are frequently cut down and ruined by frost, which is

not an infrequent visitor throughout the Summer months. It will therefore be seen how difficult it is to rear vegetables in this country. It has been said with great truth of Newfoundland, "The *ingrata tellus* scantily repays the husbandman's toil." I have noticed that the radish, lettuce, turnip, and cabbage are the only vegetables that thrive well in the North. I remember seeing the most beautiful bed of lettuce I ever saw at a Hudson Bay Company's settlement, 250 miles to the Northward on the coast of Labrador in the Summer of 1882.

Julia Bullock-Webster
1894–1895

From Julia Bullock-Webster's Diaries

—⚄—

*J*ulia Bullock-Webster (b. 1826) was a diarist and profi-
cient amateur artist from Herefordshire, England. She and
her husband, Thomas, a military man, also lived for a time
in South Africa, and she spent 1894 to 1896 in the lower Similkameen
Valley of British Columbia, near Keremeos. This extended visit with
her sons, Ted and William, who were homesteading, gave her ample
time to observe and enjoy this near-desert environment.

Her diary, excerpted here, and her watercolours (some of which
are in the collection of the Art Gallery of the Southern Okanagan in
nearby Penticton), reflect her lively interest in this new landscape,
with its unfamiliar native flora and its immense potential for horticulture. Although earlier settlers had grown wheat, those of the
1890s were producing fruits and vegetables. Eventually, following
the introduction of widespread crop irrigation, Keremeos became
known as "The Fruit Stand Capital of Canada."

—⚄—

26th Aug:st 1894

They sat me in the only chair they had to offer in the verandah &
thankful I felt to be at the end of our long journey. We could see nothing beyond a few yards. The smoke was so thick. The house is log
built. The verandah covered with a mass of hops. Looking & feeling
deliciously cool & green . . . I need not say we were all very tired.

6:th Sept. 1894

Had our Exhibition of fruit & vegetables. Spread out on the bench
against the store house. Such a grand array. Of course we got First-

Prize for everything! All looked so lovely & clean. No holes in cabbage leaves & no caterpillars to pick off! Apples an enormous size & so were the onions, tomatoes, potatoes, carrots, in short one & all in the utmost perfection.

25:*th* March 1895

Out in the morning watching Ted raking & sowing onions with a drill. The seed is in a box & through a tube sows as it goes along, another contrivance covering the seed with earth., & the hind wheel rolls it down, such a saving of time & most clever invention.

6*th* April 1895

Liz & I sowed the flower seeds in three borders, & put cotton over the beds to keep off the fowls. Watched Ted & Willie ploughing the kitchen garden. Sand working beautifully. Any where about us on the sides of the "benches" it is rich as down here, requiring only to dig a hole & plant trees (fruit) & they were sure of growing. Rich sand loam is just what they like. [If] Only one could see the whole planted with vines, peas & apple trees.

J. T. Bealby
1909

From "Our New Ranch," in *Fruit Ranching in British Columbia*

—◆—

*J*ohn Thomas Bealby (1858–1943?) was born in Lincoln-shire, England, and educated at Cambridge. He edited a geographical magazine, contributed to two encyclope-dias, translated a book from the Swedish, and wrote many books of his own.

Bealby came to Canada sometime after the turn of the century, and wrote Canada, first published in 1909, mainly for would-be vis-itors and settlers from England. In it he assessed the "wealth in rock and sand," the "spoils of sea and wood," and the potential of the "golden wheat and the big red apple." He praised the vast, open spaces, but assured readers that in Canadian cities they would find things "much as they are at home."

Bealby, with his wife, Margaret, settled on unimproved fruit land near Bonnington Falls in the Kootenay River, eighteen kilometres below Nelson, British Columbia, and gradually converted it into a productive fruit farm. With that experience to draw upon, he wrote two detailed books encouraging others to do likewise: Fruit Ranching in British Columbia (1909; 2d ed., 1911) and How to Make an Orchard in British Columbia: A Handbook for Beginners (1912).

—◆—

A broad garden path, shaded by half a score of rose arches, runs down from the front of the house to the edge of the lake, a distance of little more than 100 yards. The path is flanked by broad flower borders, behind which stand on the one side a triple row of cherry trees, and on the other a double row of Italian prunes. The walk ends at an exceptionally lofty cottonwood tree, the topmost branches of which have been broken off in some storm. It only wants that melancholy sombre fowl, the raven, to come and perch on the topmost broken branch to complete the sense of weirdness and some unholy curse which the sight of it suggests, especially when a tempest howls about its gaunt and stiffened limbs.

Behind the cherry trees are the greenhouses, standing in a broad excavation, hewn, or rather blasted, out of the sloping surface. The only level ground on the whole of the ranch was too near the edge of the lake for us to use it as a site for the greenhouses. The stoke-hole of the furnace would have had to be put down below the water level, and when the lake rises, as it does, ten, and sometimes fifteen, feet at high water in July, the furnace would almost certainly have been standing in water. Consequently, we were forced to excavate the site for the houses. As fate would have it, we made an unfortunate choice of a locality, for we chanced to stumble into the middle of a stone slide, which was, in fact, as it turned out, little better than a veritable stone quarry. Towards the upper end we had to blast out almost every foot of the ground. We shifted tons upon tons of stone, hauling them with the horses down to the boulder-strewn margin of the lake. The excavation of the site for the greenhouses occupied five men for nine weeks. We were, of course, prevented from beginning the work of construction until the whole of the site was excavated and levelled, for fear that the blasting would shatter the glass, or even smash the spars and rafters. The houses were built and glazed throughout by two young men named Arthur and William, the former an Englishman, the latter a Canadian from Manitoba. The winter was, on the whole, so mild and open that, despite the heavy snowfall, they were able to continue the work almost without interruption all the season.

MARY IRENE PARLBY
1920

From "The Woman's Garden," in *The Grain Growers' Guide*

—w—

ary Irene Parlby (1868–1965) broke new ground in more ways than one. She was an exceptional woman who accomplished much for farm women in particular, and for Canadian women in general. When this article was written, Parlby had already formed the first women's local within the United Farmers of Alberta, and had then transformed it into the United Farm Women of Alberta, an influential voice in advancing women's welfare and rights. As well, she was one year away from becoming an MLA: an office she would hold for fourteen more years. She, along with Nelly McClung and others, was a major force behind the landmark 1929 reversal of the Persons Case.

And still she found the time to garden at her home in Alix, Alberta. Parlby's spirited promotion of flower gardening was influenced by growing up in garden-loving England and by her gardening contemporaries, who actively promoted gardening as a spiritual, physical, and mental support for adults and children alike.

As we see in this piece, she also brought some of her political agendas into the garden.

—w—

In this western country when I first came to it, everything in the way of flower growing was an experiment, and as far as a great many shrubs and perennials are concerned, an experiment still; an experiment also which our benign government holds off as much as possible with its high tariff and regulations. We know now, of course, that practically every kind of annual will grow and flourish exceedingly with the most ordinary care, but farm flower gardens should really be made of perennial plants which need so little attention, with annuals merely used to fill in.

One mistake so many people make in laying out a garden is to put it all in front of the house in a series of stiff little beds, which have no artistic beauty about them. Try instead taking the already beaten lines of travel, which have been made by the tramping of feet to and fro, from the barn to the house, from the well to the house. These paths will, probably, have some pretty curves to them, unless the ground surrounding your house is absolutely level and the distance to be travelled very short. In any case try broadening them out wide enough for two people to walk abreast and then make a wide flower border on one or both sides, and if you can have flowers nowhere else, be sure and grow them around your kitchen door. Then on warm spring and summer days you can take a great deal of your work to the back porch and enjoy first the bursting of the buds, and later the colors and perfumes of the flowers. Even washing day would be a joy under these conditions would it not? and as for mending it would become a delightful occupation with the flowers nodding their friendship to you, and the butterflies and humming birds flitting from blossom to blossom. Then think what it means to the children to know flowers and love them. Think of the competition to be the one to discover the first flower which bursts into bloom in the spring. The beginning of May, along the path that leads from the kitchen door to the well, orange, lemon and white Iceland poppies flaunt proudly in the spring sunshine, and Saxifraga cordifolia, brought from England as one little plant many years ago, but now edging a long border, lifts its heavy pompous pink blossoms. Then in quick succession gay pink and red pyrethrums make a splash of color, great, gorgeous Oriental poppies glow until they almost make you want to shade your eyes from their flame-like intensity. Next to them come the beautiful, stately Iris, the poor man's Orchid, the Fleur di [sic] lis of France, in their beautiful delicate shades of lavender, white and blue. Then as the burning days of midsummer come along the beds glow with a patchwork of gaily-colored annuals, and in the evenings when the grass is damp with the heavy dew after the heat of the day, the starry blossoms of Nicotiana Affinis lift their heads and breathe out their fragrance to the night air, while at their feet stocks, mignonette and clove pinks add their perfume to the other. Can you imagine anything more restful after washing supper dishes in a hot kitchen than a few minutes spent in such an atmosphere before retiring to bed?

I have said nothing so far about the practical work of the flower garden, how to start and how to carry on, because I believe everyone has to find out these things for themselves, for what suits one soil and one locality often does not agree with another. Some things are essential. There must first of all be a genuine love of flowers. Flowers are like children, tender, sensitive souls. They need unlimited love and affectionate care to reach their best development. Just as a continual nagging and grudging attention ruins a child's character quicker than anything else, so complaining begrudging care spoils the growth and beauty of your plants. Then you must have right soil conditions especially for perennials, which need deeply trenched beds and rich soil; some again need shady spots, others the full glare of the sunshine. All these things experience teaches—sometimes at great cost.

One of my first lessons which nearly broke my heart was when in my ignorance I thought I would have an Iris border along the north side of the path up to my kitchen door, and proceeded to transplant a really good collection of plants which had taken me years to accumulate to that bed. Next year I had no Iris. The border was a shady one, and the Iris roots which cannot stand moisture had rotted away. So one learns.

Another way in which many plants were killed in my first years of gardening, was by smothering them in the winter in my efforts to protect them as I fondly thought from the fearful cold. I was soon made to realize that a heavy mulch of manure hurt them worse than any amount of below zero weather, and now I go into the woods and sweep up leaves in barrow-loads for my most precious plants, and they thrive under this treatment. This winter, lying in a deep trench waiting for spring, to be planted, are Mountain ash, Guelder roses, Syringa with their waxy fragrant blossoms, Spireas, pink and white, and other interesting things.

The sad thing for gardeners in the West is the difficulty and tremendous expense in getting really good-named varieties of the different plants. The government and the transportation companies have made it almost impossible to import them, and the local nursery gardens simply do not grow them. They say there is no demand, that if people grow flowers at all they want "just peonies" or "just phloxes," so the commercial people fill their wants and do not attempt to educate their tastes.

Some of my plants have been carried here among my clothes from England; some I have begged from friends in British Columbia; some at great expense I have bought from the States. I hope when our farmers get down to Ottawa in sufficient numbers, they will see to it that seeds and plants and bulbs come into this country as freely as the winds that sweep across the boundary; we need these things so badly in the West to help us in our efforts to make this a country of beautiful farm homes. But until that happy day comes let us at least make use of what we already have. Do not scorn to transplant the wild things that nature has given us so freely. You can make a beautiful shrubbery with transplanted dogwoods, saskatoons and cherries, with which our woods are full. Last year on the shores of the lake I found thousands of baby seedlings of spruce, dogwood, hazel, etc., not a couple of inches high, and carried home a bucket full of them. You would hardly believe the tremendous growth they made in spite of the dry, hot summer.

Then in the woods I found tiny seedling cherries with their first pair of leaves, and up they came, to find a new home along the fence, where, in a few years time there will be a bank of cherry blossom that will look like a snowdrift in summertime.

H. B. Dunington-Grubb
1935

"The Landscape Architect in Canada," in *Landscape and Garden*

—⚮—

*H*oward Burlingham Dunington-Grubb (1881–1965) was the most influential Ontario landscape architect of his day—if only because of his long career, his output of more than fifty articles for magazines and journals, and his leading role in the formation of the Canadian Society of Landscape Architects and Town Planners (renamed the Canadian Society of Landscape Architects in 1963).

Howard Grubb was born in England, received a Bachelor of Science in agriculture from Cornell University in 1908, then returned home to work in the prestigious office of Thomas Mawson, for whom, from 1908 to 1910, he executed designs for the Palace of Peace at The Hague. When Grubb and fellow landscape architect Lorrie Dunington married in 1911, they created a hyphenated surname, moved to Canada, opened an office in Toronto, and founded what became Sheridan Nurseries.

In partnership with his wife and others, he designed the grounds of many private residences. In his view, his most significant public landscapes were several designed during his partnership with J. V. Stensson: the Sunken Garden at McMaster University, and Gage Park, Hamilton; the Oakes Garden and Rainbow Bridge Garden, Niagara Falls; and the central boulevard of University Avenue, Toronto—all in Ontario.

In this article for the journal of the [British] Institute of Landscape Architects, however, he confided that practising their profession in Canada was certainly not a bed of roses.

—⚮—

A quarter of a century ago, on the eve of my departure from London, friends and relatives were sympathetic. A colonial career offers the last refuge to the inefficient, forced out, by competition at home, into the wolf infested wilderness, the ice and the snow. A much travelled uncle said that Canada might be ready for my profession in fifty years.

Arrival in the land of promise, armed with nothing more than a soiled packet of introductions, brought forth a further outburst of sympathetic but disheartening advice. The immigrant's reasons for leaving his native land were politely never referred to. A prominent architect felt that no garden was so beautiful as plain trees and grass. A bank president said that Canadians had such an inborn love of natural scenery that garden design was likely to make little progress. The first prospective client wanted the surroundings of his new Italian Villa made so wild that a wild beast would feel at home. Having borrowed enough money to come the chances of borrowing enough more to get back appeared slim. Boats seemed to be very effectively burned.

In the boom year of 1911 Canadians were so preoccupied with unearned increment that gardening imagination reached no further than a few beds of geraniums planted by the local florist. An attempt was made to keep the wolf from the door by trying to show real estate speculators that the gridiron was not the only method of laying out streets. The words "garden cities" and "town planning" helped to carry the landscape architect over the period of waiting for the emergence of a more garden minded public.

The last quarter of a century has seen the development of considerable culture and civilization in this country. Canada is beginning to grow up. The arts have become more firmly established. Our best architecture compares favourably with that of other countries. Even gardening shows signs of becoming popular and, amongst a certain circle, even fashionable. Instead of the lowly geranium one finds to-day the newest varieties of delphinium, paeony and iris. Gardening and horticultural societies are attracting an ever-increasing membership. For the first time this year garden clubs are arranging public visits to better known gardens in aid of charity. Here and there isolated people are to be found who actually include an item for garden development when estimating the cost of their new home. The fact that this fund is invariably appropriated by the architect for panelling or tile roofing does not alter the significance of the original intention. It is possible, however, that even English landscape architects may occasionally have the experience of arriving on the scene after the house and its furnishing have swallowed up the last five pound note. People here are just beginning to grasp the idea that gardens are an expensive luxury and that a small sum spent on finally sodding the place down is not going to be good enough for the home of the future.

I doubt if you people at home have the slightest idea of the difficulties encountered by landscape architects in a climate like this. The winter of 1933–34 destroyed old established apple orchards. Shrubs like common privet were frozen to the ground, resulting in dead hedges in every city. The only evergreens we can grow here are a very short list of conifers and even the Austrian Pine may not survive in Montreal. Roses and perennials are often carried off wholesale in spite of every possible protection. And then, the insects—but no, I won't start on the insects. And yet people persevere.

English people would scarcely believe how short our planting season can be. In this country it is almost possible to jump from winter into summer overnight. During the latter part of April, 1934, we were advised by a local nursery that our order for shrubs would be delivered as soon as the ground thawed out sufficiently to make it possible for them to be dug. After the ensuing ten days of midsummer heat shrubs were so far advanced in leaf they could only be moved with great difficulty. Our autumn planting season should last at least two months, but the risks of planting, just before our arctic winters close in, are so great that most people prefer to wait till spring. Unfortunately they wait not only till spring to do their planting, but till the last minute of spring before they consider even the question of layout. The Canadian landscape architect works day and night for six weeks in the spring; snores gently through the short, hot, summer; finds his autumn golf interrupted by the occasional job, and hibernates during the winter.

After covering the greater part of England last winter I came back with the impression that you must be rehousing your entire population. A new house going up here is such a rare occurrence that it forms the principal topic of conversation at tea parties for weeks and if some attempt at a garden should be included the excitement is maintained at fever heat for months; but in spite of all drawbacks landscape architecture is a delightful profession. A common interest in gardens establishes many friendships and although the great days when Sir Humphrey Repton spent his life travelling from one country house to another are gone, we are still able to find some scope for our limited powers of imagination and watch the growth and development of our modest schemes.

Garden design is a profession for the safe and prosperous world in which people of my age were brought up. It can hardly be expected to bloom during the winter of economic change through which we seem to be about to pass. I think that the private garden of the immediate future in every country is likely to be small in size, of strictly limited cost and more horticultural than architectural in its composition, but some small gardens are lots of fun.

Holland Cox
1940

From "Prince Rupert Gardens," in *Canadian Homes and Gardens*

—⁂—

*H*olland Cox wrote this article twenty-six years after the completion of the Grand Trunk Pacific Railway from Edmonton, through Jasper and Prince George, to the site of Prince Rupert on the upper coast of British Columbia. Although the government's intent had been to establish a town that would rapidly become a second major port and rail terminus, the anticipated volume of incoming freight never materialized and Prince Rupert remained "merely a little fishing village" for many years, while Vancouver flourished to the south.

Sadly, Elizabeth Simcoe's description of Upper Canada in the late-eighteenth century and Cox's description of Prince Rupert in the early-twentieth century suggest that there had been little change in the attitude that one had to clearcut the forest in order to make room for the advance of so-called civilization. Gardens are part of that civilization, however, and as Cox reported, the gardening spirit flourished in Prince Rupert.

—⁂—

When the Canadian Government decided to carve a town out of solid rock and trees to form the most northerly railway terminus, Prince Rupert, on Kaien Island, B.C., at first glance the town resembled nothing so much as a forest after lumbermen have finished with it. Nothing was to be seen but raw stumps dotted thickly everywhere; streets were plank runways from one ridge to another, and the streets ran drunkenly up hill and down, or swerved to avoid rocky obstacles. Of gardens, vegetable or flower, there were none. A more desolate scene could not well be imagined. Those settlers and officials whose lot it was to go first into this crude wilderness roughed it in tents or shacks down by the harbor.

A few years passed and houses commenced to appear, with open drains running alongside. A tentative effort to produce beauty was made here and there, but most gardening was done in flowerpots, tin cans and wooden boxes indoors. Occasionally a bolder spirit, more beauty-loving and stubborn, hacked out the stumps or used them to train some vine, but the average dweller was too easily discouraged with conditions to attempt much, for, before a piece of ground could be utilized it had to be stumped, drained and sweetened with lime. Muskeg and rock everywhere offered incredible obstacles to success and, too, the climate, whose rainfall may be one hundred inches annually, had to be reckoned with. Winters, strangely enough, in that northern latitude, are very mild, there being little frost and snow; but summers are rarely hot, though light lingers in the sky until after ten at night, and the interval between night and day is short, so that, with long hours of sunshine and abundant moisture, growth is exceedingly rapid and lush. Prince Rupert was called "merely a little fishing village."

But the plank bridges rotted with the years, and new streets, permanent and costly, had to be constructed in the ravines or cut through solid rock. With these improvements and the slow disappearance of that bewildering forest of stumps, civic pride awoke and the inhabitants took to gardening *en masse*. Never in a place of its size have more gardens been made under such difficult conditions, and Mr. Pullen, editor of the Prince Rupert *News*, gave every encouragement through his paper and by example. His small cottage stands on a plot on Third Avenue (the main thoroughfare) from four to eight feet below street level. At the back the land rises sharply to a high ridge leading to the next street on a cliff which overlooks the town. Gardening under such circumstances calls for real ingenuity and knowledge of soil and plant.

With infinite patience he formed a small lawn and terraced the lower part of the hill, using flat stones in winding pathways to reach the upper levels. Friends generously donated seeds, bulbs and cuttings and now it is a common sight to see groups of visitors standing on the sidewalk, admiring the colorful patchwork quilt which he calls his Community Garden. Mr. Pullen does not aim at the rare and exotic— he has stuck mostly to the older favorites of other times and places, and one will find in his plots many perennials, and these, with some annuals, produce bloom from early spring until after Christmas.

FRANCES STEINHOFF SANDERS
1948

"Oasis on the Roof," in *Canadian Homes and Gardens*

—⚡—

*F*rances Claire Steinhoff received training in landscape architecture at the Lowthorpe School in Groton, Massachusetts, but soon returned to her native Canada. In 1934, in Toronto, she was one of the nine founding members of the Canadian Society of Landscape Architects and Town Planners.

Her career was primarily as a garden journalist. As early as 1932, she was writing about private residential gardens for Canadian Homes and Gardens, *and she was its garden editor from August 1939 through September 1948. By the time of her last contribution in November 1948, her by-line had appeared on nearly 175* Canadian Homes and Gardens *articles, and on dozens of her monthly column, "Canadian Gardening Illustrated."*

Early in 1946, her by-line changed following her marriage to Frederick Sanders. By early 1948, she had moved to Vancouver, and by the end of that year, her writing had disappeared from Canadian Homes and Gardens. *Her landscape architectural friends also lost touch with her; but as Humphrey Carver, another CSLA founder, observed in 1984, "I'm sure she had a beautiful garden."*

In "Oasis on the Roof," she encouraged postwar apartment dwellers to take gardening to new heights.

—⚡—

Three stories up in an apartment building on a strategic site in Vancouver, overlooking city and surrounding mountains, is one of the most attractive roof gardens we have discovered in all Canada.

The owners were happy to have pictures taken by Canadian Homes and Gardens in order to help others plan their own roof garden.

A stairway with wrought-iron railing leads from the main lower apartment to the penthouse which they had constructed on the roof. This is large, and has one entire wall of picture windows. The building stands on a steep hillside, giving a view across treetops and houses to Vancouver's waterfront skyline and across Burrard Inlet to include North and West Vancouver and the mountains.

Double glass doors open onto the roof garden which faces east and north and is entirely open to the sky. There were structural problems, like having a wooden flooring with spacing for drainage, and a sturdy railing—painted white to match the building. The dominant feature of the roof garden is a generous pool, where goldfish sun themselves, and there's the refreshing tinkle of falling water from a central foundation.

The pool was designed by the owner from one he observed in his travels, and built according to his measurements in the maker's shop. It was then raised by derrick up the three stories—quite an engineering feat! It is rectangular with curved ends and broad coping. In the centre a hollow pipe spouts water that falls in gentle spray.

Banked around the pool are pots filled with soft-yellow marguerites, one of the most charming summer flowers and in bloom from early spring until autumn.

The garden furniture is modern and inviting, the chairs upholstered in sunproof materials, an umbrella table, magazine tables and covered swing—all done in a soft blue, with white trim. Occasional striped cushions introduce the cherry red trim.

Tubbed cedars make effective accents in the corners. Petunias in a white frame add further gay color.

The combination of penthouse and roof garden provides an all-year outdoor retreat. Kitchen equipment nearby makes it ideal for outdoor entertaining.

LAURA BERTON
1954

From *I Married the Klondike*

——✀——

*L*aura Beatrice Berton's *(1878–1967) northern adventure began in 1907 with the ringing of the telephone and an offer to teach in the Yukon, in the Dawson City school. With great charm and humour, Berton recounted in this autobiography her twenty-five years of hardships, courage, colourful characters, and joys of living and raising a family in Dawson City. Her husband, a civil engineer and jack of all trades, was also an avid gardener. One of their children, the renowned Pierre Berton, became an enthusiastic gardener only after he and his wife moved to a new home in Kleinburg, Ontario, in 1951. Before that, as he wrote in "Force of Nature" (City & Country Home, October 1985), he had sworn he would never again pull weeds as he had in his parents' garden.*

Although small flower and vegetable gardens such as Laura Berton's were often found in the Yukon, few surpassed the horticultural heights of Kate and Otto Partridge's garden at "Ben-My-Chree." By the 1920s, they had created a showplace garden on the border of Yukon and British Columbia. Tourists came in droves to see three-metre-tall delphiniums towering over a picture-book garden that seemed to be transplanted from England. One journalist, writing in 1931, noted that he was "spell-bound, for we had expected nothing like this, wilder wilderness, perhaps, but not a garden in it."

——✀——

Because of the perpetual light, those plants that would grow at all in the Klondike grew to enormous proportions. We had pansies four inches across, sweet-pea hedges ten feet high with as many as six flowers to a stem, and asters as big as chrysanthemums. The east side of our house was covered in the summer with canary vine which ran over the roof. Frank, with a scientist's curiosity, measured its growth one June twenty-first. It had grown five inches in twenty-four hours. All the annuals grew and flowered swiftly, but the perennials, except for delphiniums, which survived the hardest winters, were another matter. We did raise fine Canterbury bells and hollyhocks, but only by keeping them in the cellar from fall to spring.

Most of our seeds were planted in flats in March from earth stored over the winter in the cellar. They were transferred into dozens of old tins and set against the windows until the ice was out of the river in May. Then into the garden they went. The vegetables grew as rapidly as the flowers and matured so quickly that they were wonderfully tender and sweet. One of our neighbors grew a cabbage that weighed fifty pounds and we raised a cauliflower which weighed eleven pounds ready for the pot. Green peas grew well, but beans we couldn't grow at all. Our finest crop was spinach, which we gathered by the bushel and bottled for winter use.

FRANK LEITH SKINNER
1967

From "Problems and Objectives," in
*Horticultural Horizons: Plant Breeding and Introduction at
Dropmore, Manitoba*

—⟋⟋⟍—

*rank Leith Skinner (1882–1967), one of Canada's fore-
most plant breeders, introduced more than 248 plant
hybrids—including trees, shrubs, perennials and bulbs—
into Prairie cultivation. One hundred forty-four of them were new,
improved plants.*

*He might have become a full-time rancher and farmer, had not
weak lungs and a cattle accident in 1911 turned his childhood love
of gardening into a lifetime vocation. As he was convalescing in the
warmer climate of Vancouver Island, he began reading horticultural
books and collecting seeds and plants to experiment on. Those island
rambles became the basis of his sixty years in horticulture. In
Canada, this self-taught hybridizer became known as the "Luther
Burbank of the Prairies."*

*In 1925, Skinner formally established the Dropmore Hardy Plant
Nursery and began to commercialize his endeavours. By this time he
was also working tirelessly toward legislation granting patents for
plant hybrids. (A plant patent would prevent unscrupulous nursery
operators from propagating a breeder's new varieties without financial compensation.) As well, he promoted vigorously, and against
much opposition, the labelling of nursery stock by place of origin, as
an indication of plant hardiness.*

—⟋⟋⟍—

In pioneer days on the Canadian prairies, the main concerns of the
settlers were the establishing of homes, the production of food, and

the purchasing of day-to-day necessities. Little thought or time could, at first, be given to the improvement of home surroundings apart from providing shelter for buildings. But even as the interest in growing trees, shrubs, climbers, and herbaceous perennials began to increase, the settlers had a very restricted choice of materials.

Most of the settlers had come from regions of milder climate, and very few of the horticultural plants of their homelands were sufficiently hardy to survive on the Canadian prairies. Plants from the mild regions of the eastern and western parts of North America were likewise deficient in hardiness. It was necessary then to depend mainly upon plants native to the prairies until more suitable material could be introduced or bred by individuals or institutions.

As I have shown, I myself began the search for suitable plants in my earliest years in Canada. However, in retrospect, I must say that it was impossible for me, at that time, to visualize that an activity that began as a hobby and personal interest would develop into an extensive hardy plant nursery based mainly on my own horticultural productions.

Our greatest problems in developing and raising horticultural plants are due to our climate. The long, cold, dry, windy winters of our prairies, and the short, hot, and sometimes equally dry summers, make it impossible to cultivate, with any degree of success, the varieties of trees, shrubs, fruits and flowers that are commonly grown in the eastern part of North America and in Europe. Nor are even those horticultural varieties of our native Canadian plants that have been adapted for cultivation in the moister climate of Europe any better suited for our prairie conditions.

Fortunately for us, in eastern Asia there are to be found growing wild, many species of trees, fruits, and shrubs of ornamental and economic value that are extremely hardy and at the same time closely related to varieties that are cultivated in Europe and the eastern part of North America, and have been raised to their present state of perfection by many centuries of cultivation.

Here on the Canadian prairies we have, for example, no native species of apple, pear or lilac, but all of these genera of plants have species that grow wild in eastern Asia where the climate is at least as cold in the winter as it is in the prairies of western Canada. The reason for this is that the prevailing winds in winter come from the neighbourhood of the Lena River Valley which has the reputation of being the coldest spot in the Northern Hemisphere, with a January mean temperature of −40° Fahrenheit. These northwesterly winter winds give much of Manchuria, Korea north of latitude 38, and the island of Hokkaido very cold winters, and much of the woody vegetation of these areas has the ability to withstand as low temperatures as, or even lower than we have on the prairies of western Canada. For this reason the trees and shrubs of northeastern Asia have proved very valuable for use as hardy parents in breeding work with the less hardy but better quality varieties developed in Europe and eastern North America.

So it soon became evident to me that many valuable plants from eastern Asia should, by themselves, or by combining with species from other regions, contribute to the diversity of our material.

CAROL STAIRS
1979

From "Uptown Radichetta," in *Harrowsmith*

—✺—

When she wrote this article about "a pocket of Mediterranean lushness in the cement landscape of Montreal," Carol Stairs was assistant editor of the McGill News—*and a gardener. Raffaele Cristofaro was one of the tens of thousands from Italy who had come to Canada—particularly to Montreal and Toronto—in the post-World War II period. They, along with fellow immigrants from many other countries, added exciting new dimensions to a horticulture that until then had been dominated by British, French, and American traditions.*

Unlike earlier pioneers, homesteaders, and fruit ranchers, Cristofaro was not clearing and planting hectares of virgin land in a new township or settlement area. Instead, he was restoring—through equally hard work—the tilth and fertility of small patches of badly mistreated and heavily compacted urban soil. He, too, was a groundbreaker. His wise and gentle methods for dealing with the various friends and foes of his burgeoning garden suggest that he, if anyone, could turn a concrete jungle into a paradise.

—✺—

When Italian-born Cristofaro bought his semi-detached brick duplex in Montreal's Snowdon district 12 years ago, the tiny backyard was nothing but a stone and gravel two-car parking lot. "Was no green like this," he smiles. "I said, 'I want no more car!' The first year was not so nice, but every year we plant and grow and plant and grow and it's getting always better. It just takes time."

The garden is now a plot of Mediterranean abundance in the city cementscape, so lush and productive that it feeds Raffaele, his wife, their son and three married daughters during the summer. But can such a hemmed-in little spot produce enough for winter storage?

"Ah! Too much! We freeze beans; tomatoes—make jar for sauce—make pizza!" says the exuberant Cristofaro. When frost threatens the Montreal area in the fall, the pace becomes especially hectic, as the couple hurries to harvest all the vegetables before they are killed. "My wife, she wants to lose nothing, so we take inside."

Every possible square inch is utilized—Cristofaro has even found room for a pear tree. *Scarlet Runner* beans clamber to the top of the corner telephone pole and cascade down its guy wires. A ladder is needed to harvest the crop. Heavy clusters of blue grapes intertwine on the latticed patio awning giving "shade, Italian style." It's just the right kind of shade, Cristofaro explains, to shelter a cool drink and a quiet game of cards.

With all of his own yard, except the narrow paths, under cultivation, Cristofaro recently approached his neighbour about an unused, foot-wide strip of grass that bordered the driveway. Told that he could plant anything "as long as it was green," the gardener planted a 20-foot-long, stunningly beautiful scarlet-flowering hedge of green beans.

Born 64 years ago in Campobasso, Italy, Raffaele discovered early in life that working with the soil suited him. "You look better, you eat more," his mother commented whenever he had been working outdoors. He left school early to work on his cousin's land. "It was always the farm," he remembers fondly. In 1952 he made the decision to move to Canada, despite his father's advice that it was "too cold in Montreal." It did turn out to be too cold for Cristofaro's favourite types of grapes, but the country boy persisted in his new land, and in 1956 felt secure enough to bring his wife and five children to Montreal.

The young immigrant also brought his simple but effective gardening skills with him. "First, in the fall, I clean everything and put some peat moss or manure and then I turn over. Then we wait for spring. We start to plan—here I want to put this, here I want to put that." He had always bought both manure and peat moss from garden supply stores, but last year he went out to the country and bought some horse manure from a farmer. This he mixed half and half with peat moss, one large bag of each, and the mixture was turned into his beds.

Cristofaro refuses to use insecticide or chemical fertilizers, even if it means a poorer crop. "You're supposed to spray, but I leave. If the year is good, I eat something natural." His grapes have occasionally suffered from infestations of worms, but they are not his favourite type [of grapes] anyway. A reminder that the south of Europe is far away, these blue grapes are wild and somewhat sour tasting. Now, despite his knowledge that "it takes time to grow grapes—about 10 years," he is starting some new vines that will bear sweeter, green fruit for the patient gardener.

His natural talent with plants extends to crop rotation—"I change around every year. It's better for the soil,"—and care with watering. Because diseases are easily spread on wet leaves, he avoids the garden after a rain shower. "When it rains, I don't touch. The plants get hurt. When is dry, I water."

His watering system includes an above-ground stone wishing well, and an in-ground pond made of an old bathtub—"I make new bathroom last year. I think first to throw away the old bathtub, but I put here!" These two ponds collect rain water and allow it to be warmed by the sun. This water is fresh and unlike tap water, is warm and unchlorinated. Cold tap water, he says, gives plants a cruel shock.

Cristofaro prefers not to start seedlings indoors—"it's too much work; the room, the light no good"—and thanks to the sheltering and warming effects of buildings, factories and automobiles that extend the urban growing season, he is able to seed directly in his garden about May first. "In spring I put in ground in corner where is sunny and rich soil." These seedlings often have to be covered at night with plastic or boxes to protect them from frost. Then, when the young plants are strong enough, he moves them to the proper location in the garden. He begins to pick tomatoes by early August.

Many of his seeds are bought from W. H. Perron (a Quebec seed house) as he likes to try one or two new varieties a year, such as this year's yellow peppers, but most of his old favourites, like *San Marzano* tomatoes, basil and zucchini, are guarded by the reminder, "*I primi sono per la semenza.*" ["The first is for SEED."]

With the exception of olives and wheat, the gardener grows virtually everything that thrives in his native Italy. "I have tomatoes, cucumbers, beets, carrots, Swiss chard, yellow beans and green beans. Also green peppers, sometimes red peppers, and this year banana peppers. Also basil. When my wife makes a jar of tomatoes, she puts two or three leaves of basil on the top; when you open up it smells so fresh! And chicory. It grows under the snow. It is tender at first and you eat like lettuce; after, you cook. Can grow corn here too, but the squirrels, ah!" He throws up his hands in despair.

Squirrels, unfortunately, do not read. A far more pressing menace than the eager fingers of children too young to understand signs, or visitors who are not afraid of dogs, squirrels and raccoons tend to keep a city gardener on the lookout. But Cristofaro is a passive resister and rather than take measures against the squirrels, he lives with them harmoniously. He has given up on corn, and plants their favourite treats, such as newly sprouted tomato seedlings, away from the areas they frequent most.

Evidently, his programme works. Although squirrels scamper through the garden, a stroll through the neatly arranged, weedless rows reveals further delights: parsley between the cabbage and tomato plants, zucchini and celery, and rucchetta and radichetta for spicing up an Italian salad. The former, known also as rouquette, is a peppery, pungent herb; the latter is a type of chicory, a salad green that is a Mediterranean favourite.

"I cut maybe 10 times and it come back. The first year I let grow high like this with nice blue flowers. I take seed."

Since he works the four to midnight shift with the City waterworks department, Cristofaro is able to spend the best part of the day in his garden. And he does. "Everything I do," he says, "is just because I like it." Evidence is everywhere that here his best and happiest hours are spent.

The wishing well, surrounded by fragrant rose bushes—in themselves an achievement in the eastern Canadian climate—is topped by several whimsical wooden birds that he whittled and painted himself. These birds may be reminders of the more lush countryside of Italy, but they are also unable to peck holes in tomatoes, or dig for worms around young seedlings. The carved birds, securely and permanently perched, scan their own small refuge of greenery.

Cristofaro smiles with satisfaction, and leans on his long-handled garden fork. "The way I see it," he says, "try always to get it better."

PERCY JANES
1980

"A Newfoundland Garden," in *Light & Dark*

—⁂—

*P*ercy Janes is a Newfoundland poet, novelist, and short-story writer, who was born in St. John's and raised in Corner Brook. After serving in World War II, he travelled extensively, settled in England for a number of years, but then returned to Newfoundland in 1975.

Janes was the first recipient of the Lydia Campbell Award for writing, presented by the Newfoundland and Labrador Arts Council. In 1984, he was made an honorary member of the Newfoundland Writers' Guild. A prolific writer, he has a distinguished list of publications, including novels, such as Requiem for a Faith; short-story collections, such as The Newfoundlanders; and poetry that has appeared in magazines across Canada. Light & Dark was his first collection of verse.

Janes, in this poem, expands the garden beyond a place of soil and plants, into the larger arena of human endeavour.

—⁂—

Rock
and shovel
strike out sparks
that will not warm
this frozen ground until
our April showers of snow,
May gales and shivering fogs in June
are plucked away, and winter veers to scorching sun
without the grace or interception of a gentling spring.

Dig
like dogs
for spud growth
and turnip greens!
between parentheses
(Victoria to Races Day)
plant and hoe and trench, and think
to reap, as August evening coolly drawing in
before September's threat of frost, may turn our greens
to yellow limp, and rot our spuds to pulpy mushroom ooze.

God's
bitterness
upon this land?
perhaps his irony,
to let such labor bear
so little fruit, but from the toil
make bodies like our enemy the rock;
and yield a subtler harvest to our souls,
tempered in patience and low expectation that may serve
to help us endure in rougher gardens than the spud-and-turnip field.

MIDGE ELLIS KEEBLE
1988

"It Grows Beautiful Weeds," in *Tottering in My Garden:
a gardener's memoir with notes for the novice*

—◊—

*Tottering in My Garden began as a few pages of advice for
her friends and children, and grew into a book first published in 1988. Midge Ellis Keeble's charming account of
her seven different southern Ontario gardens is firmly in the tradition
of "garden autobiography." She not only teaches, but also delights —
through her vivid, often humorous, anecdotes of the gardening life.*

*Keeble came to gardening only after marriage, children, and her
first house. Before that she had been a singer, radio announcer, and
schoolteacher.*

*Gardening is shown needing patience, perspiration, a sturdy
back — all tempered by liberal doses of humour. With infectious zest,
Keeble writes that mistakes happen. Her readers can take comfort
knowing that they are not the only gardeners who have planted daffodils upside down.*

*Today Keeble continues to garden on nine hectares of countryside
outside Orangeville — tending a twenty-four-metre perennial border, a
large vegetable garden, fruit trees, and a terrace garden.*

—◊—

On the twenty-fourth of May people in this climate, if they are cau-
tious, finally bring their plants out of the greenhouse, open their
packets of seeds and set them in the good earth. On our first twenty-
fourth of May, it was all too apparent that we had no good earth in
which to set anything. I had ordered a small load of cow manure
and a small load of topsoil, which had been dumped at the front of
the circle contained by the driveway. Anxious friends had brought

me cuttings and Mary had contributed the mock orange that was crowding her driveway. This we had dug out with a large root-ball in which strange little green things were growing. As there was no place to put them, we simply heeled them into the pile of topsoil.

The land still lay bare. Fine dust blew about where it had been scarified by the bulldozer, and the circle was still undisturbed cow pasture. Only now did I begin to realize where we were and what we had. We were on top of the Niagara Escarpment in Dufferin County. Our property had been bought as Crown land in the early 1800s by the McBrides and hadn't been plowed since the glaciers had harrowed the ground, leaving great granite stones behind them. Mr. McBride had cleared out trees where our house now stood and planted fruit trees, which were destroyed by a blizzard. But he hadn't plowed. Much, much later, local farmers had turned their cows loose on our hills to eat the wild grasses, and, while they were at it, they had chewed down the young shoots coming from old apple-tree roots. By the time we came, the cows had been long gone and young trees were shooting up about six feet high from the old roots. A neighbor said there had never been an orchard here and they were wild apples. Then why were they precisely twenty feet apart and set in the classic contour pattern to be used on hills? We cleared out a few shoots and left them alone.

No time to worry about apples. The real problem was the earth or lack of it. It wasn't just that I couldn't get a spade into it. No one could. No one ever had.

Nancy C. said, 'What you need is a plan. Then each year do one part of it. And face the facts. You can't do it yourself.'

I called Walter. I had tried to tell him the problems, but all he had heard was 'a house in the country'. He came roaring up in his truck, all smiles, but when he got out of the truck, his face fell.

'Why did you build this tall house here? It is sticking up like a chimney. It should be cradled with trees!' His hands waved, planting a veritable forest of trees.

I told him about the need for a plan, something to make house and land more compatible. He nodded and began a tour, striding about, growing less and less buoyant, and at last picked up a handful of the ground. 'What is this stuff?'

'It's like pit-run, Walter, what they use to surface the roads—it packs down hard.'

He let it drizzle out of his hand. I had never expected to see a look of despair on his face, but there it was. 'How can we grow anything in this?'

'It grows beautiful weeds.'

He stopped short and stared at me, then decided to ignore such nonsense. 'I don't know. I am going to have to think about this.' He drove away and I thought at the time he might never come back, but I *should* have known.

He came back and brought with him the strangest assortment of tools and machinery I had ever seen. There were wooden rakes with long tines set about four inches apart and he set his team to work with these, pulling off rocks the size of baseballs and only scratching the surface.

'You're not going to till it?'

'Golly no. We'll just get more rocks.'

While that was going on, Walter brought forward what I think was a tractor. On the back of it was an immense paddle wheel, big enough to drive a show-boat down the Mississippi.

'There may be some good stuff over here,' he called. He stationed his contraption over by the cedar-rail fence and set the great wheel flying while the tractor stood still. Turf, rocks and dirt flew in all directions with the wheel reaching down deep. When he'd worked up a patch about twenty by twenty, he said, 'That's your vegetable garden.' Then the tractor was brought up beside the kitchen door. Here the plasterers, carpenters and stucco men had dumped everything, including their lunch bags. Again the wheel churned until all the area up to the foot of the ridge and the full length of the house was loose. It was appalling stuff, but it was loose.

Now, while his men went to work with their rakes on what were to be the vegetable garden and the side garden, Walter slung a big canvas bag over one shoulder, filled it with pasture mix, and went striding over the bare ground, flinging out seed in great arcs as he walked and looking strangely biblical.

'I used to do this when I was a lad,' he called.

When I went over to look, he told me that there was a lot of good clover in it, which puts nitrogen into the ground.

'Will it bring back the wildflowers?'

'Who knows?' He looked out over the bare earth and then his familiar look of confidence returned. I still hold fast to what he said then.

'The land heals itself.'

At the end of the day, I stood by the truck as Walter prepared to drive off and gave me my last instructions. 'You play around with that for awhile and see what happens. Let me know. See over there? I've left you some of my own good topsoil.' The truck started to move away and then he couldn't help himself. He popped his head back out the window and called, 'It grows byootiful weeds!'

Taking heart, I bought an assortment of vegetable seeds and Gene brought me tomato plants. It was now June, a little late to be planting and, as well, the ground was too lumpy to be raked. I pounded it with a mattock, put the seeds in and hoped for the best.

Gordon came up with the idea for the side garden. Use the left-over chimney bricks to design a parterre; cover the paths with gravel and use some of Walter's beautiful topsoil to fill the beds. But what to plant in the parterre? The beds had only a top-dressing of good soil, so it couldn't be anything that sent down deep roots. Herbs. I looked up herbs. Herbs like a poor soil. If that's what they liked that was what they were going to get, and wouldn't it all look charming with little green mats growing in the circles and triangles?

Did you know that dill grows five feet high, that sage and hyssop turn into three-foot woody shrubs? Nothing was less than a foot, even the basil and lemon balm. The thyme replanted itself in the gravel paths. I had a herb garden but couldn't find the parterre. Canterbury bells and borage frothed along the wall of the house, humming with bees. The vegetables grew and the clover came up lush and green. It was chaotic but thriving in 'this stuff'.

I still wanted a plan.

The hills rolled off in every direction of the compass, not a straight line anywhere, and paths were appearing where we walked to the woods or to the top of the long ridge. I couldn't think where to begin. Help arrived in the form of Jon, Liz and David. Each went about it in his own way. Jon said to plant the circle enclosed by the driveway to grass. 'Then, where the topsoil's been dumped along the front of it, you can have a real flower border. Plants are growing in it now.' When I went out to have a look, I found the funny little green things that had come riding in with the mock orange were now unmistakably phlox and delphinium.

Liz set herself to the task that was obviously waiting to be done and weeded the parterre and the vegetable garden. 'Never mind. It's all going to be beautiful. You'll see.' Her faith would move mountains and inspired me to gather bushel baskets of the mustard weed the 'dozer' had stirred up.

David, who believes that the taking or giving of advice is a monumental waste of time, simply took a pick and shovel to dig great holes and helped us manhandle the mock orange into them. After that he sent me a copy of *Findhorn Garden*. The message, none too subtle, was that only a miracle could save me now. He had seen all too clearly what lay below the surface: a gravel pit.

We all thought the grass circle was a good idea, but how to get it in?

A strange little magazine kept turning up once a month in our rural mail-box. It was a chock-a-block with the most extraordinary ideas, some of them hilarious, I thought. It was called *Organic Gardening*. One evening I sat leafing through this while Gordon read the paper and Jon read a book. A picture caught my eye. A determined elderly woman was standing beside a large red tiller and behind them both was a luxuriant green market garden.

'Gordon, there's a picture here of a tiller.'

No reply.

'The woman who uses it is eighty. Her name is Mame.'

He didn't even rustle his paper.

'I'm only sixty-two.'

Silence.

'If she can use it, I can use it. It tills up hard turf.'

'What?' Jon was up and sitting beside me. 'Let's see that.' He read it all carefully, then moved over beside his Dad and started talking about bolo tines in the rear, precision gears, electric start and one-hand control. Man talk.

The Troy arrived in the last week of June. It was a little late to be putting in a lawn, but the tiller was there and we had to try it. At first we kept both hands on it, then one hand, then no hands. The area was flat and the machine rolled along turning up rocks, a few Coke bottles and more rock. When we finished, we had an indescribable mess of rocks.

'We'll have to get that off before we till again.'

I went looking for one of Walter's stone rakes, but no one had ever heard of them. In the end, we bought a rake with long tines and cut out every other one. It worked, but it wasn't easy.

We spread manure and tilled again: more rock and more raking. At this point I was all for spreading the grass seed, but Jon—and I still can't believe this—harnessed himself and his father to heavy boards with ropes and the pair of them dragged these back and forth until they were satisfied that it was level. If you're wondering why we didn't hire someone else to do all this, all I ask is, who else would be that crazy?

The seed was spread and watered and lo, a fine green whisker appeared. The topsoil was spread around the front of the circle and the phlox and delphiniums placed with the few annuals that could be found so late in the season.

We didn't have a garden, but the bare ground was gone, the pasture mix was lush, and now we knew a garden was possible. I called Walter with the glorious news. 'Plants will grow here!' He said he would come to us first the following spring, with a PLAN.

Someone once told me that you should never decorate a house until you've lived in it. 'Give the house time to tell you what it wants,' she said. I began to wonder if that would work with a garden. And I didn't have to wonder for long. Late July and August came with burning blue sky, hot winds and endless, endless sun. The garden didn't *tell* me—it shouted for shade and screamed for water; the plants were shrivelling in the heat and so were we. We were spending the summer out in the country and living inside. We couldn't wait for a plan. We ordered six mature trees and a swimming pool.

CLAUDETTE BURTON
1990

From "From Russia With Love: Doukhobor traditions in
Canadian gardens," in *Harrowsmith*

—〰—

*C*laudette Burton provides an interesting glimpse into the
connections between gardening and the Doukhobor religion. Gardening was said to give this community the
means of acting out two mainstays of their faith: toil and a peaceful
life. However, the religious grounding of their cultivating did not
stamp out horticultural rivalry. Often there was intense competition
within the community to be the first to produce a vegetable crop. To
illustrate this, Burton was told what her informant called a typical
gardening story that involved two practical jokers who "pretend to
till a patch of the cold spring garden to tempt competitors to plant
too soon." Another common theme in Doukhobor gardening was
their love of singing prayers and special songs. In earlier days, gardeners were always singing in their fields—especially at planting and
harvesting time.*

—〰—

Whenever she tends her garden, Julia Ozeroff sings. "To help create
the right feeling," she explains. As a Doukhobor, a member of a
much-misunderstood sect of Russian Christians who settled in western Canada, Julia celebrates a way of life, honed in difficult climates,
that combines vegetarianism with hard work and practicality with
joy. As she works, Julia sings some of the traditional Russian words
cherished by her faith and tells me, "You can grow a good garden
only if you truly love what you are doing."

Louise Konkin, another member of the Doukhobor community,
was all astir when I visited her in early April. Our meeting had been

arranged through a mutual friend, so both Louise and I felt more than a little awkward. A lean young woman with energy to spare, she was in the midst of washing her already clean floor but insisted that I enter and, she added, to never mind taking my shoes off. The voluntary breaking of these two cardinal country-house rules was a sure sign of her nervousness. I reassured her that I had come just to see her greenhouse and gardens, so we moved outdoors into the spring sunshine.

Louise lives in New Krestova, a tight village of frugal plywood houses closely nestled along the fertile bottomlands of Gander Creek, whose waters flow into the Kootenay River between Castlegar and Nelson in the southeastern corner of British Columbia. Here, 30 or 40 years ago, turmoil fuelled by differences between the Russian speaking Doukhobor immigrants and their Anglo-Saxon neighbors led to distrust and tension still evident in the settlement, so I make a point of centring all my attention on the gardens. One thing I soon notice is the amazing orderliness and neatness of Doukhobor gardens, characteristics deriving in part from the belief that a garden is an expression of a woman's ability to keep a good household (it was largely women with whom I spoke) and in part from the Doukhobor tenet that one should not take charge of any life unless one will take care of it.

"There is nothing special about my garden," Louise claims modestly as she guides me around her property. Snuggled against the *banya* (steam-bath house) to capture its excess heat is her greenhouse, where good-sized tomato and cucumber plants are growing. Under the walkway are decomposing kitchen wastes kept indoors to protect the compost from marauding bears. Chicken manure has been tilled into the outdoor garden, and a cold frame has been set up for the field tomatoes. The last stop on the tour is the root cellar, where a lighted match reveals, in the dark and chilly air, shelves still overflowing with last year's canning and bins more than half full of root vegetables.

This store of food represents more than just a harvest: it helps maintain a culture as much as the health of the individuals within it. Some of the potatoes, a Russian staple, will go into *pyrahi*, the Doukhobor version of perogies; the cabbages can be used for goluptsi (cabbage rolls) and for a type of borscht based on cabbage rather than beets. Dishes such as these can be traced back to the origin of the Doukhobor religion on the steppes of the Ukraine during the 17th century. Later, near the Black Sea, a region of balmy climate and river bottomland ideally suited to farming, the people earned the reputation of being excellent growers of grain, vegetables and livestock—at that time, meat was an important part of their diet—but persecution resulted in several migrations to new and often more hostile territories. Finally, an unlikely alliance of Leo Tolstoy and the Society of Friends (Quakers) intervened with an international appeal for humanitarian aid, which resulted in a mass migration of more than 7,000 people to Canada in 1898 and 1899. . . .

Speaking to Ellen Lundh, my interpreter and her granddaughter, Vera [Streleoff] said that when she was a little girl here, "we grew mostly hay, potatoes and fruit trees because the water was good. Lots of apple, cherry, plum and pear trees. There was a pipe, a big metal pipe that went over the [Kootenay] river to bring water down from the mountains.

"People from the other villages would come and help us plant and harvest the potatoes. During haying, they would come too. We all worked in the fields and gardens, except some of the men who had to work outside. There was a boss—sometimes a man, sometimes a woman, it changed every year—who helped organize the work and distribute the food. But everyone decided what was to be grown in the garden. It was a consensus. Everything was done communally. Times were better then. People took care of each other."

Some crops were grown only in the best places and then distributed to the other villages. For instance, millet and lentils were specialties of the Slocan River Valley, and today, cabbages, potatoes and onions are still grown on a commercial scale by two Doukhobor families in Grand Forks. Wheat came from the prairie villages, which received lumber and fruit in return. Strawberries and raspberries were extensively cultivated around the present town of Castlegar and were so successful that a jam factory was built in Brilliant around 1910 to process extra fruit. The Doukhobors developed an excellent reputation for the quality of their preserves. Vast orchards were planted wherever possible, and the Grand Forks area soon became known as the Valley of the Fruits. The fruit was usually dried for the winter. One woman recalls "racks and racks of pears drying in the hot sun."

With most duties of the fields and households being shared and rotated, every young person acquired all the skills of growing, cooking and preserving the huge quantities of food required to keep the 60 residents of the village for the winter, plus extra to give away. Many adults have memories of not being allowed to go swimming until the garden chores were done. One elderly man says, "I can remember filling a coffee can full of potato bugs, picking them by hand, listening to them plink in the bottom, plunk as it got fuller. The can had to be full before I could go and play."

LAYING OUT
THE
GROUNDS

—m—

WILLIAM CLAUS
1806

From William Claus's Garden Book for 1806–1810

—⚏—

*W*illiam Claus (1765–1826) was born in New York and fought for the Crown during the Revolutionary War and the War of 1812, attaining the rank of colonel. In 1796 he became deputy superintendent of the Six Nations at Fort George near Niagara (now Niagara-on-the-Lake), and in 1800 became deputy superintendent general of Indian affairs for Upper Canada, a position he would hold for the rest of his life. His second house at Niagara, begun in 1816 following the burning of his first in 1813, still stands.

Although busy with Indian affairs, Claus also became a justice of the peace in 1803, a member of the Legislative Council in 1812, and a member of the Executive Council in 1818. Yet he still found time for an intricate garden, and kept detailed garden records in a series of small notebooks—three of which have survived.

He recorded more than the names of the plants he grew. He also mentioned the people from whom he received them, the parts of the garden into which he put them, and the horticultural tricks with which he nurtured them. In these selections from 1806, we gain a sense of how he laid out his grounds.

—⚏—

Mar. 21st
Put out along the Centre walk Several cuttings of the white & black Currents from Mr. Crooks also in other parts of the Garden & in the Nursery one slip of Mrs. Servos' yellow clingstone from Mr. Crooks —

Mar. 26th
Sowed in the Asparagus beds Celery, Cauliflower, Salad Radish, &
early Sugarloaf.

Apr. 15th
Sowed a bed of Early pea from Mr. Nevill, between the spinage &
asparagus beds. put an Egg plum under the apple Tree to the right of
the Gate

Apr. 16th
Sowed 4 beds of White onion seed from Albany & set out 2 layers
of the Carnation

Apr. 21st
Sowed the Guinea pepper in the long border to the left of the Gate—
in the Watermellon Square one bed with red Beet & long orange
carrot, and in next to the above with round spinage & Mr. Prices
parsnip and a large bed next to the last with early Dutch Turnip
Salad, white & red Turnip Radish.

Apr. 22nd
Sowed next the Gate to the left 3 rows of grape seed & a row of
Orange Seed

Apr. 24th
Grafted from Col Smiths tree & the small one next to it on two
Stocks of Apples near the Bee hive in the front Court.
    Sowed a row of Small pepper from Mrs. Blackwell in the long
border to the left of the Gate.

Apr. 25th
Sowed in the long border to the left of the Gate Celery & Cauliflower
of my own seed, 4 rows of peppers, Brown lettuce from Albany & the
Salmon, white Turnip & Salad Radish

Apr. 28th

Grafted on a tree next to the red Clingstone in the long border one of Dr Kerrs Newtown Pippins.

May 1st

Sowed one bed of Salsafy in the old W. Melon Square.

May 2nd

next to the above, sowed one bed Carrot & one bed . . . pea.—Along the new Walk by the bees on the right, the Lima Bean & on the left the . . . running bean.

May 10th

Sowed in the Grape bed next to the house Green Kale, Sugar loaf Savoy & Imperial Cabbages & Radish

May 12th

Sowed the Red Potatoe from St. Joseph in the left hand square.

May 13th

Sowed in the Grape Vine bed, Battersea Red Cabbage, Lavender, Green curled Endive, Brown lettuce & Salmon Radish. in the Water Melon Square between the peas & onions, one bed of round Spinage. in the new Water Melon plot Nine Hills of the Blackeyed Water Melon Seed. Sowed some Celery under the Locust Tree in the Nursery

May 21st

Sowed Musk Melons in the Square where the cabbage and WM— planted in a border below the assparagus bed 5 rows of Curled parsley

May 23rd

Sowed in the Grape bed one hill of five seed of Water Melon from China—& in the old Musk Melon square two hills one 6 & the other 7 seed of a Red Water Melon from Busherville. Sowed under Miss Adlams Window 4 Rows of Apple Seeds from John McNabbs apples. sowed in a small keg 3 seed of the Indian shot.

May 24th
Sowed 5 hills of Blackeyed Water Melon with those sowed on the 13th inst.—in border next Mr. Powell's fence in the Onion bed 3 seed of the Dwarf Nusturtion and 3 in the border at the head of the asparagus bed—

June 3rd
Planted the Corn that old Basstutic gave me, behind the Lima Bean in the Garden.

June 5th
Sewed some . . . fine salad in the assparagus bed. & in the border by Julia's beds.

June 21st
Sowed some of Mr. Price's Lettuce in the Turnip bed.

July 9th
began to cut the hay in the field Sewed salmon Radish in the asparagus bed next the apple Tree. Sowed a bed of Prusian pea next the asparagus bed. cut about one Ton of hay on the lot.

MARY GAPPER O'BRIEN
1828–1830

From Mary S. O'Brien's Journals

—⟨w⟩—

*I*n 1828, Mary Sophia Gapper (1798–1876) and her mother
travelled from England to Upper Canada to visit family
members settled at Thornhill. Mary stayed on, married
*Edward O'Brien in 1830, and moved with him to Vaughan Township.
In 1832, they moved once more, to Shanty Bay on Lake Simcoe.*

*From 1828 through 1838, Mary kept a series of journals describing her life and that of her friends and relatives. Indeed, on October
17, 1828, the day after arriving at her brother's in Thornhill, she was
already expressing her strong interest in the landscape.*

*Like Catharine Parr Traill, Mary transplanted trees and shrubs
from nearby woods, and cultivated wild fruits. Like Elizabeth Simcoe,
she looked—sometimes in vain—for familiar aesthetics in an unfamiliar landscape. (While Simcoe favoured the picturesque, Mary
seemed to prefer "the romantic & sublime.")*

*Like many gardeners in a new world, she introduced familiar landscape-design elements from the old: lawns, shrubberies, and clumps
and plantations of trees. Yet she also thrilled to the sight of Canadian
forests carpeted with wildflowers, and collected their seeds to send
back to England.*

—⟨w⟩—

1828 Oct [17]
All Southby's fields are covered with stumps so thickly that the many
he has destroyed are scarcely missed & the worst part of the story is
that the next estate towards which the front of the house looks is
covered with dead trees which make no very becoming veil to the

fields and forest; beyond the ground is sufficiently undulating to be graceful when it is cleared & cultivated but at present we cannot boast much of the prospect. Southby says that the stumps do not interfere with the tillage of his farm but there is still much to be done to bring it to its due productiveness.

1828 Oct 31
[A]fter breakfast Bill threw a sunshine over the gloom on my spirits . . . by calling me to help him lay out his garden and looking at me as full of glee in his gardening prospects as he used to do . . . Went out to walk, met A. & took him into the woods to pull up some trees to finish my first clump. S. & M. came to help us plant them.

1828 Nov 6th
S. & A. went into the woods to get some gooseberry plants of which they find there a species remarkably good to be used green, they grow in marshes & with them a species of strawberries very much like our scarlets; these two plants are therefore to occupy jointly a bed in the lowest part of the garden. There is also a wild plum which is deemed worthy a place in the garden for the sake of having it handy for here nothing is ever used unless it comes handy . . . [I] could not resist Bill's invitation to accompany him and Mary to fix the boundry of his kitchen garden on which he has been hard to work.

1829 Apr 30
[P]lanned a plantation in the garden which is to be commenced tomorrow.

1829 May 1st
[A]mused myself in the interim with Mr. Hamilton's assistance in promoting the tidification of the *lawn* . . . . After dinner we went into the woods to get trees & shrubs for our plantation & returned laden—Mary with a little tree as tall as herself across her shoulder, looking like a fairy genius of the vegetable world in the exercise of her functions.

1829 Nov 5th

The kitchen garden is fenced, that is one comfort but we shall be in a mess all the winter if the lawn fence be not finished also & the posts must be put in before the frost or it cannot be done at all.

1830 June 25th

I challenged E. to go and examine it [the wheat crop]— we found that there was no cause for apprehension & as we were then close to the meadow, E. thought it as well to go & look at that; this is also our fruit garden containing raspberries, strawberries, currants & plums— It is watered by a beautiful trout stream . . . running out of the forest thro' a poplar copse which is just now covered with some of the prettiest white flowers which have something the air of anemones— Then he wanted to look for cedar poles so we crossed the fence into the swamp & from thence returned thro' the wood having walked all round the estate.

1830 June 29th

My gardening had made me so tired as to render lying down an intense pleasure.

ASA PARKER
1851

"Fencing," in *The Canadian Gardener; Containing
Practical Directions for the Kitchen and Fruit Garden; and
also a Brief Treatise on Field Culture; Adapted to the
Climate and Soil of Canada*

—※—

*When Asa Parker wrote this eighty-five-page book with
its twenty-eight word title, he had been gardening
near Aylmer, Quebec, in the Ottawa River Valley, for
ten years, and had been encouraged by neighbours to share his
knowledge of growing vegetables and "such fruits as can be easily
propagated in a new country." He intended to continue his experiments, he said, and to produce a second treatise on fruit and ornamental trees. He apparently never did, and it was James Dougall, in
1867, who wrote English Canada's first book on fruits of all kinds:
The Canadian Fruit Culturist.*

*Parker's book gave general directions for siting, laying out, and
planting a kitchen garden, followed by short essays on each of an
ambitious number of vegetables, small fruits, and medicinal and culinary herbs. His stated preference for hedges, in this section on fencing, was timely. The Canadian Agriculturist was also recommending
live fences, especially for deforested areas.*

—※—

A good fence is essentially necessary, although too often neglected.
How often do we see garden crops destroyed for the want of proper
or good fences. Should the farmer not have time to perform the work
necessary for a good garden, it is to be hoped, that he will not neglect
making a substantial fence, so that he may enjoy the fruits of his
industry, from a garden which he has perhaps but partially cultivated.

As to the material of the fence, I will leave it to the judgment of the owner; but were I to command the means of making an ornamental fence, as a matter of course, I would make or plant a hedge. As few however command the means of making a brick or stone wall, I would recommend the north side to consist of boards, as on the south side of the same grape-vines and other useful and ornamental shrubs could be reared.

LINUS WOOLVERTON
1889

From "A Few Hints on Landscape Gardening," in
The Canadian Horticulturist

—⁓—

inus Woolverton (1846–1914) was, at various times, an examiner in English and classics, a fruit grower, a fruit experimenter, an executive secretary, a civil servant, an editor, and the author of two books on fruit and numerous articles. Yet except for his years at university, he lived his entire life on land that his great-grandfather had purchased in 1802 in Grimsby Township in the Niagara Peninsula of Ontario. He read and corresponded widely, belonged to provincial and national organizations, and travelled throughout the province and to various cities in the United States.

In 1886, Woolverton succeeded D. W. Beadle as secretary of the Fruit Growers' Association of Ontario and editor of The Canadian Horticulturist. *Over the next eighteen years, he guided that monthly periodical into the twentieth century with a firm hand. The subscription base grew, the contributions from readers outside Ontario became more frequent, and the number of articles on ornamental horticulture, landscape architecture, and city beautification increased.*

When no one else took on a topic he thought was important, Woolverton did so himself—as with his four-part series on landscape gardening, in which this was the final instalment.

—⁓—

The distance from the main road at which a house is to be built should be governed by its size and by the extent of the grounds by which it is surrounded. Similar considerations also govern the disposal of the approach, or carriage drive, by which access is had to it from the main road, and both these considerations are too often entirely lost sight of by those who plan their own grounds.

Manifestly in the case of small village and city lots it would be in poor taste to attempt to introduce those curves in walks and drives which grace the park-like surroundings of an elegant country seat; and, indeed, in most such cases the straight lines are the most suitable because most economical of space, and encroaching least upon the precious green sward.

Unfortunately, many a fine mansion, owing to a lack of taste on the part of the owner, is built so near to the road that no opportunity is left for the beautiful in the arrangement of the grounds, and the house itself appears to the greatest disadvantage; and all this notwithstanding the possession of broad acres which the wealthy proprietor might have drawn upon to extend his house grounds. Where, however, they are admissible, gentle curves in the walks and drives are more in keeping with our modern idea of taste than the straight lines, and the stiff geometric style of gardening of the ancients. Our model is nature itself, in which we see the curve predominates, and the trees and shrubs are not in straight lines, but grouped in ever varying shapes and forms. In such a case, then, the disposal of the approach is a study, and should be made to enter the grounds amid dense groups of forest trees and shrubs, so arranged as to conceal the house itself until the best point of view is reached, after which there should be little to attract the eye away from this object. But though curves are desirable they should not be introduced too freely or without at least some apparent reason; as, for instance, a group of shrubbery, a large tree, or perhaps an elevation, about which an easy ascent is desirable.

It is recommended that the entrance from the public road be not too abrupt, but at an easy angle, so as to give the approach as much importance as possible. It is also important that the carriage way should not skirt the boundary too closely, for that would betray the limit of the estate, and impart a sense of confinement, which is not in good taste; indeed, all such division lines should be concealed from view as much as possible, not by stiff, formal rows of evergreens or other trees, but by groups so arranged as to conceal objectionable features when viewed in passing, or from the windows of the house. And just here another important point should not be overlooked, viz., that these blocks of trees and shrubs be also so disposed as to leave open to view, especially from the side and front windows, any distant scenes which are interesting to look upon, and with this object imaginary lines should be drawn across the lawn, along which nothing should be planted which would obstruct the view.

Probably nothing in our country so offends the eye of the cultured foreigner as our picket fences, or "palings," as he calls them, and certainly when one considers them, even when painted up in the most suitable colors, they are a blot upon our landscape, tiring the eye with stiff formal lines of wood. Neither is there the same excuse for their employment as formerly, for the introduction of wire fences has enabled us, by using a neatly turned post, to put up a fence where it is needed that will be almost invisible.

The drive is an extension of the approach which can be used to great advantage by our wealthy farmers, whose well cultivated fields and beautiful orchards invite the attention of the visitor. A drive-way of such a kind need not be kept with such scrupulous care as the approach, with its even edge of closely shaven sod, but may be itself a strip of green sward, just large enough to be easily kept cut with the mowing machine, and along it may be planted choice specimens of plants, trees and vines. It may be planned to lead through the most attractive portions of the farm, and will prove, according to the experience of the writer, both a delightful walk and a charming drive, much preferred by every member of the family to the public road.

On a closely shaven lawn we see little need of cutting walks, for by them the cost of caretaking is largely increased, and, if overdone, they are rather a blot than an ornament to the landscape. Still, when leading to a much frequented spot, as to a flower-garden, or to a retired summer-house, or to an attractive promenade, it is in good taste to lay out a walk, curving about real or artfully placed obstacles in such a manner as to bring into view the most attractive features of the grounds in graceful succession. . . .

By a little attention to such points as these our readers, who have some natural ability in the way of design, may have the pleasure of planning out their own home surroundings in such a way as to be almost above criticism, for even the professional gardener must admit that to form all plans upon any one model would be an unpardonable blunder on his part.

W. T. Macoun
1912

From "Lady Grey and the Gardens at Rideau Hall," in
The Canadian Horticulturist

—ɯ—

illiam Terril Macoun (1869–1933), one of the major figures in Canadian horticulture, began working at the Central Experimental Farm in Ottawa in 1887 as "a labourer in the Botanical Division." Nine years later he had become curator of the Arboretum and Botanic Garden, and by 1910, he was Dominion Horticulturist, overseeing the work of the twenty-four farms and stations in the system.

In addition to his administrative duties, Macoun pursued extensive breeding programs for potatoes, and originated the 'Melba,' 'Joyce,' and 'Lobo' apples. Macoun was characterized as a tireless worker for the betterment of gardening. He was actively involved in most of the horticultural movements of his time: He promoted school gardening, served on local beautification committees, led food production campaigns during World War I, and judged flower, fruit, and garden competitions. Macoun also held office in a great number of horticultural organizations, was a popular commissioner on the Ottawa Improvement Commission, and wrote articles and lectured throughout North America on an amazing variety of horticultural and agricultural topics.

—ɯ—

With the departure of Lady Grey from Canada lovers of flowers and gardens have lost a warm friend, and one who will long be missed. Wherever Lady Grey went in this country she impressed her love of flowers upon those whom she met and encouraged many to improve and beautify their homes. During her sojourn in Canada there has been a more marked development in gardening than in any previous period of Canada's history, and while there has been a number of influences at work, she has played no small part in bringing about the widespread interest which is here to-day.

A concrete example of the way Lady Grey lent her influence was the "Lady Grey Garden Awards," a garden competition which under her patronage has been held in Ottawa for the past six consecutive years, and for three years before by Lady Minto, who inaugurated it. During these nine years no less than one hundred and twenty-four different gardens have been entered in competition, most of them during the past six years. It is believed that this garden competition has done much to improve the gardens in Ottawa.

The true horticulturist, however, must have a garden of his own if he or she is to be of the greatest assistance to fellow gardeners. In this respect Lady Grey is a true gardener. Belonging to a family noted for their love of flowers, she has not been content to see others plan and plant, but while residing at Rideau Hall has done both herself.

It has been the writer's good fortune to have had many conversations on gardening with Lady Grey and to have been shown her treasures at Government House by herself. What has impressed me more than anything else has been her ability to remember the names of new plants. How few Canadians, even among our most enthusiastic horticulturists, are like her in this respect? How much more interesting it is to know the names of plants we grow than to merely know that they are phloxes or paeonies or irises.

The effects in a garden depend so much on color, contrasts in color, and the blending of colors that there is a boundless field for resource in the planning and planting of a garden. Good taste in this respect is all important in gardening. It is unnecessary to say that Lady Grey had this in the highest degree and it is unfortunate that she was not able to remain in Canada long enough to bring about all the changes in the gardens and grounds at Government House which I know were in her mind. She had in a large degree the desire which all enthusiastic horticulturists have of getting new things of merit for her garden and of giving to others interesting plants which she had.

She paid many visits to the Experimental Farm to take notes on plants which pleased her, and wherever she went she endeavored to obtain new and choice things.

Lady Grey showed an especial interest in Canadian wild flowers and before she left had brought together quite a large number of the more ornamental species at Government House. So keen was her desire to see Canadian flowers growing in their native wilds that she visited out of the way places to do so. One instance of which the writer had personal knowledge was a trip to see the showy lady's slipper (Cypripedium spectabile) in a distant bog. Neither heat nor mosquitoes daunted her, but pulling on a pair of rubber boots she entered the swamp and saw these lovely flowers in great abundance.

A little has been said of Lady Grey's influence on horticulture in Canada, and of her knowledge and love of flowers. It remains to record some of the things she accomplished at Government House itself. When she came to Ottawa the conservatories at Rideau Hall were small and comparatively uninteresting, but through her influence a fine range of houses was built in which are grown practically all the cut flowers used at Rideau Hall, and many other ornamental plants. . . .

There had been little done to make a good herbaceous border at Government House. Lady Grey took it in hand and after several years hard work she had the satisfaction this year of knowing that her work had not been in vain. In the past the plants suffered during dry weather, but she had the border subirrigated by means of tiles, which has been very effective in keeping the soil moist and the plants have made much more satisfactory growth since. Two years ago she planted grape vines between the two borders and made a pergola or archway of the vines. . . .

Many fine herbaceous perennials are now planted in this border, which will long bear the impress of Lady Grey. Much effective planting has been done in recent years on another border, the one with the palm house in the rear, and the smaller borders about the conservatories. The Hall itself has received more attention than ever before . . . [And] climbers have not been neglected.

One of the most satisfactory and pleasing bits of planting which Lady Grey planned was the planting of thousands of bulbs of narcissi and tulips, in the grass along the roadside and in the park belonging to Government House. Everyone was welcome to walk in and see these charming flowers when they were in bloom in the spring. The great masses of them everywhere in abundance, their striking contrasts of color and their setting among the trees, was a delightful picture. The planting of bulbs was, however, not confined to Government House grounds for in Rockliffe Park, near by, many children helped to plant the bulbs of tulips and narcissi, which for several years have been a striking feature of the park in spring.

The last improvement which Lady Grey effected at Government House before she went away was the removal of an arbor-vitae hedge which restricted the view on the west side of the grounds and hid the trunks of a fine row of hard maples, spoiling the effect. With the removal of the hedge there is a more extensive view and when the planting which was planned is completed there will be a pleasing vista with white pines in the distance. When the hedge was removed a terrace or parapet was made with steps leading down to the level of the maples, which is also a marked improvement.

The results of Lady Grey's work on the Government House grounds and gardens will be that those who follow her will endeavor to maintain the standard she has set and possibly cause still further improvements to be made.

FREDERICK G. TODD
1929

"Where Nature Is Abetted," in *Canadian Homes and Gardens*

—⁂—

*F*rederick G. Todd (1876–1948) was Canada's first resident landscape architect. He was born in New Hampshire, and after apprenticing in the prestigious Olmsted firm near Boston, he moved to Montreal, where he conducted his practice until his death.

Todd's 1903 preliminary report to the Ottawa Improvement Commission, although never fully implemented, was the first comprehensive plan for the nation's capital. His projects also included towns and subdivisions from Newfoundland to British Columbia, urban parks, memorial parks, and private gardens—of which "Hillside," mentioned in this 1929 article, was a typical example.

Among his designs that still survive are Assiniboine Park in Winnipeg; Bowering Park in St. John's, Newfoundland; and the Garden of the Way of the Cross for St. Joseph's Oratory in Montreal. Todd applied one basic conviction to all his designs: that nature was an active partner in all his undertakings.

The 1920s and 1930s were the heyday of country estates in Canada, when anyone of social pretension wanted "a place in the country," preferably landscaped to perfection. Some owners went beyond clipped hedges and rose gardens, to also establish hobby farms where they could enjoy, at a distance, the sight of contented cows or gently baaing sheep.

—⁂—

On the Southern slope of Mount Bruno, the country residence of Lady Meredith, of Montreal, nestles comfortably against the Oaks and Birches of the hillside; quiet and dignified, yet so expressive of the friendliness and charm of its owner that the simple harmonious beauty of lawn, flower border, and woodland lingers long after more extensive and ornate gardens are forgotten. Lady Meredith's knowledge of floriculture is so well rounded, and her appreciation of simple landscape beauty so keen, that the expert's task resolves itself into pleasant discussion and co-operation—different from the landscape architect's general experience.

Approached by the beautiful winding drive through the Mount Bruno Golf Club Links, a bird's eye view of Lady Meredith's property, about twelve acres in extent, would show it divided almost in halves by a steep escarpment. The lower portion is almost entirely occupied by a mature Apple orchard, while the steep slope and upper half is for the most part covered with a splendid growth of Oak, Birch and Maple.

The house, designed by Messrs. Edward and W. S. Maxwell, was located on the upper level, well back from the edge of the escarpment, in order to provide a pleasing foreground for the extensive views over the Richelieu valley to the Green Mountains beyond. In the Spring this view is over a sea of Apple bloom which is exquisite in its loveliness.

At the outset it was decided that the natural beauty of the place was to be the guiding spirit for all landscape work, and this was adhered to throughout. The house stands some two hundred feet from the semi-private road at the boundary of the property, and, contrary to usual practice, it was decided not to break up the privacy of the grounds by extending the drive to the house, but to approach the house by a flag walk.

An English paling fence with an arched entrance was constructed at the road, and from this point the flag walk leads to the house, flanked on either side, for much of the distance, by shrub and perennial flower borders. The flags in the walk were purposely left well apart in order that grass and small rock plants might grow between them and harmonize the walk with the surrounding lawns, and among the stones at the outer edges of the walk were planted groups of Snow drops and other Spring flowering bulbs to welcome the owners on their first visits in the Spring.

Broad sweeping lawns were arranged about the house, and their smooth undulating surfaces were kept free from beds of flowers or shrubs, save in one or two instances where it was desirable to limit a particular vista. Shrubs were planted about the base of the house to unite it more pleasingly with the grounds, and about the borders of the lawns broad masses of shrubs were arranged in an irregular manner, punctuated at important points by small trees. In places these borders were allowed to project sharply into the lawn and at others deep bays were formed, thereby creating a contrast of sunlight and shadow which greatly increased the attractiveness and apparent extent of the lawn.

One of the most attractive features of the entire place is the rugged natural wood which was left in direct contact with the house on the north and east sides. To preserve these woods in all their native wildness, and to accentuate these qualities and reveal them most effectively, was one of the pleasures of working on such a place.

Woodland walks were suggested and so located as to exhibit to the best advantage some particularly fine tree, or stony crag, and other points of interest. No stiff formal walks there, but irregular wood paths made level for comfortable walking and so carpeted with fallen leaves as to be hardly distinguishable from the rest of the floor of the woods; indented here with a clump of wood fern, and there with a group of Hepatica or other wood flowers; in some places passing underneath a broad spreading Oak standing in the open wood where a seat is found comfortably arranged; at other points curving sharply between masses of native Hemlock which masked unsuspected beauties beyond.

N. DE BERTRAND LUGRIN
1931

"Canada's Most Famous Garden," in *Canadian Homes and Gardens*

—❦—

*N*ellie de Bertrand Lugrin (b. 1874) of Victoria, British Columbia, was the daughter of one journalist, Charles Henry Lugrin, and the mother of another, Charles Lugrin Shaw. From 1921 through 1938, her fiction appeared frequently in The Canadian Magazine *and* The Chatelaine. *Her occasional nonfiction—in these periodicals, the* Canadian Geographic Journal, *and* Canadian Homes and Gardens—*usually focussed on British Columbia subjects, as did her books such as* The Pioneer Women of Vancouver Island, 1843–1866, *a series of biographical sketches of early settlers. Lugrin embellished several of these sketches with tantalizing details of early plantings of fruits, shrubs, and flowers.*

Jennie Butchart began her garden on Vancouver Island in 1907, reportedly saying to her husband, "We've made it ugly. Now let's make it beautiful again. Let's put some flowers in there." She later said she knew nothing about gardening at the time.

By 1915, her gardens had expanded to fifty-two hectares, and were visited by 18,000 garden lovers a year. Even into the 1920s, the energetic, unpretentious Butchart could occasionally be found serving free cups of afternoon tea to garden visitors.

—❦—

A little more than twenty years ago that paradise of bloom, known throughout the continent as Butchart's Sunken Gardens, was non-existent. Primeval forest, with the marks of Indian trails, covered the acres where the present house stands and the upper gardens now spread their panoply. There was a deep ravine with a rill of water running through, the coy Maiden-hair hugging close to its banks, and the wild flowers a carpet of beauty all about. At the upper end of Tod Inlet was a disused lime kiln, a relic of the earliest settlement of this part of the Saanich Peninsula on Vancouver Island; and the only dwelling in the vicinity was an ancient log cabin, so moss-encrusted that it looked as though it had grown there. It was at Tod Inlet that the little stream entered the salt water in a bright cascade.

Then came the devastating hand of man. Where the lime kiln stood were found large and valuable deposits for the making of cement. Hence an important commercial undertaking with an enormous mill, tall smoke stacks, the whirr of machinery and the ravishing of the forest.

It became, instead of a sight to enrapture the senses, a bruised and broken stretch of land: ferns, Lady-slippers, Erythronium, Wild Honeysuckle and a score of other wild flowers were swept away; and, where the limestone was quarried, a great hole was dug, which grew in depth and height and horror until, looking down into it, it seemed abysmal. Naked, grey sides reached up for a hundred feet or more, and at the bottom were sickly patches of water, like great eyes yearning toward the sky. From having been a happy, lovely picnic ground where, every week, little crowds used to gather, coming all the twelve miles from town or from the different districts of Saanich, it was soon a forgotten desolation.

But if man had destroyed it, it was for woman to heal and restore. When Mr. and Mrs. R. Pim Butchart built their home near the cement works, the sight of that wrecked bit of forest land distressed them, particularly Mrs. Butchart. Something ought to be done about it, especially the hideous hole where the quarry had been. For some time she pondered over it. Then came the great idea.

To give all that ravished beauty back a hundredfold. To make of that sheol of nature's hopes a living well of refreshing loveliness. In her mind's eye she could picture it—the vast, cool greens of it, the drifts of color. There was a gaunt grey rock thrusting up out of the slime in the midst of the abyss. This should figure in her marvellous scheme.

It was a tremendous undertaking as far as the old quarry went. There was not an atom of soil left there in which anything would grow. All of that must be hauled to the spot, sand and gravel and rich black loam. And where once there had been the music of running water, running water and its song must be brought back. To be able to accomplish a marvel like this was a joy supreme, and from its inception, Mrs. Butchart whose idea it was, superintended every bit of the work. As it grew, and the first thin veil of color showed in patches, she knew that she was doing more than making a sunken garden for herself and her family, that it would be a shrine for all the world to see.

The first sunken garden was not more than half the present in extent, and the upper garden has grown into very much larger proportions than those embraced in the original conception. Nor are plans yet complete. Each year sees some addition, some pleasant innovation that will add to the infinite variety and furnish amusement to the thousands of visitors who enjoy the hospitality of Mr. and Mrs. Butchart throughout the twelve months. Even in the winter the garden has much verdant beauty, and along certain paths or in sequestered nooks one will come upon some little surprise of bloom.

No chart has ever been made of *Benvenuto*, for the reason that it was not developed according to any preconceived plan. In the first place, in order to ensure a plentiful water supply for irrigation and ornamental purposes, the little stream was dammed up at its outlet and furnishes all that is needed and more. This, in itself, is the biggest asset, for without plenty of water nothing could thrive, particularly in the sunken gardens.

One enters *Benvenuto* by way of a drive which follows a pleasant curve for three hundred feet or more from the main road to the inner gates. This drive is lined with Hawthorn trees and terraced borders of bloom varying according to the season. Beyond these borders lie, to the right and to the left, the wide sweeps of the seed gardens, from May until October wonderful mantles of changing color. There are ten acres of them, and all of the flowers to be found within the garden proper bloom here in a luxuriance that is bewildering to the eye. These ten acres offer no diversity of design or shape. They are merely wide, flat stretches, getting the full of the sun and sheltered by the woods and hills from any overcold or boisterous wind. This commercial plantation was started about five years ago, the outcome of endless requests for seeds from the *Benvenuto* garden.

The gates of *Benvenuto* are never closed. There is a notice to the right which advises motorists to park their cars in a very large, gravelled space close by which has been made for them; and, throughout all the tourist season, a detachment of police are there, to see that this is done, and that order is preserved in the two long lines of cars which continuously wind in and out of the first gate.

Once within, a double drive leads around a large Rose-embowered lawn. This lawn is studded with a group of wide-spreading Maples, while around one half of the Roses climb on trellises and on the other are trained to fall in festoons from tallish poles. The right-hand drive takes the owner and his special guests to the house, which is directly ahead of the gate. The Butchart home is low and rambling, cheerful with many windows, and liberally draped with vines. It is so unique within that it is worth a whole story in itself, but nothing of this is evidenced from the exterior, which is unpretentious and simple. It has its own small quota of private garden, enclosed by a white latticing, a charming place of modest dimensions with a fountain, a Lily pool, a tea-house and a revelry of flowers, chiefly Roses.

To the left of the gates, the land rises rather steeply and is traversed by a pathway of flags up to and around a waterfall, the first of the many water delights. Where the two branches of the road rejoin, the garden finds its natural diversion, for the original contour of the land has been followed whenever possible. Sweeping away to the right are lawns and shrubberies, a log tea-house, the croquet and archery lawns, the new Rose garden, all of which one glimpses, as one crosses the main lawn to the Japanese garden.

Where the ground drops gently to the Inlet, this exquisite whimsy of horticulture finds its place. Dwarf trees and shrubs of Japan are used, featuring little bronze Maples, drooping Elms and the Plum. There are tiny winding waterways, miniature bridges, stepping stones across streams and occasional summer houses. For the edification of youthful visitors, little figures of gnomes and leprechauns and rabbits and frogs and other creatures of the woodland are scattered about under the trees. It is loveliest here in the spring and early summer, for first comes a cloud of Primroses and Forget-me-nots, up from which the myriads of bulbs spring into being as though it gave them birth; and, a little later, there is the marvel of the

Japanese Iris in its delicate shades of blue and the tiny forests of Maidenhair fern; while all along the lower pathway, where the trees meet overhead, the Lilies-of-the-Valley crowd one another in an orgy of bloom.

Returning from the Japanese garden, one takes a leisurely way to view the formal beauties of the Italian garden, which is charmingly placed for the view from the window of the sunroom in the house. A new water feature has been added recently, though perhaps it is not to be considered as part of anything so dignified as the Italian garden. But it lies immediately adjacent to it. It is a very large and ornamental duck pond, enclosed with a gay, flower-hung fence, and it has, besides the pretty sheet of water, a charming, almost palatial house for the lucky ducks.

The new Rose garden, which one enters through the new Rose-embowered pergola, is developed about a circle of fine, green turf, against which the blossoms show to the best advantage. The bushes have been planted in a shallow, continuous terrace and a narrow border of Box hems them in at the foot; a trellis of climbers forms a wall behind them. There are wide paths of grey flags, broad stone steps at four sides, a drinking fountain. A well with a wrought iron top, and bucket and chain complete, has a circular stone seat around it, and a stone wall partially enclosing it.

One takes one of the paths on the left-hand side of the entrance drive to reach the most famous part of *Benvenuto*, and, on the way, passes by the apiary [sic], where are housed a dozen varieties of pigeons, golden pheasant, grouse, lordly peacocks and other birds. Thence on, until a defile between high banks is reached. These banks for two months of the year are cloaked with Primroses, Bluebells and Narcissi and to describe the effect is beyond the power of words in any language. Walls of bloom high above one's head, and so close that one can touch both sides at once with the outstretched hands. A fitting entrance to the miracle of the sunken gardens!

That one-time vault of death and destruction has become an incredibly radiant place of shimmering greens and rainbow colors. Against its steep sides vines have been hung and ferns festooned, and waterfalls course down here and there. Where the winding path leads downward, alpines of every kind flourish happily among the rocks—the lively pink of the Dianthus, rosy mauve of Violas, grey foliage and rose and white flowers of the Candy-tuft, the soft tints of the Alyssum, the more showy Anemones, the Aubretia in sheets of violet, rose and lavender; the wee, trailing golden blossoms of the Saggetalis and the exquisite, clear blue of Gentians.

On the floor of the garden, flagged walks laid in firm, green turf lead one through a maze of bloom to the tall pyramid of rock which centred the old abyss. It is clothed now from head to foot with blossoming shrub and flower. Around its base is a forest of the taller garden perennials, Delphinium, Foxglove, Hollyhocks, Campanulas, Cosmos, Poppies. A steep path leads to the very top where may be had a marvellous view of the whole of the sunken garden.

Water plays its charming part, the water from that same little stream which enlivened the green of the woods a half century ago. It tumbles over the side of a cliff to form a gay, little rivulet which leads along to a series of small lakes, lakes stocked with fish, graced by drooping Willows and bordered with flowers, the blue of Forget-me-nots, the gold and crimson of Tulips, the vivid pink of a Japanese plum, or the soft rose of the Almond tree mirrored within it.

The sunken garden holds the sunshine like a great cup. The steep high walls shut away all sound from without. No wind, except the soft breeze of summer, finds its way within. So still, so flooded with color and perfume, that one's senses are almost intoxicated into the belief that it is not real at all, but just a marvellous vision that must presently vanish.

It takes at least a half-day to see *Benvenuto* in its entirety. An entire day is much better. But even then ones goes away a little bewildered by the endless diversities of the garden and its opulence of bloom.

W. L. Mackenzie King
1931

From William Lyon Mackenzie King's Diaries

—⚏—

*W*illiam Lyon Mackenzie King (1874–1950), Canada's *longest-serving prime minister, found great solace in his gardening and landscaping activities at Kingsmere, his country estate. For nearly fifty years, he revelled in designing this landscape that rested on the firm foundation of the Canadian Shield in Quebec's Gatineau Hills, today about a thirty-minute drive from Ottawa.*

King's country estate, the focus of his nonpolitical life, became not only a refuge and a status symbol, but also an enormous canvas for him to fill with flowers, trees, roadways, and European-inspired ruins. Over and over in his voluminous diaries, King wrote that his country activities "filled me with delight." Kingsmere was certainly a focal point for his flights of romantic imagination and his profound response to the landscape.

In this diary selection, we eavesdrop on King, who, with characteristic energy and thoroughness, is enthralled by a new landscaping challenge.

—⚏—

August 26, 1931
I planned too a balustrade for the front lawn which I have had in mind for some time—have asked for sketch & estimate on same. Something is needed to give proportion to the front of the house— an upper lawn evenly laid will be a great improvement to get the necessary earth from round about will be a real job.

August 27, 1931

I spent considerable time during the day looking over numbers of 'Country Life' & 'Houses & Gardens' to get ideas for front lawn. There is great need of centering the garden.

August 28, 1931

Cummins and his man Campbell came out to take measurements for a balustrade on the front lawn. Joan came over and the four of us worked on measurements for some time. It was amusing to see the many optical illusions as we worked on the different levels of the lawn, and tried to centre the garden from the oblique and position of the verandah. The large stone in the centre of the lawn & the elm tree were the deciding factors, next to the rose garden & its bird bath & little figure in the centre, first the place was——then it changed to——, and next to——. We took a good deal of time to guess at heights & levels—& and putting up white furniture, tape measures, pickets, etc. By two o'clock we had completed the preliminary survey. Mr. Cummins was very kind & genial in his willingness to wait etc. The design of balustrade I took from a number of Country Life.

September 2, 1931

It is a difficult business to arrange to centre a garden obliquely from a house but that has been the task. I think I have succeeded very well, but have had to trust my eyes more than follow rules, save as to preserving proportion . . . I was at last able to explain to Campbell (the turner) what was wanted in making the balustrade bars look like a vase on a stand, he sent a satisfactory turning during the afternoon.

September 5, 1931

The other delight, and it has given me a real thrill, is the first two sections of the balustrade which are now set temporarily in place and give an entirely new appearance to the lawn, the front of the house, the gardens & the grounds. They are quite lovely. I seemed to have secured just the right dimensions, the whole effect is going to be 'incomparably beautiful' at least that is the way I feel about it.

September 6, 1931

The morning sunlight was very beautiful on the new balustrade, and throughout the day with shadow & sunshine casing each other over the lawn and the forests and fields beyond the effect was too beautiful for words. The distant blue was particularly blue and I have seldom seen the view from the upper lawn more lovely. When that is completed by the balustrade, & levelled, it will give a commanding position for the whole scene which will be very fine indeed.

September 10, 1931

Cummin's man at one o'clock brought out more of the balustrade and I had all of the men shifting about the different sections to see how they would best appear. Finally I let the men go ahead with a line further down the lawn than at first planned . . . Joan & I stayed and talked on the lawn. It seemed to me the balustrade was too low.

September 11, 1931

I spent the forenoon revising the location of the balustrade, its openings etc. I came to the conclusion that it was too far into the garden, it lost the intimate touch with the house and crowded over too much towards the garden & the tree . . . notwithstanding . . . the foundation laid in part in cement, I brought it about five feet nearer the house and decided upon another plan of approach of the garden, by steps leading down from the centre . . . I feel satisfied now the right locations have been obtained, & so I had the work proceed on those lines.

September 12, 1931

Spent the forenoon with the men making final arrangements of the location of the balustrades. Oddly enough I came back in the final adjustment to just the spots I had decided upon before placing the order, the only change being holding the sided openings over towards the extreme end instead of the centre, which I was keeping undecided till I saw the effect of the balustrades in place.

September 17, 1931
The foundation of the balustrade except the top layer of stone is near completion. It has taken a very long time.

September 18, 1931
[S]tone work of the balustrade. It is having the capping put on and the effect is very good.

September 25, 1931
[H]ad a word with the painters regarding the terrace balustrade. They were finished their first coat and all put in place today. They are quite lovely and in the moonlight and the effect is too wonderful for words.

LORRIE A. DUNINGTON-GRUBB
1938

"The Artist in the Rock Garden," in *Canadian Homes and Gardens*

—⚉—

*L*orrie Alfreda Dunington-Grubb (1877–1945) wrote this piece four years after she, with husband, Howard, and seven others, had founded the Canadian Society of Landscape Architects and Town Planners. She was by this time well-known in gardening circles, having joined the new Rose Society of Ontario in 1913, spoken on rock gardens to the Toronto Horticultural Society in 1917, and having written about garden design for national periodicals since 1921.

Lorrie Dunington grew up in England, India, South Africa, and Australia; studied at the Swanley Horticultural College in England; and become "the first female landscape architect to practice her profession in England." She was lecturing to the Architectural Association in London when she met Howard Grubb.

Soon after their marriage and arrival in Toronto in 1911, she spoke on "The Modern Home and the Garden City Movement" at the annual meeting of the Ontario Horticultural Association, but her own interest in town planning gradually gave way—at least in her writing—to the reading public's greater interest in gardening.

She may have been the first female landscape architect to practise her profession in Canada. But she was not the first—or the last—to criticize inartistic rock gardens.

—⚉—

So much has been written on rock gardens that the subject seems to have been worn threadbare. Surely the very last word has been said on the disposition of the stones, the composition of the soil, and the most suitable plants for their embellishment. Apparently little remains to be added from year to year except lists of newer or rarer plants for the joy of the truly enthusiastic gardeners. But these latter, may we add, are as rare as the plants they seek. Yet when one looks around our cities at the overwhelming number of badly constructed rock gardens, one is tempted to wonder how much of what is learnedly set forth in print is ever read, much less studied, by the general public. In these hectic days people have no time to read. All they want are pictures. Yes! Show them pictures! But, alas! even these make little impression, otherwise how could such a tolerance or indeed indifference exist for what passes, by name at least, for rock gardens?

Such monstrosities, in fact, have rock gardens become, as the inevitable result of their popularity, and the supposed ease with which they can be constructed, that to embark on what the writers of the 18th Century might have described as a "critical dissertation" on such, would leave the critic utterly exhausted from overmuch condemnation. The most superficial observer, however, need not journey far to find excellent examples of what not to do. In our cities, our residential sections are crowded with them, and they are rapidly extending to the suburban and rural areas. It will suffice to mention the chief offender which, unfortunately, also happens to be the type most in evidence. This is the one whose function is to hold up a bank on the street front of the property, adjacent to and paralleling the sidewalk. The bank may be quite low or it may be five or more feet high. On a very shallow bank, flat stones or even pieces of old concrete pavement are laid flat like crazy paving, and mostly the plants are conspicuous by their absence, though occasionally a few are to be seen.

When banks are higher and steeper, small rocks or thin stones are stuck on edge in a promiscuous fashion like nuts on a fancy dessert. A "collection" of rock plants is obtained from a local merchant and planted in any available spaces. The owner of the property is seldom responsible either for the construction of the rockery or for the selection of plant material. A cheap contract price has probably been offered by a third-rate "jobber." Indeed the owner usually knows so little about gardening that he fails to be dissatisfied with his bargain even the first season. It looks all right to him. The plants put on a brave front and do their best to flower, but they play a losing game from the start. Cats, dogs and children alike are attracted by the fascinating little runways up and down the bank and long before the summer is over the plants are in sorry plight. Only the most robust will survive the first winter. The following spring the bare places are usually filled with unsuitable bedding annuals which inevitably do badly, and after that the owner gives up in disgust and says he does not think much of rock gardening. And can one blame him?

Such sidewalk banks certainly present a problem. Treated with turf they are difficult to cut and maintain and any alternative treatment is readily seized upon as a solution, but such is not found in a load or two of inferior stone scattered over harsh subsoil from cellar excavations.

The neatest and most serviceable way of dealing with front boundary banks is by retaining the soil with stone or brick walls, and to plant a low growing hedge, preferably evergreen, on top to enclose the front lawn. However, where money is a consideration, a Japanese Barberry hedge will make a good substitute. If the hedge be allowed to grow out over the top of the wall and is kept clipped flush with the front face, there will be no trouble keeping children from running along the top.

The foregoing is a description of rock gardening at its worst and is not intended to disparage or throw ridicule on a form of gardening, but merely to serve as a warning to those who know vaguely that something should be done, but who are unconscious of the desirability of a little expert advice as to how to do it. The only way to abolish these freaks is to educate the public, by means of really fine examples of executed work to realize that very considerable skill is needed to produce satisfactory results.

Fortunately, there is a small minority of real gardeners who are both discriminating and appreciative, but whose approach to the subject is much more from the standpoint of the horticulturist than that of the artist. Their chief interest is in a type of gardening which will provide ideal growing conditions for a certain group of plants and shrubs, namely those which are found in nature on mountain ranges, alpine slopes and high pastures. They proceed to imitate, on a small scale, and as faithfully as possible, the native habitats of such vegetation. They are not primarily concerned with the relation of garden to house or the part that the rock garden should play in the general garden scheme. Their interest is centred almost entirely on the growing of the plants themselves and in their rarity. In order to obtain the desired result, a suitable portion of the grounds is selected which is open to the sun and free from the drip of trees. A series of elevations and depressions is artificially created and partially covered by rock surfaces to simulate a mountainous area in miniature, water being sometimes introduced as diminutive falls, pools and lakes. Finally it is planted with alpine and sub-alpine flora, in as great a number of species as obtainable.

The first consideration being that each variety shall have the aspect and soil conditions best suitable to its individual needs, the main framework of the planting usually consists of standard varieties planted more or less haphazard, without much regard for the general effect, as seen from a distance. From then on, the owner, with a true collector's instinct, begins to develop an out-of-door horticultural museum, or in other words, an alpine herbareum. Rare plants are obtained from trade sources or by exchange with other enthusiasts and are tucked away in safe corners, many so small as almost to demand a magnifying glass to view them.

Undoubtedly the collecting urge is strongly developed in most of us. The forms it may take are legion. It can run all the way from stamps and antiques to plants. And what more utterly fascinating and absorbing an occupation can one have than plant collecting, whether it be in one's own garden or in the wilds of Turkestan? Nevertheless it is an art apart and should not be confused with landscape design. That does not mean that the two arts are necessarily antagonistic to each other but that the former should be subservient to the latter in the general garden scheme. It is not sufficient that the position chosen for the rock garden is ideal for the well-being of plants. It must also have a scenic value in the garden arrangement. The disposition of the plants should be such as to stand out from the distance in bold masses of harmonizing or contrasting colors. The forms of the flowering shrubs and evergreens should be studied for pictorial effect. Indeed, it is the painting of a picture with living pigments.

Broadly speaking its naturalistic style suggests that the rock garden should not be too closely associated with the formal lines of architecture and probably, where the grounds are sufficiently extensive to permit it, the happiest placing would be at some distance from the house and at least partially hidden from it. A meandering walk through shrubberies might lead the unsuspecting visitor to a surprise view of it in all its full glory and pageantry of bloom. Not many properties, however, are large enough for such an arrangement and something less ambitious must be attempted.

When it is necessary to place the rock garden near a building, it never looks better than when used to support and decorate a steeply falling or precipitous bank on a ravine lot. With a narrow formal terrace next the house, the rock garden with sparkling cascades and clear pools may fall away sharply beneath it, to be lost gradually in the woodland scene below. Thus, many a lovely picture can be created.

KERRY BANKS
1980

From "The Most Honourable Gardeners," in *Harrowsmith*

—ຈຈ—

*K*erry Banks is a Vancouver-based writer specializing in environmental issues. Since the 1970s, his articles have appeared frequently in numerous periodicals, including Canadian Business, Canadian Geographic, Chatelaine, City Farmer, Equinox, Harrowsmith, Maclean's, *and* Owl. *This is an excerpt from the first in his two-part series about the horticultural expertise of Chinese-Canadian home and market gardeners in the Vancouver area.*

Vancouver's quiet Chinese residential area, near its bustling commercial district, is the oldest and largest such community in Canada. The original block of this Chinatown, having narrowly escaped massive urban renewal during the 1960s, became the site of the Chinese Cultural Centre during the 1970s and, complementing that, of the Dr. Sun Yat-Sen Classical Chinese Garden, opened in 1986. This garden, based on those of scholars' residences in the city of Suzhou during the Ming dynasty (A.D. 1368–1644), is a serene and elegant tribute to the man known as the "Father of Modern China," and—as translated from two scrolls sometimes hanging in the Main Hall at the garden's entrance—to "the accomplishments of the past ages" and "the greatness of Chinese culture."

—ຈຈ—

A friend of mine once tried to interest her next door neighbour, a Chinese gardening wizard named May Wan, in planting some tomatoes in her very Oriental garden. Mrs. Wan shook her head and laughingly declined, "No. Too slow. Too slow." It is not unusual for

Vancouver's Chinese gardeners to get three complete harvests from their cabbage and mustard crops within a single growing season, with thinned seedlings finding their way onto the table within a couple of weeks of sowing.

Virtually all Chinese greens are rapid producers, easily outgrowing our traditional leafy vegetables. *Gai Choy* (Chinese mustard) is ready for harvest in only 40 days, *Bok Choy* (Chinese white cabbage) in 50, while western cabbages require at least 60 days. Like most Chinese vegetables, these are cool-weather crops, ideal for the cold frames, greenhouses and gardens of the north, and perfect for both spring and fall plantings, especially here in Vancouver, where the coastal April-to-October growing season complements vegetables that have a rapid growth rate and a hardy resistance to cool temperatures. Chinese greens planted as late as September in Vancouver still have ample time to develop before any danger of killing frost.

My next-door neighbours, the Chongs, grow *Bok Choy* and *Gai Lan* (Chinese broccoli) right through to late November. Yet even this extended season is not enough for Mr. Chong, an almost compulsive gardener who, in addition to his backyard vegetable patch, maintains the most immaculate, weed-free front yard flower garden in the neighbourhood. (My rather wild-looking front yard is a compelling challenge to Mr. Chong, who cannot resist tidying up its rim with a row of the tiny, daisy-like flowers he favours.)

Some Chinese do cultivate other vegetables in addition to their traditional favourites, but they tend to choose only those crops that conform to the requirements of fast growth and good yields. Kohlrabi, Scarlet Runner beans, green onions and Jerusalem artichokes are particular Western favourites among Vancouver's Chinese. The latter, a North American relative of the sunflower, was known by the Indians as "sun root" and grown as a staple food. The Chinese call it *Kuk Oo*, "daisy tuber," and plant it along fences and in corners of their yards where this extremely hardy perennial dependably produces large crops of edible potato-like tubers that can be dug up in winter as needed.

This horticultural tradition of selecting the most productive vegetables extends also to the Chinese growing methods. They have learned to garden in three dimensions; underground, on the ground, and in the air. Next to a short-term vegetable like a cabbage, they plant a root crop, and next to that, something like a squash which will grow skyward if supported. By making the most effective use of a planting space, they use less land, which in turn means less fertilizer, less water and less labour.

Many of Vancouver's Chinese use raised beds, a method used in China long before it was "discovered" in the west. The soil is arranged in long rows about six inches high, with a surface width of three feet, tapering down to a four-foot base. Or the raised soil may be contained within boards. Between the mounds, space is allowed for narrow, foot-wide walking paths. Once these mounds are made they are permanent and easy to work, requiring less bending and crouching than a "flat" garden does.

The raised beds also provide efficient drainage in the rainy, West Coast gardens. Even after a heavy rain, water drains from the beds, collecting in the pathways. Fertilizer can be concentrated only where it is needed. The soil never becomes compacted in the rooting area as all traffic is confined to the pathways, and while the surface of the mounds becomes richer over the years, the soil on the pathway gets poorer and harder with time, so that eventually it discourages the growth of weeds.

But sometimes even more space is required than that provided by the growing beds. The Chinese do not restrict themselves to planting in the ground, but will use any sort of container that is feasible for holding soil. I have seen cookie tins, fruit boxes, wooden crates, buckets, egg cartons and cardboard milk cartons used as moveable planters. Even discarded bathtubs are put to use, for growing the emerald-green aquatic plant, *Chee Koo* (Arrowhead). The enamel antiques are filled with a mixture of mud and water and the edible corms are then harvested from the tub. . . .

The Chinese habitually rotate their crops to minimize the chances of disease or insects returning to damage the same crops in successive years. Beans and peas are rotated to beds where past production has been poor, so that their nitrogen-fixing qualities will improve the soil. *Chang Fa* (scallions) and *Suan* (garlic) are grown throughout the garden to repel insects and moles. The Chinese also cultivate an edible variety of chrysanthemum which they call *Chung Ho* or chop suey greens. They say that its roots discourage nematodes and its flowers seem to be unattractive to unwanted flying insects.

Nancy Pollock-Ellwand
1987

"A Homestead Restored," in *The Prairie Garden, 1987*

—⚏—

*N*ancy Pollock-Ellwand is an assistant professor in the
School of Landscape Architecture at the University
of Guelph, Ontario. She has been involved in a num-
ber of research projects, including an inventory of heritage cultural
landscapes, a study of the ethics surrounding the treatment of cultural landscapes, and an exploration of connections between natural
and built elements in the landscape. She is presently examining the
new Ontario planning legislation with respect to its implications for
landscape conservation. When she wrote the Motherwell homestead
article, she was working in Winnipeg as a period landscape architect
for Parks Canada.

Some recent preservation efforts have focussed on historic buildings in their organic environments. Thus, the landscapes surrounding
these buildings are beginning to attract more attention than in previous years. Parks Canada is a leader in conservation activity at the
national level. The careful restoration of the Motherwell farm grounds
is a good example of the exacting textual, visual, and horticultural
research that Parks Canada undertakes in order to restore a Canadian heritage landscape.

—⚏—

William Richard Motherwell (1860–1943) claimed his 160-acre parcel of Saskatchewan land for $10.00 in 1882. Of that original claim
8.3 acres, which represent the core of the Homestead, were purchased
and restored by Parks Canada from 1968 to 1983. Motherwell and
his Homestead were commemorated for several reasons.

As a native of Lanark County in Eastern Ontario, Motherwell was typical of a significant western migration of people in the 1880s who came from overpopulated rural areas in Central Canada to seek their fortune in the promising frontier of the West. Motherwell, however, not only succeeded in establishing a prosperous farming operation but went on to distinguish himself in Canadian politics. He became known as the "Grand Old Man of Canadian Agriculture" after many years of service as a community leader, elected official, and agricultural minister in both provincial and federal governments.

In addition to Motherwell's association, the Homestead was obtained and restored because it exemplifies the most current scientific methods advocated by government agencies and agricultural researchers of the period. The landscape stands as a model of the principles taught to farmers at the beginning of the 20th century in order to succeed in conditions particular to the prairies.

The 1983 opening of Parks Canada's Motherwell Homestead National Historic Park in southwestern Saskatchewan (100 km east of Regina) marked a significant development in the Canadian restoration movement: as much importance was placed on the restoration of the landscape component of this historic property as on its structures. Parks Canada recognizes that the historic landscape is just as effective a means of interpreting the story of this man and his times as are the site's historic buildings.

The restoration of the landscape at Motherwell Homestead was an interdisciplinary effort comb[in]ing the talents of historians, archaeologists, curators, landscape contractors, site staff and landscape architects. During this four-year undertaking, energies were devoted to all phases of restoration: research, design, and implementation. Attention was turned to all aspects of the landscape including the gardens, shelterbelts, regrading, resodding and seeding, fence, trellis and hotbed reconstruction, as well as to the construction of newer facilities to accommodate Park visitors (i.e. parking lot and pathways).

It was, however, the establishment of the plant material—the shelterbelts and gardens—which posed the most challenging restoration problems and it was in creating this "vegetative" framework that the most money and time were devoted over the years.

Originating from the smaller-scale and more verdant landscape of central Canada, Motherwell brought a sensibility for this landscape image to his new Prairie home, as did many of his fellow homesteaders. A common thread is still evident today as one travels the concession roads of southern Saskatchewan. Those early settlers tried to recreate the ambiance of the homes they left behind. A consistent expression is found in the region's tinroofed architecture; rows of shelterbelt trees planted to lessen the effects of prairie winds; excavated ponds (known locally as "dugouts") built in an attempt to provide a reliable source of water; cleared, cultivated, and fenced land; and experimentation with familiar plants which could survive the shorter growing season of the Plains.

Motherwell, however, went beyond this and created an even more sophisticated development with his prairie claim. Giving over a sizable portion of his property to "unproductive" uses like ornamental gardens and a lawn tennis court, Motherwell was projecting his success as a farmer and prominent politician. The restoration of this historic site has once again brought Motherwell's story alive.

Parks Canada purchased the property from the Motherwell family in 1966 but it wasn't until 1980 that restorative action for the landscape was actually taken. The task was made more difficult as the result of an unmonitored "clean up" of the site in 1970 in which much of the original and unrecorded plant material was removed. This situation was further complicated when new trees were planted without respect to historic species or location.

The first and largest challenge in the restoration of the Homestead was to reconstruct the planting configuration. Without original trees to refer to, three other sources proved most helpful. Firstly, a 1971 survey plan compiled by John Stewart which based identification on remaining stumps, gave information concerning species, location, and diameter, (useful in the determination of age). Secondly, results from archaeological root sampling helped confirm some species identification missed by the Stewart survey. Microscopic analysis of root slices helped to determine the unknown species. Finally, a plethora of historic photographs was found to be most useful in discovering the c. 1912 plant listing and locations.

After reconstructing the shelterbelt plan, a second controversial removal of the incorrect vegetation had to take place. The following growing season, new seedlings were obtained from the same source as Motherwell used: the Indian Head Experimental Farm.

Predominantly Manitoba Maple (*Acer negundo*) shelterbelts surround the property. Internal rows of Russian poplar, acuteleaf willow, chokecherry (*Prunus virginiana*) and cottonwood (*Populus*) with ornamental caragana, White spruce (*Picea glauca*), and American elm (*Ulmus americana*) serve to divide the Homestead into four quadrants. Segregating different Homestead functions into various quadrants (residential, food growing, water supply, and workyard) was recommended practice of the time.

Historic treelines were reestablished in the original locations with the same four-foot spacing that had been advocated by agricultural authorities at the turn of the century. Even though prairie horticulturists are now recommending eight-foot spacings as the optimum for tree belt plantings, the historical spacings were used. Parks Canada decided to use the historical spacing for the sake of authenticity even though the closer spacing will necessitate a more intensive maintenance and tree replacement program.

All "period" trees needed for the replanting—except the Russian poplar—were readily available. Fortunately, the Russian poplar could be obtained from a "library" of older species at the Indian Head Experimental Farm arboretum. Cuttings were taken for propagation of some 200 Russian poplar seedlings which will be planted on-site when mature enough.

Numerous gardens sited all around the Homestead served a variety of purposes from food production to fodder and decoration. There is no doubt that a vegetable garden was planted as soon as possible by Motherwell as a vital source of food. But the ornamental areas did not begin to appear until 1907, when Motherwell evidently had more available capital because of his appointment to the Saskatchewan Commission of Agriculture.

Motherwell papers, which included invoices from seed companies and correspondence with western-based agricultural agencies, proved a valuable resource in reconstructing the gardens. Motherwell's letters to other farmers concerning their experimentation with plants for productivity and hardiness in prairie conditions proved most helpful.

Much information was derived from plant identification in historic photographs as well as from the review of nursery catalogues of that period (e.g. Patmore Nurseries, Brandon, Manitoba; and Steele Briggs Seed Company, Toronto). In addition, government research bulletins and agricultural journal articles of the period proved excellent sources, as did personal reminiscences of family and former employees.

As a result of this research, a list of possible plants for the vegetable and ornamental gardens was drawn up and distributed to seed and nursery suppliers throughout Canada and the United States, as well as in a few places in England. Consequently, 60% of the gardens were planted with vegetables, flowers, fruit, and ornamental shrubs typical of Motherwell's time. Growing contacts within the heritage plant suppliers' world will ensure the increasing authenticity of the gardens from year to year.

A more complete and truer history can be told today to visitors of the Motherwell Homestead because of Parks Canada's fulfillment of its commitment to full landscape restoration. This renewed prairie farm landscape provides not only a compatible setting for the restored barn, house and outbuildings, but more importantly, it stands independently as a living artifact of a man's life and times.

DES KENNEDY
1994

From "Planning," in *Crazy About Gardening*

—⚶—

or a man who, once he left his childhood home, thought he had escaped gardening forever, Des Kennedy writes zestfully about the prodigal's return. For twenty-four years, he has been gardening and writing on an island in the Georgia Strait off the coast of British Columbia. In addition to gardening, he has written on environmental issues and rural living for many magazines and newspapers, such as Harrowsmith, Nature Canada, *and* The Globe and Mail.

His humorous, yet thoughtful, writings are well within the literary tradition of mad, keen garden writers who are perfectly aware that they live in a precarious world at the capricious mercy of an early frost or an overly exuberant wind. But these writers want to share the joys, the sorrows, the disasters and successes of the gardening life with equally afflicted humans. Kennedy does this with a charming wit and verbal flair based on a solid foundation of gardening experience.

In this selection, he touches on a familiar theme in Canadian garden writing: the tendency of nature to have its way in our gardens — often with happy results that we are all too pleased to take credit for, especially in front of garden visitors.

—⚶—

I was meandering around the garden one late July morning not long after sunrise. For several weeks the weather had been scorching hot and the earth seemed almost seared. Under my bare feet the pathway stones felt warm and dusty dry. A few melancholy delphiniums hung on still; the monkshood looked to be having a dark night of the soul;

chronic fatigue syndrome seemed to grip the remaining old roses. I paused at the bottom of a flight of flagstone steps. Near the top of this wide stairway a cluster of white muskmallows was blooming brilliantly, lit up like candles by a slanting shaft of sunlight. On the next level down, emerging from gaps between the flagstones, grew a crew-cut cluster of feverfew, its compact, lime-yellow leaves and single white daisy-like flowers a vision of freshness and vitality. Another step down, a white and yellow splash of ox-eye daisies completed the setting. All three of them were volunteers, opportunistic self-seeders happy to adapt to Spartan conditions. All are considered coarse and unrefined, meadow weeds really, even though feverfew was once a particular favourite in Victorian gardens. Nobody had planned their appearance here on the steps. Nowhere was this little nomadic trio delineated in a planting scheme on graph paper. There had been no prior discussion about the aesthetic of their asymmetrical triangle, reflecting from the art of Japanese flower arranging the trinity of earth, humans, and heaven. And yet here they were, elegantly descending the stone steps, forming a perfect small arrangement of fresh green foliage and cool, demure whiteness of bloom.

It's a sobering realization that a fair bit of what passes for clever planning at our place is more the result of the lunchbucket work of dependable volunteers and happy accidents. In spring more than a few of our self-celebrated plantings are rescued from dull contrivance and made brilliant by the spreading foam of clear blue forget-me-nots, their countless tiny yellow-eyed flowers brushing the garden with a hazy, lovely wash of blue. Or there will be single incidents, such as last spring when three spears of a pure white volunteer foxglove perfectly intersected the white flowered dome of a 'Mme. Hardy' rose. No designer could have done it better.

In June, when delphiniums and larkspur lift their flowering towers together, massed common foxgloves, volunteers all, stand boldly erect in the background, their blooming spires well over two metres tall, heavy with pendulous flowers—creamy whites and purples, pinks and mauves freckled with magical small runes. They are a perfect blue-collar counterpart to the aristocratic refinements of delphiniums. Together they raise their colourful arms skywards in a massed egalitarian choir of praise.

In the full sun of summer, volunteer poppies pop up all over the place, equally indifferent to soil conditions, weather, and whatever clever planting schemes we may have envisaged. Iceland, Shirley, and opium poppies sow themselves in brave little colonies and wave their brilliant pastel papery flowers like the multicoloured flags of assembled nations.

At our place there's no happier naturalizer than the California poppy. A perennial that behaves like an annual in our climate, it sows itself with astounding profligacy. By late summer they're everywhere, covering dry banks and awkward corners with their ferny blue-green foliage and masses of satiny flowers, coloured from pale yellow to rich custard gold. You can't get much closer to paradise than to walk through whole meadows of these blooming beauties along the sea cliffs of Oregon and northern California, with the Pacific surf thundering far below.

The magic of the gardens I like best seems a combination of happy accidents, lusty volunteers, and the bold experiments of adventuresome gardeners. There's an easy blowziness, a natural nonchalance about these places. The plants seem clustered together for their own enjoyment, in combinations that flatter each plant, its immediate neighbours and the garden as a whole. The casual correctness of these magic places is, of course, illusory. Over time they've no doubt seen more trial and error than a circuit court. Their gardeners are themselves strange hybrids: part artists, part technicians, part graduates of the "wait and see" school of landscape design. When something doesn't work, out it goes and in goes something else. And when it does work, when everything falls into place and the best-laid plans come to fruition with a carefree precision, an impeccable grace and correctness, then the gardener stands easy for a moment and all's right with the world.

GARDENING

IN PUBLIC

—᠁—

EDITOR OF
The [Colonial] Pearl
1839

From "The Improvement of Halifax," in
The [Colonial] Pearl

—⚏—

*T*he voice of the newspaper editor was a loud one at times
in Canadian landscape history. Editors often used their
positions of influence to bring improvement ideas to the
public. Although the editor of The Pearl did not know it at the time,
his call for the general improvement of Halifax's streets was one of
the early examples of what would later be called the City Beautiful
movement. As well, his desire to green up the city centre with a landscaped public square predated the city-park movement that would
sweep North America later in the century.

The city square is as old as settlement itself. Often it began as a
dirt- or grass-covered area where the military practised drills or assembled for speeches and other ceremonies. But the urge to landscape
these spaces for public use was a phenomenon of the nineteenth century. This urge, fostered by nineteenth- and early twentieth-century
city improvers, was often unabashedly connected to the desire to
impose the splendours of European and American city design on our
Canadian soil.

—⚏—

One matter, in the ornamental way, should be particularly remembered, this is the improvement of the much neglected "Parade." Here
is a spot, in a central situation, which affords excellent opportunity
for something similar to the squares of embellished cities everywhere.
Those who have visited London or Paris, or continental cities, know

what delightful places these openings form;—the regular lines of good mansions,—the fine level spaces, so pleasing to the eye, after being pent up in crowded streets,—the shrubs, and trim walks, and flowers which adorn the centres, and which form most agreeable retreats for the nursery maids and children of the surrounding houses. Much need not be attempted for the Parade, and yet much might be effected,—and the area might be preserved to the inhabitants, instead of being scrapped away as some of the original space has been. Let a spacious oval grass plot occupy its centre, relieved by some of our native, beautiful shrubs; let a gravel walk bound this; let each of the angles of the area be occupied by a group of evergreen trees, the whole speckled by some of the hardier flowers, and surrounded by a neat, substantial fence. Thus, at a small expense an improvement could be effected, creditable to the town, pleasing to all who looked on it,—and particularly embellishing to the houses in the vicinity, which would soon assume a much more respectable appearance, and rise in value. One boundary of this area, would be the College front,—the other, the road in front of St. Paul's, removing the Engine-house tresspass,—the third and fourth, the Post office, and upper side, lines, greatly improved,—and thus "Parade Square" would be an ornament to Halifax.—Suppose this done, and the splendid fortifications at Fort George completed, where could a more romantic and picturesque street-view be found, than that seen from the foot of George's street; the spacious and fashionable and busy thoroughfares, the expanse and verdure of the Parade,—the street beyond, rising the hill,—and above all, the green glacis of the fort, the old Town Clock in its new position, the battlements and the flag staffs. Already, the soldiers pacing along the battlements just mentioned, dwindled to pigmies by distance yet distinctly traced against the sky, and looking down from their quiet post on the bustle of the town, form part of a very picturesque sketch;—what the view will be when the fortification works are completed; and the Parade contributes its foliage, may be imagined.

EDITOR OF *The Canada Farmer*
1868

"Railway Gardens," in *The Canada Farmer*

—⚉—

*W*hen this editorial was written in the mid-1800s—probably by W. F. Clarke—the era of railway gardening in Canada was just picking up steam. A British-inspired import, railway gardens were few until the Canadian Pacific Railway began corporate gardening on a large scale, around 1900. By the 1920s, the company-supported gardens dotted the nation along nearly 26,000 kilometres of track.

These gardens were not maintained solely for beautification. The 1868 editorial touches on what was later commonly acknowledged: that railway gardens had a public role to play in encouraging beautification of farm and town. Indeed, one of the reasons for the CPR's enthusiastic support of their railway gardening program was the fever of city beautification that was sweeping eastern Canada at the turn of the century.

However, the company also wished to "fill up" the Canadian west and to create revenue from passenger and freight traffic. Railway gardens advertised prairie fertility, and demonstrated that the west was a "civilized" place to live.

By the 1930s, many of Canada's railway companies had gardens at their major stations, a few horticulturists or landscape architects on staff, and programs firmly in place to supply seeds and plants to station masters.

Unfortunately, due to decreasing revenues and the need, in many cases, for large parking lots to accommodate the growing number of passengers' cars, the railway garden began to die out by the late 1950s. Hardly any can be found today.

—⚉—

The Grand Trunk Railway Station Master at Guelph, G. A. Oxnard, Esq., has set an example the present spring which we should like to see imitated all along that and the other lines of railway in the Dominion of Canada, having laid out and tastefully planted, at his own expense, a beautiful little garden adjacent to the Passenger Depôt. It is astonishing what a change this has made in the whole contour and influence of the place. Whereas before the scene had only an air of business and was purely utilitarian in all its belongings and surrounding, there is now an air of refinement and an appearance of beauty and elegance, whose influence is felt by all observers. The stone station-house and brown sheds have assumed a look of enhanced respectability, being affected by the garden very much as a man is, who already dressed in a good, substantial suit, gives himself the finishing touch by putting on a good hat and a nicely fitting pair of boots. Passengers who are waiting for belated trains beguile the weary moments by admiring the shrubs and flowers, and travellers beginning or pursuing a journey, get a glimpse of rural loveliness which reminds them of home. The town artisan beholds with pleasure the little enclosure, and thinks how easy it would be to get up such a scene of beauty in front of his own cottage door. Giles from the country, where grass and trees are abundant, reflects how readily he could make a pleasure garden on a far larger scale, and beat the little railway parterre hollow by a spacious lawn, an extensive shrubbery and spreading flower-beds on his own farm. Wives and daughters besiege husbands and fathers for leave and help to do something equally pretty where they live. The little railway garden is thus not only a source of pleasure, but an educator. Railroads have educated us into promptitude, punctuality, and push; they have exerted mighty moulding influences on business; it is possible for them to give that dull scholar, the public, some lessons in aesthetics and be an educator in the direction of rural improvement and home adornment. The question, will it pay? by which all railroad affairs are mainly settled, may, we think, be proved to be entitled to receive an affirmative answer without resorting to any very far-fetched argument. If people catch the contagion of taste and refinement, they will build better houses, import articles of adornment, freight shade, ornamental, and fruit trees, and travel more under the influence of a desire to see the far-off loveliness of nature and art.

If these improvements are made, it must be, we understand, at the cost of the station-masters. Being subject at all times to promotion and removal, the encouragement to engage in this sort of thing is not great. Might not Railway Companies apply a stimulus in some way, either by affording inducements and facilities in this direction, or by giving a prize annually for the best laid-out and neatest-kept garden along their lines? At water stations it would be easy for companies to apply what would be the most striking feature in a railway garden, namely, a fountain. This could be fed from the tank and the flow carried back to the well or reservoir, so that there would only be the pumping to provide for—a comparatively small item.

Railway gardens are very common in England. Some of them are extremely pretty, and fix themselves in the recollection of the transient traveller. We have very distinct and pleasant memories of some we saw during a tour in England nearly seven years ago. Railway gardens are also becoming numerous in the United States. There are some very handsome ones in the vicinity of New York. On the line of the Erie Railroad, also on the Lake Shore Railroad between Cleveland, Ohio, and Erie, Pennsylvania, there are many tasteful depôts. An American exchange, referring to this subject, but more especially urging a better style of depôt building, remarks: "It is not to be supposed that all railroads can immediately rush into such landscape and architectural exercises; for it is a prime principle with them to make everything pay. But we submit whether pretty depôts, surrounded by nice lawns and gardens, do not go far toward making a road popular; and if popular, of course it pays."

There are very few railway gardens in Canada, but we hope the station-masters may have a run of horticultural fever, and then there will soon be more. Kingston and Brampton are the only places on the line of the Grand Trunk Railway where we remember to have noticed gardens. The Great Western Railway at Hamilton is beautifully ornamented in this way, and some time ago there was a very pretty little garden at Harrisburg, but the station-master during whose reign it flourished seems to have had a Gothic successor, who officiates

"Near yonder spot, where once the garden smiled.
And still where many a garden flower grows wild."

We hope more attention will be given to this matter by railway
people.

H. A. ENGELHARDT
1872

From "Graveyards and Cemeteries," in *The Beauties of
Nature Combined with Art*

—◊—

*H*einrich *Adolph Engelhardt (1830–1897) was born in
Mühlhausen (Germany) and studied civil engineer-
ing in Berlin. After military service, he immigrated to
Baltimore in 1851, and became a landscape gardener working—it
was said later—on important cemeteries in Richmond, Virginia, and
Raleigh, North Carolina.*

*He arrived in Ontario around 1870. He must have had either good
recommendations or an impressive portfolio, for he soon obtained
work from the Ontario Department of Public Works, designing and
supervising construction of the grounds of two large institutions
then under construction at Belleville and Brantford, and drawing up
a plan to improve the grounds of the aging legislative assembly building in Toronto. Still during the early 1870s, he designed Belleville
Cemetery, Union Cemetery in Port Hope, and Mount Pleasant Cemetery in Toronto; and settled in Toronto, where he superintended the
development of the latter through 1888.*

*His 174-page book was the first on landscape design published
in Canada. "I have the pleasure to send you one of my littel works,"
he wrote in one complimentary copy. "[I]t is short (I will not say
sweet) but to the point. It will . . . set you to thinking in progressing
with the work at the Cemetery."*

—◊—

It is most earnestly to be desired that every city, town, and village,
may have, at no distant day, *one* cemetery, where all, of whatever
creed or denomination, may rest side by side. The narrow limits

around our churches and chapels must no longer be used as burial grounds, and should at once be made pleasant for the worshiping assembly, and suitable places for burial be secured beyond the limits of town or city.

The site for a cemetery should be well chosen, at some distance from the turmoil and bustle of active life. Yet should be always easy of access. If the site chosen possesses natural advantages, such as hills and dales, groves and creeks, so much the better, but the improvements should agree and conform to the natural features of the place.

The main roads should be laid out with due regard to turning, and not too many of them. The smaller paths should be from North to South, and the graves from East to West.

The custom of enclosing the graves is very awkward, and should not be encouraged, but monuments of notable character should have an enclosure. Too many fences and enclosures will cause a general confusion, and greatly mar the harmonious appearance of a cemetery, the character of which should be unique; cemeteries should also be well provided with seats and shade trees, characteristic and emblematic.

The buildings, such as chapels and vaults, should be of appropriate design, not gloomy, but tasteful and modest. The vaults may be either below or above the ground, but in either case they must be built in a proper and peculiar style, according to the entire arrangement of the cemetery.

If, for instance, the cemetery be surrounded by a wall, then ornamental monuments and vaults, erected, either of brick or stone, and facing inside will produce an agreeable effect. Slabs of marble or stone may be inserted in them as well as other emblems, so also should the gates or the whole entrance be of such a structure as to be ornamental to the place.

The soil should be of a dry nature, such as clay, and not rocky. The graves ought to be set neatly in short turf, or flowers of white or blue, and in every respect be chaste and plain.

AGNES SCOTT
1900

From "Notes by the Marchioness," in the
Ottawa Daily Free Press

—⚹—

The Marchioness was the pseudonym of Agnes Scott (who died sometime in the early 1930s), a society reporter and member of an influential Ottawa family who had entrée into all levels of Ottawa society, from gatherings of the business elite to government soirées and to Rideau Hall.

In her often witty and occasionally sardonic columns for Saturday Night *and the* Ottawa Daily Free Press *(written at a time when journalism was finally opening up to women), Scott reported on the capital city's most important social events, including garden parties.*

Garden parties have been a common social event on Canadian lawns from the mid-1800s to the present day. Some were held for purely social reasons, others for fund raising for charitable causes, and still others for political vote gathering. During such occasions, more than the garden was on view. The calibre of the guests, what they wore, and who was invited and who was not were all marks on the social yardstick against which to measure one's worth. The annual Rideau Hall garden party was one of the most important social events in the capital—made all the more prestigious, up to the 1940s, by the presence of royalty.

—⚹—

Fawn was the favorite last Saturday afternoon at the garden party at government house; fawn in cloth, in crepon, in mousseline and in silk. It was not exactly fawn either, but a cross between grey and that shade of tan formerly known to fame as café au lait. It is a becoming color and combines nicely with pink, blue or mauve. Many of these materials in fawn had a "panne" finish, which is quite the most fashionable of finishes, and all the gowns—that is nearly all the gowns—were handsome ones.

Owing to the coolness of the afternoon many women had sufficient strength of mind to withstand the fascinations of muslins and linens, which over-worked dressmakers had managed to send home just in time, and to appear at the garden party attired in cloth gowns of tailor make. There were a number of pretty diaphanous summer creations to be seen, but the woman in the cloth gown looked and felt more comfortable than her sister in muslin. Her Excellency the Countess of Minto wore fawn cloth with some white silk and lace in the front of the bodice, in which a cluster of pink roses was fastened. There was a becoming touch of blue in her toque and over her shoulders a very lovely boa of soft grey feathers. Their Excellencies received in the anteroom, from which the guests passed down to the garden. Exquisite pink roses, suggestive of New York, were massed at one side of this room; in jars on the refreshment table of the tea room there were many more of the same roses. The racquet court, with its red and white walls, was the tea room proper, but refreshments were also served in a couple of marquees at the upper end of the garden, where a green hill stands out from a circle of fir trees. The Guards band was stationed on the lawn below the main terrace; the music they played during the afternoon was rousingly patriotic, and thoroughly in keeping with the sentiments of those present. In honor of Mafeking, flags were everywhere flying gaily to the breeze. Everybody spoke of Mafeking and of Colonel Baden-Powell, the hero of Mafeking. It seemed somehow as if this garden party had happened on just the right day, and was a festivity intended specially to celebrate the good news. The flowers certainly did their best to make it a brilliant affair. They came out in all their glory, reds and yellows predominating in the lovely parture of tulips that few people at the party missed seeing. Sir Wilfrid and Lady Laurier were among the distinguished people present. Lady Laurier wore a becoming gown of grey silk, with embroidery appliqued on the skirt, some white in the bodice and a grey hat.

D. P. PENHALLOW
1907

From "Shade Trees for Our Cities," in *The Canadian
Horticulturist*

—◊◊—

*D*avid Pearce Penhallow (1854–1910), a distinguished authority on Canada's paleobotany, was appointed, in 1883,
professor of botany at McGill University in Montreal. He
held this post until his death at sea while on a voyage to England.

Penhallow, a fellow of the Royal Society of Canada, contributed
many articles in various journals on botanical and horticultural topics,
and published both Plant Life and The Botanical Collector's Guide in
1891. He also published an extensive overview of the history of
Canadian botany from the time of the settlements in New France
through the late 1890s.

In this article, although the botanist does peek through, Penhallow
is speaking as one of the City Beautiful "evangelists" who were a vocal
part of the Canadian scene from the turn of the century until World
War I.

By the late 1800s, planting trees had become a popular approach
to greening up bare streets. Winnipeg, for example, began a munici-
pal program of street tree planting in 1896, and by 1908, its Board
of Works announced that it had planted 20,000 trees along 138 kilometres of the city's streets and boulevards.

—◊◊—

The question of shade trees for our cities and towns, is a many-sided
one, which has engaged the most careful consideration from a very
early period in our history. Shade trees, as well as properly kept
shrubs and flower beds, exert a powerful reflex influence upon those
who are habitually associated with them in their daily lives. From

this point of view it is therefore not difficult to determine that the extent to which trees are cultivated, and *the intelligence expended in properly caring for them*, may be safely adopted as an index of the relative progressiveness, culture and civilization of a town.

In discussing the relation of shade trees to purposes of street ornamentation, there are three factors of leading importance which should be taken into consideration: Their productive value; their esthetic value; and their educational value. . . .

It may reasonably be contended from these statements, that a city which is abundantly supplied with shade trees will, in general, be distinguished by the greater purity and more bracing quality of its atmosphere, and it would seem to me that the relations thus developed, are too often overlooked or even ignored in considering the part which trees play in urban life.

There is another respect in which trees manifest their protective influence, as found in the extent to which they minimize the effects of excessive heat. Any one passing from a narrow and crowded business street devoid of trees, to a residential street provided with shade trees, becomes sensible of a gratifying difference in temperature. This difference is not altogether dependent upon the relative height and the crowded character of the buildings, though it is a large factor; but it is due, in the main, to the influence of the trees themselves. The trees not only give the pedestrian direct protection from the rays of the sun, but they so shield the pavements and buildings as to prevent the absorption and reflection of heat, affording to the buildings in particular, such a degree of protection as to give to the inhabitants a sense of refreshing comfort.

Of the esthetic and educational value of trees, much might be said, but it may be sufficient to point out that to bring up children habituated to association with those forms of vegetation which typify great beauty and grace of form; which represent the embodiment of plastic strength and great virility, is to insensibly shape their moral natures in such ways as to develop character and self-reliance, as well as an appreciation of those more gentle graces which contribute so largely to the characteristic qualities of the cultured and refined. Nor can we doubt that an abundance of well-cared-for shade trees operate as an attraction to visitors and as an actual incentive to settlement.

The naturally fine shade trees of Montreal constitute one of the features most commented upon by strangers, and it is the same feature which lends such charm to Toronto, New Haven, Washington, Buffalo, Detroit, and many other cities.

Turning our attention briefly to more practical considerations, it is obvious that it is the part of a wise civic policy to see to it that a form of property which possesses so many potentialities for good; which possesses so large a measure of intrinsic value; which constantly enhances in value with increasing age through a long period of time; and which also involves a considerable initial expenditure, should be most carefully protected, not only against the far too numerous enemies which Nature herself has provided, but against man himself as the very worst of all the foes with which shade trees must contend. . . .

Since the introduction of telegraph, telephone and electric lighting wires throughout all the thoroughfares of our cities, shade trees have ceased to have any recognized status. A tree which has developed a fine form through the growth of half a century is suddenly deprived of its top or other essential parts and left a maimed and shattered wreck whose mutilated stumps of former members reach up their ragged ends as if in mute appeal for vengeance upon the vandals who have been guilty of such an outrage. The case is somewhat aggravated when an enterprising citizen plants a fine tree, perhaps at considerable expense, and watches with fondest care its gradual development into an object of beauty and utility. Some day he arrives home from his office to find only a wreck of that in which he has taken so much justifiable pride and pleasure. Trees which have been dealt with in such a manner, should be removed at once, for they can never become what Nature designed them to be, and their presence cannot fail to exert precisely the opposite effect to that for which they were intended, because of the false standards which they illustrate.

C. ERNEST WOOLVERTON
1909

"The Value of Parks," in *The Welland Telegraph*

—⚍—

*C*harles Ernest Woolverton (1879–1934), the son of Linus
and Sarah Woolverton, was born in Grimsby, in the
Niagara Peninsula of Ontario. In 1898, he entered the
three-year horticulture program at the Ontario Agriculture College,
where he studied landscape gardening.

Woolverton was likely Canada's first native-born landscape architect, for soon after graduating from OAC in 1901, he began advertis-
ing his Grimsby-based practice. Indeed, although Woolverton was
never as successful as Frederick G. Todd of Montreal, the two were
the pioneer practitioners of landscape architecture in Canada in the
first decade of the twentieth century.

Woolverton gained experience in large-scale design during
1907–09, when he worked for Warren H. Manning, a Boston landscape architect whose office was busy at the time with projects in
Boston; Philadelphia and Wilkes-Barre, Pennsylvania; and Munising,
Michigan.

When Woolverton returned home, he tried to convince officials
in several Ontario cities, including Welland, that he could assist them
with parks planning, but without success. Finally, about 1929, he
received a commission to design Elgin and Russell Street parks in
Sarnia. His other known landscapes were all residential.

—⚍—

Some doubtful one may ask right here, "What have parks to do with
the residential district? What have they to do with the development
of our city, we want manufacturers and we don't care about parks?"
Now, look at here, my friend, let us lay aside all sentimental reason

why parks are of value to a city or a town, and at once proceed on a business basis. For example, there is a strip of land [in Welland, Ontario] lying between the canal and the river which, I am informed, is owned by the Government and leased by one or two gentlemen and used for horse-back riding. All well and good. But let us suppose this strip could be leased by the town and laid out with a wide bridal [sic] path running down the centre and footpaths along the side divided from the bridle path by masses of attractive shrubbery and trees and planted so as to form long sheets of color in their flowering season in place of the dismal outlook which now presents itself from the southern side of the river. What effect would this have on the land adjoining it and across the river? Would it not immediately jump in value, and would not your factory owners and men of means fight for the ownership of a lot facing such an attractive view? This would mean then an increase in the taxable value of the adjoining land and would be borne by those willing to pay for it as they feel that the influence of that beauty is sufficiently beneficial to make the investment good.

I know of a great many cities in the United States that spend hundreds of thousands of dollars on the improvement of waste areas. Why? Because it is of some sentimental value to the people? O, dear, no, but because it pays. So in a smaller way may Welland improve her residential districts by improving the surrounding waste land.

This of course, should be done in a systematic way, for it will not prove in the least satisfactory if it is gone at by a haphazard method. First, a board of Park Commissioners should be selected and a certain annual appropriation be set aside for their use. The commission should have some definite and comprehensive scheme of improvements before them and adhere closely to that scheme, for nothing will cost the city more and lead to a more intricate mix of affairs than the continual changing of plans by the different men annually in power.

CECIL M. SIMPSON
1915

"A Prince Edward Island Garden," in "The Beaver Circle,"
in *The Farmer's Advocate*

—◊—

*T*he school garden movement was especially active from
the late 1890s up into the 1930s. Influenced by American
and European theory and practice, the Canadian school
garden was promoted for two reasons: to keep country children on the
farm and to "reconnect" urban children to the natural world. As well,
both groups, according to contemporary education theory, would benefit from having a concrete basis for the three Rs. That is, math could
be learned by measuring a garden plot, English grammar from writing
about the gardens, and so on.

The movement was vigorously championed by the graduates and
faculty at the Ontario Agricultural College (now the University of
Guelph). The OAC was an extremely influential institution up into
the 1930s.

School gardens were also supported by local horticultural societies, which included such gardens as part of the City Beautiful movement. Some urban school gardens were cultivated on vacant lots.

As well, provincial education departments issued teaching bulletins to help teachers, and provided plant materials, seeds, and small
grants for other supplies. In many provinces, the school garden was
a standard curriculum item.

Some schoolchildren, such as Cecil Simpson of Bayview River,
Prince Edward Island, cultivated their school gardens at home.

—◊—

Dear Puck and Beavers,—As I was successful last year in winning the Garden Competition I felt like trying again, but was almost discouraged with the late, cold spring and also the condition of the ground.

As my garden had been ploughed and harrowed and kept well weeded last year, all the work necessary was done with a garden fork and a rake. In winter it is used for a sheep pen so needed no manure, only a little nitrate which I sprinkled around the plants. The first work was to clean up the ground as it had been littered up by the sheep in winter.

The first week in June I dug and raked it and then made it into beds. All of the plants which would transplant had been started in a hot bed and the rest were sown in the beds. Though it was so late in the season, the ground was still cold and damp and the plants did not grow much until the warm weather struck, which was in the latter part of August. My garden was about equally divided between vegetables and flowers. On the west end were the sunflowers, sheltering the sweet peas in front of these were dahlias and chrysanthemums. These were my tallest flowers. From these a walk divided the garden into two parts, the walk was bordered on one side by flowers and on the other by vegetables.

For vegetables I selected early turnips, beets, beans, radish, carrots, cucumbers and tomatoes. The flowers were in two long beds and consisted of nasturtiums, five varieties of poppies "all colors," asters mixed colors; phlox, stock, schizanthus, gaillardia, candytuft, balsam, pansies, and pompon dahlias, which was quite a variety of flowers.

The garden afforded us all a great deal of pleasure, and was visited by many of our friends who all carried away bouquets. The tables of our Red Cross picnic, at which $300 was realized, were decorated with flowers from it, and also the church on Rally Day.

Accompanying the letter is a photo of myself and garden, which was taken September 2nd. The work was all done by myself.

HENRIETTA WOOD
1917

"My Garden—1917: A Dream," in *Agricultural Gazette
of Canada*

—⚊—

*H*enrietta Wood won first prize in the vacant lot
gardening poetry contest of 1917. The contest was
inaugurated by the energetic W. T. Macoun, the
dominion horticulturist of the experimental farms system, to support
the vacant-lot campaign that year. When Wood was not gardening,
she was earning a living as a stenographer.

In Canadian cities and towns, the promotion of gardening on
vacant lots—which were often weed- and rubbish-filled eyesores—
began around 1910. At first, it had more to do with charity than
beautification. Vacant-lot gardens were promoted as a way the poor
could help themselves by growing their own food. But as the City
Beautiful movement gathered strength, vacant lot gardens began to
be sheltered under its broadening umbrella as yet another way to
beautify built-up areas.

By 1916, vacant-lot gardening associations, filled with eager
members from every class of society, were active across Canada.
Many organizations charged their members a small fee to cover rental
costs plus, in some places, ploughing, fertilizing, and a few seeds.

As the effects of World War I began to be felt, the vacant-lot garden movement was transformed once again—this time into "greater
production campaigns" urging gardeners of all kinds to raise vegetables for the war effort. In the selection after this one, Dorothy Perkins
describes one of these "greater production" gardens.

—⚊—

Rain-softened and sun-warmed, it stretches fair
Prepared to yield a wealth of all good things.
In neat, well-ordered rows the seedlings pierce
The rich brown mould, and seek the sunlight.
Swift fly the days, and soon with eager hands
I cull the radish, ruddy tinted globe
Of pungent crispness; and green-gold lettuce;
And that scented darling of the garden,
The spring onion.

The happy days glide on.
Behold my Vacant Lot, vacant no more.
Here grow my cabbages, dew-pearled at dawn.
There stands my corn, beplumed like knight of old.
Look on my cauliflowers, white as snow;
Potatoes, soon to yield a khaki host
To rout the hordes of hunger; and carrots,
Beets and parsnips, and many more fair growths
Depicted in the catalogues. All these
Adorn my garden.

Hark, the alarm sounds! The vision fades.
'Tis morn; 'tis March. Deep lies the snow upon
The unbroken sod, hiding the couch-grass,
Snake-like roots and many a weedy foe.
A thousand million tiny enemies,—
Worm, weevil, beetle, bug,—in ambush lie.
To win my harvest I must surely bear
A thousand aches in my poor stooping back,
And cramps in bending limbs, and sun-skinned nose,
And countless freckles on my now fair arms.
O say, thou preacher of domestic thrift,
Dost think that I can conquer?

DOROTHY PERKINS
1918

From "The Kitchen Garden and Production," in
The Canadian Garden Book

—⚏—

*D*orothy Perkins was the pen name of Adele H. Austin, who, as a very young woman, served as treasurer of Austin and Company, Ltd., her family's wholesale jewellery business in Toronto. She had a half-acre garden, with a fifty-by-fifty-foot space devoted entirely to "eats." She must have been a rose lover, for she joined the recently formed Rose Society of Ontario in 1914, and chose as her pen name the popular pink-flowered rambler rose introduced by Jackson and Perkins in 1901.

If Annie Jack's The Canadian Garden *was the first book of its kind by a Canadian woman, Dorothy Perkins's* The Canadian Garden Book *was the second. In it, Perkins carried on imaginary, often high-spirited, conversations with her readers: "How can we . . . live near to nature? . . . Create it at home. In what way? By gardening!" At the same time, she gave them sound horticultural advice and constant encouragement.*

In the passage presented here, she describes the large community garden in Toronto—on Oriole Parkway just below Oriole Road, where she lived—organized by a group of women in aid of the war effort.

—⚏—

Last year when the cry went forth to "Produce or Starve" women foresaw disaster ahead. Were not we willing to play the role so often seen in fields in Belgium, in France, in those happy pre-war days?

Early in the winter a sub-committee of the women's thrift banded themselves together to aid production. Weekly they met to discuss plans and means of meeting the enemy half way. In May it was decided to rent a farm of nine acres and put into practical use their adopted slogan, "Produce or Starve."

The soil was poor, hand-seeding machines refused to work, and so this veritable desert was hand-seeded, bit by bit, row by row, by women. Aching backs, tired bodies and souls were urged on to still greater efforts. Most of eight acres were seeded by two women, while the balance was done by voluntary help.

The scheme of planting is one to be recommended to other productionists, for the rows were planted straight through, planted in "twenties". First came corn, the beets, parsnips, onions, carrots, squash, and then the salads, cress, radishes and lettuce. Several two-foot paths ran lengthwise. When all was planted surveyors marked off in cross sections twenty different plots.

Twenty different women's patriotic clubs re-rented from the committee at $5.00 a plot. Many workers learned for the first time the difference between an onion and a bean; learned that pea-pods form from the dainty white flowers. Learned that parsnips do not grow from the base up, but vice versa. Many for the first time since leaving home and entering the cruel cold world re-learned that peace and contentment come through living and working in the open.

There were girls in every walk of commercial life among the club members. Even two sections were given over to tired mothers from a downtown settlement. Smart signs on the different allotments signified who the willing workers were. Each club had the privilege of disposing of their own produce, as the captain of the club saw fit. Some sold their produce to cafeterias, others supplied military hospitals with fresh vegetables, others sold privately to boarding-house keepers, but the money resulting from any sales was always turned in to the captain, who kept the season's books.

The committee engaged an instructor, an old retired market gardener. He was there daily from 2.30 until 8 p.m. to answer questions and solve problems which were bound to crop up. His dry humour and ready wit helped many a rank amateur to forget her tiredness in the joy of producing.

'Twas truly an inspiration to visit that great gardening school on Oriole Parkway. There, nightly, one saw many overalled figures, bending over their allotment, digging, hoeing, thinning or gathering up ripened vegetables. Fancy seeing some 150 or more women toiling diligently, doing their bit, helping to oust the soaring prices of food-stuffs by production!

At the entrance to "the farm" a delightful garden had been laid out in landscape design as well as for utility. An old one-time well was filled in and happy pink geraniums greeted one. Following a central path in place of a sun-dial, the same effect was produced by a central flower-bed filled with cannas, kochia, snap-dragons, pansies, while the rest of the garden, some 50 x 50 feet, was filled in with flowering perennials—all donations. It was in a marquee at the side of this war garden that the Red Cross served tea to the "farm hands". Usually the workers came to work direct from business and were glad to have tea served from a spotless flower-decked table, which was temptingly set with fresh salads from the garden.

Was the committee's production campaign a success? Yes, decid-edly so. Almost nightly the workers returned home laden with thin-nings of beets, carrots, etc. Some clubs supplied a down-town store with pepper cress, and every sale helped in some way to win the war.

Tall corn waved a welcome, and walking down the central path one's eye was gladdened by an artistic sense, again revealed in this large community garden. Brilliant orange nasturtiums smiled up at one and accentuated the whiteness of the tufts of sweet alyssum which snuggled closely to the cool brown soil. Here and there clubs had planted tall, feathery cosmos, golden anthemis and bright happy old-fashioned bachelor buttons. We wondered what the common grey-leaved cabbages thought of this rare chance of mingling with the aristocrats of flowerdom.

Off on a rising upland peaceful cattle browsed or wandered down to a tiny brook which threads its way just beyond an old snake fence. Swinging from a delicate twig on the bough of a nearby tree liquid notes from Canadian vesper sparrows floated like a benedic-tion over the scene. Wending our way homeward just as the work-ers were resting from their labours, preparing to fold up their tents for the night, a great full moon broke loose from behind some clouds. The same beautiful moon that shines on scenes in Flanders, that, perhaps, will shine brighter some night over there and tell our lads how we women are helping to send them food by the "Produce or Starve" campaign.

What did this community garden yield in returns? Slightly over $1,000 in money, filled the patriotic workers with health, hope and a greater determination to save our lads from hunger in each coming year until right downs might, with greater production, whether by community gardens or home gardens.

F. Leslie Sara
1934

From "Rockery Holds Peace and Charm," in
The Calgary Daily Herald

—ɯ—

*F*rederic Leslie Sara *(1896?–1940) emigrated from England to Calgary in 1913. Carrying on a boyhood interest,
he soon became active in Boy Scouting in Alberta, first
as a local Scoutmaster and later at the district and provincial levels.*

He was a respected naturalist, whose weekly editorial for The
Calgary Herald, *"What Nature Shows Us," was often reprinted in
other newspapers. He was known to CBC radio listeners through his
broadcasts on wildlife and Ducks Unlimited. He had a keen interest in
the native peoples of Alberta, knew many of their chiefs, and attended
their ceremonies. At the 1939 Calgary Stampede, the Stony tribe made
him a blood brother. Somehow he also found time to travel Alberta
and Saskatchewan representing several lines of hardware.*

*Sara's description of Calgary's Reader Rock Garden illustrates his
appreciation of ornamental as well as natural settings. (Indeed, on the
afternoon before this piece appeared, Sara's wife, Dorothy, had enter-
tained more than fifty at a garden party on the lawn of their own
riverside home.)*

*William Reader created his garden between 1913 and 1943, and
Sara described it in its heyday, when it contained some 4,000 species
of herbaceous perennials. A sidebar in the* Calgary Herald *article listed
people throughout the world—including F. L. Skinner of Dropmore,
W. R. Leslie of Morden, and F. Cleveland Morgan of Montreal—from
whom Reader had received plants.*

—ɯ—

Were one to describe it without disclosing its location, few would realize and fewer believe, that situated in the midst of Calgary is a garden which from earliest spring to the killing frosts of late autumn is a paeon of beauty; a lovely little sanctuary where amid the cool cloisters of a sheltering grove, myriads of gorgeous blooms nestle between the sheltering rocks; where ferns caress the mossy sides of a tiny stream that wanders merrily through this glade, falling with the tinkle of liquid music into the deeper pools, and bubbling out over a marsh where the kingcups run their riot of green and gold.

Everywhere, one is struck by the beauty of color, the subtle scent of this wondrous bouquet, the rapture of bird song and a peace that possesses. To walk in it is a solace, the memory of which lingers long.

Outstanding among Canadian gardens, and acknowledged as one of the most unusual collections of Alpine flora with specimens from many corners of the globe, this rock garden, part of Calgary's park system, is situated adjacent to the home of Parks Superintendent W. R. Reader, branching off from the main driveway leading through the Union Cemetery. The inception of this beauty spot, the planning and direction of it all has been a hobby of Mr. Reader, and citizens may be justly proud of the fame it has brought the city.

Twenty years of work on the part of the parks superintendent and his staff have gone into the making of it—

> "For such gardens are not made
> By saying 'Oh, how beautiful!'
> And sitting in the shade."

And at the start Nature did little beyond providing a bare hillside scarred with channels where the rain had washed the soil away and possessing no more possibilities for landscaping than the slopes leading up to Crescent Heights. First came the planting of trees, mere saplings that gave little promise of afforesting the bald benches, and a modest scheme of rockery was commenced on a new cut in the hill that gave access to the park superintendent's residence.

So steep was this cutbank that nothing but rockwork would retain the sliding soil, and to cover its barrenness, seeds of quick-growing plants that would withstand the blazing heat of the sun beating on the rocks were scattered.

Even by the second year visitors marvelled at the riot of color which the masses of yellow anthemis, the poppies, lychins [sic] and delphiniums produced, and as time advanced and the shelter belt of trees along the brow of the hill added protection, the rockery was extended, and choicer and more varied alpines were added, until today this portion of the garden contains in its hundreds of specimens, one of the finest collection of plants that ordinarily make their habitat nestling among the rocks or dotting the alpine meadows of the mountain peaks.

During these years plans were being made for the development of the larger rock garden on the slope below the driveway. Here the gradient was not so steep, a natural declivity offered possibilities of a bosky dell through which the tiny stream now flows, and an old sand pit lent itself to the scheme of providing pools and a boggy swamp for the marsh plants.

Trees planted on this slope made steady progress, and as the grove of poplars and spruce grew, the ground beneath them was carpeted with blue forget-me-nots, with sweet rocket and aqualegias, which soon ran riot in this sylvan glade.

Making a rockery is not the indiscriminate dumping of a heap of stones on a pile of earth; every rock and boulder has to be set with consummate care, not alone to give the appearance of having "grown" out of the ground, but at angles which will attract moisture to the crannies and pockets of soil in which the plants flourish. Thousands of tons of stone, each piece picked for its surface, or the beauty of its lichen-covered face, had to be used; many of the boulders were a truckload in themselves, and besides the local-supply, interested citizens donated choice rocks from as far afield as Banff, Drumheller or Cochrane.

Beyond the area set aside for the marsh, which had to be treated with a liberal application of peat and spagnum moss, no special treatment was given to the soil, ordinary prairie loam being used, enriched annually by a light mulch of straw manure which protects the plants during the winter from premature budding when the warm chinook winds blow in from the West.

Choice shrubs and some of the rarer trees were planted in points of vantage, and the space between the rocks filled with alpine plants. Seeds of tiny saxifrages and other creeping plants were sown in the crevices of the flat flagstones which form the paths, to spread and form a living outline for each stone. And where the winding paths crossed the little brook at many points, adequate access was provided by a flat stone slab, an ample stepping stone, or a bridge of rustic wood.

Thus was the garden made; made, but not completed, for each season sees new specimens being added to the collection of about 4,000 species which Mr. Reader has accumulated. Alpine plants from all over the world have been sent him by visitors who have gloried in this garden and the "mountaineers" of the floral world are here gathered in one happy family in the City of the Foothills.

COLLIER STEVENSON
1943

From "Flowers for Morale, Vegetables for Victory: Here's
the Logical Slogan for 1943!" in *Saturday Night*

—ɯ—

*C*ollier *Stevenson of Hamilton, Ontario, wrote in* The
Canadian Horticulturist *before becoming an established
journalist in the United States. He returned to Canada
in the early 1930s. For some fifteen years he worked as an editor
for Consolidated Press Limited, Toronto, publisher of the monthly*
Canadian Home Journal *and of the weekly* Saturday Night. *By 1949,
he had written for these two periodicals more than fifty articles
about home gardening, home building, and home improvement, in
addition to directing and writing the* Canadian Home Journal's *regular department "The Modern Home."*

*Stevenson appears to have retired from journalism in the 1950s.
His heaviest output had been during World War II, when, in addition
to illustrated gardening features for* Saturday Night, *he conducted
its "Wartime Gardens" department. Both Stevenson and Frances
Steinhoff [Sanders] (the latter writing in* Canadian Homes and Gardens) *advised wartime gardeners on the efficient home production of
nutrient-rich vegetables and fruits.*

*But in case victory gardening alone seemed too much like work,
both journalists also urged their readers to beautify and enjoy the
home landscapes to which gas rationing might confine them.*

This 1943 piece is typical of Stevenson's breezy style.

—ɯ—

Gardens are in the news—more so probably now than they have
been since the good old "horse and buggy days" when lawn fêtes,
strawberry festivals, croquet and slow-paced tennis games were

highlights of the summer season. For, with gasoline and rubber shortages holding non-essential driving down to a minimum, many an ardent golfer, many a chronic week-ender, many a long-time summer resorter now will have to turn to gardens and to gardening for fresh air and warm weather exercise.

Gardens, though, are in the news for a still more important reason—the raising of vitamin- and mineral-rich vegetables, both for nutritional and economic advantage to Canada. Physical fitness, developed by a well-balanced diet, is a "must" today—and vegetables are an important part of the diets recommended by our highest nutritional authorities. Economically, of course, the growing of vegetables in home gardens is equally sound, as it releases labor, relieves transportation facilities, supplements our national supply of food-stuffs.

Luxury gardening is out "for the duration"—that's by way of a warning against over-enthusiasm on the part of this year's crop of garden beginners, who may be inclined to plan too lavishly, to buy supplies beyond their actual needs. Canada has a sufficient supply of seeds this year, not enough to justify the slightest wastage. Only home-owners, therefore, who are serious and who are willing to give requisite time and energy to their gardens should attempt to grow vegetables. Another word of caution is in order here. It is futile to attempt the raising of vegetables in other than sunny, well-drained areas, whether large or small. Under ideal conditions, indeed, the vegetable plot should have the benefit of direct sunshine for a minimum of six hours a day; and, to get the full advantage of the sun, the plot should be so planned that rows will run north and south.

Now, what to grow? That's where the real fun in studying seed catalogues comes in—and it undoubtedly will be a revelation to the garden neophyte when he discovers the variety of vegetables that await his selection for a 1943 Victory Vegetable Garden. So out with pad and pencil, all you budding vegetable growers. Luxury gardening is out. True enough, but luxury in this sense applies chiefly to prodigal wastage of materials and man-power, certainly not at all to the garden beauty which is so efficacious in upbuilding and maintaining morale on the homefront. The inference is clear, however, that to relieve the labor shortage home-owners should take over as much as possible of the actual work required to keep their gardens in good order. And that really ought to be no great hardship—for, after all, a strenuous session with a lawnmower is but the equivalent of eighteen holes of golf, a down-to-earth weeding job a parallel to an hour's workout in a gymnasium!

Though there still may be snow on "them thar hills," it is not too early to be planning right now this year's garden very carefully on paper. Early planning, in fact, always is advantageous, not only because the memories of last year's mistakes still are clear, but as an incentive to ordering any desirable new seeds, bulbs, plants, shrubs, vines or trees while stocks are ample.

H. FRED DALE
1972

From "Apartment Gardeners Find A Way," in
The New York Times

—⚏—

H. Fred Dale retired in October 1993 as the gardening
columnist of The Toronto Star. He had begun there
in 1946 as a cub reporter just out of the University
of Manitoba, and by 1961 had taken over the gardening column.
Over the next nearly thirty-two years, he would write 3,328 gardening columns for The Star, four garden books, several booklets, and a
questions-and-answers column for Canadian Gardening.

Dale grew up in Winnipeg, and began gardening early by helping out in his English-born grandfather's garden at Winnipeg Beach
on Lake Manitoba and in his parents' large backyard garden in a
developing suburb, where neighbours gardened on still-vacant lots.

His interest was "in abeyance" during university, but once in
Toronto, with his own young family and bungalow-sized lot in the
suburbs, he began cultivating every available space, indoors and out.

Dale's garden horizons expanded considerably when, as a 1967
Centennial project, the family bought a forty-hectare farm, with
room to plant out all the trees and shrubs he could propagate. In this
piece written five years later, he reported on a new wave of efforts to
match available land with landless gardeners—vacant-lot gardening,
1970s-style.

—⚏—

This summer 26 garden plots on private land in Toronto were tilled,
planted, watered, weeded and harvested by tenants of nearby high-
rises. To the north and east of this metropolitan area of 2 1/2 million

people, other city dwellers rented plots of land which they visited and tended on weekends.

This all seems like a throw-back to the allotment and Victory gardens of World War II to middle-aged folk like myself. But to these young people and young families, it is a rediscovery of the land and the pleasures of growing your own, while still working and living in one of the fastest growing cities in the world.

While city fathers like to note the growth of Toronto from provincial cowtown (one nickname is still "Hog Town") to metropolis in 50 years, and greet each new high rise as a personal achievement, it sometimes takes the simple human touch to make the city more liveable. Such a touch came this year from Mrs. Beatrice Fischer. She and her dentist husband own a large property in expensive north Toronto.

She got the germ of the idea when an artist acquaintance wistfully mentioned his love of gardening but his lack of access to land. After all, there is only so much you can do with pots and an apartment balcony.

With full agreement of her husband, Mrs. Fischer offered him the use of a 50 x 50 foot plot of black loam soil on her property. He took up her offer and commuted, bringing his newly acquired garden tools by car. Mrs. Fischer watched him becoming tanned and relaxed over the summer.

With a long winter to mull it over, she decided she would like to offer two acres on her property to apartment dwellers who yearned to garden.

This was in early May and her problem was two-fold: How to get the two acres marked off in 50 x 50 foot plots, separating them from each other; and how to accomplish this before May 24, planting time.

She enlisted the aid of Lotte Dempsey, a writer of items about town for the Toronto Star. Emil van der Meulin [sic], a landscape architect and university lecturer, and his students came to the rescue. A neighbor offered a small piece of his property, adding another six garden plots to the 20 on the Fischer property.

Now came the problem of how to choose or even contact would-be gardeners. To solve it The Star printed the following invitation below one of Mrs. Dempsey's articles on the project: "If you are interested, write to Operation Green Thumb, care of the Toronto Star. Letters will be passed along to Mrs. Fischer and you'll hear from her. She's firm about high-rise tenants getting first choice."

Within 10 days Mrs. Fischer received 70 applications. One was from the wife of a university professor who not only had no balcony, she did not even have enough light for plants. A girl of 13 remembered living in a house as a small child and wanted to have a garden again. A mother of a small boy wanted him to be able to wiggle his toes in the bare earth as she had while growing up on a farm in Northern Ontario. A woman television producer thought she should have a garden to educate her son: He thought tomatoes grew underground like potatoes. Three country girls, now roommates in an apartment, wanted something to counteract the effects of "nothing but cars and concrete all around."

A couple of senior citizens had always raised tomato plants in their apartment to give away to real dirt gardeners but they couldn't grow them to maturity and now they hoped they might be able to.

Mrs. Fischer selected 25 people or groups and by Victoria Day holiday weekend, they were at work planting seeds. Marlene Klamt and her husband, Eckhart, planted eggplant, cantaloupe and beets; Mel Cescon, a second-year medical student, planted corn, tomatoes and cucumber. Mr. and Mrs. Jeffrey Daines planted lettuce, tomatoes, beans, cucumbers, beets and carrots, as well as some flowers to cut for their apartment. She is a music teacher and he is a law student. The anticipation of fresh garden vegetables they could pick and cook within minutes, or eat raw, predominated among the group, that included single and married, a novelist, experienced gardeners, complete novices, professionals and blue collar workers.

The summer was a very uneven one, periods of heavy rains alternating with droughts, and cold weather with hot. To combat the drought an engineer and a handyman among the group set up an irrigation pipe. With Mrs. Fischer's permission, they connected it to her outdoor tap. The coldness, no one could help. Though it delayed ripening, it didn't chill their spirits.

Eventually the harvest began, salad greens, root crops, peas, then the beans, corn, tomatoes, some fresh new potatoes, cucumbers and the pumpkins and winter squash to come in a few weeks. The annual flowers are blooming well and one gardener even has a couple of everblooming strawberry plants that he can pick periodically.

CAROLE GIANGRANDE
1987

"Political Gardens," in *Harrowsmith*

—⚒—

*C*arole Giangrande is a well-known radio broadcaster and
journalist who has published widely on scientific issues.
She was a fixture on the CBC in the 1970s and early
1980s, where she was a popular interviewer and farm commentator
on CBC Toronto's "Radio Noon." She is the author of The Nuclear
North: The People, the Regions and the Arms Race *(1983) and* Down
to Earth: The Crisis in Canadian Farming *(1985).*

*In this article, Giangrande grabs complacent gardeners, quietly
weeding the vegetable patch, and thrusts them onto the front lines of
political and environmental activism. Her voice, while a fresh one for
the 1980s gardening movement, does remind us of other horticulturally minded reformers—especially those strident voices in the
early 1900s who cried out, "Missionaries of beauty are needed in this
crusade against ugliness!"*

—⚒—

We gardeners try our best to be orderly people. We keep yearly
records on weather, bugs and crop yields. We make encouraging
notes about next year's harvest, reminding ourselves which crops the
cabbage fly ate and how many tomato plants are too many. Next
year's garden will be better, we say, and it almost always is. Not for
us a disorderly world, let alone one that from time to time threatens
to put an end to our harvests for good.

That explains why each year the task of planning and working
the garden feels more important than ever before. Garden diagrams,
coloured labels and seed packets have all become frail protectors of

sanity, as we confront environmental pollution, technological disasters and escalating global violence. Chernobyl is on my mind as I begin to think about this year's garden—I no longer assume that Mother Nature will put up with our nonsense forever, but like every other gardener, I will plant and harvest and find a place for melons where the beans were last year. Each small step in cultivating a garden feels like a victory, ground gained against a sense of widespread social chaos that has begun to feel like the norm.

On the other hand, isn't this thrill of victory just a bit of clever self-deception? As anyone with political savvy knows, back-to-the-land as a political statement went out with tie-dyed shirts and love beads. Today, faced with the realities of acid rain, toxic chemicals and—the final bane of all gardens—nuclear war, we harbour the notion that nurturing a patch of land does nothing to stop their onslaught. Only political action can make a difference. Gardeners live in cloisters erected by history and myth and demolished by the cold light of the present: while the arms race kills the hungry, the country dweller, awash in home-grown produce, remains smug, privileged and well fed. Gardening is essentially a private act and not a political one.

Or is it? Perhaps the idea that gardening cannot be political has more to do with style than with reality. The unhurried gardener in jeans and a John Deere cap is worlds away from noisy street confrontations. In the garden, we are forced to learn patience: cultivating, planting, weeding, biding time, hoping and waiting. When we work our land, we seldom make it to the big marches, even for worthy causes we support. Demonstrations always seem to occur in spring and fall; good walking weather but unfortunately timed to conflict with planting and harvest.

The gardener who labours with a social conscience, then, may fall into the assumption that real political activism is defined by the hard edge of protest, usually with an urban cast. Until recently, very few city activists have seen gardening and social protest as mutually supportive activities. Most view small-scale food production—the well-wrought plot in the landscaped backyard—as a pastime for the privileged few.

A growing number of people, however, are beginning to regard urban agriculture as a small but potent step toward social change.

One such person is Michael Levenston, the founder of Vancouver's City Farmer, a unique group set up to teach urban people how to grow their own food. Since 1978, City Farmer has begun several projects, including a Demonstration Garden at Vancouver's Energy Information Centre, and a garden dug out of the asphalt playground at Lord Roberts Elementary School in the city's West End.

The student gardeners are learning practical lessons in citizenship, literally from the ground up. "Every issue they're learning about in gardening is related to environmental concerns such as pollution or pesticides," Levenston explains. As kids make these connections in the classroom, they are apparently finding they have a role to play in the food system—not just as consumers but as active participants. It is a good political starting point for people of any age.

Another person who knows this is Moura Quayle, assistant professor of plant science at the University of British Columbia. She recently completed a 50-page document she hopes will prod Agriculture Canada into doing a thorough national survey. Quayle sent questionnaires to city planners across Canada to determine their attitudes toward community gardens; she also queried the gardeners themselves. She found gardens scattered all over the country. "The rise of community gardens had a lot to do with the climate of the 1970s," says Quayle. "People were concerned about food additives and conservation. There is a carryover of this into the 1980s, but gardening now has more of an economic base." People, she found, garden for many reasons, not only for low-cost food but also for the pleasure of mixing with other people, an opportunity often lost in the isolation of big-city life.

Quayle's report urges all levels of government to assist people who grow their own food by providing research and information about small-scale agriculture. There are some obvious reasons why this approach should become a priority for urban planners.

For some of Canada's urban poor, growing food provides both improved nutrition and a sense of self-respect. This is the case in Toronto's Regent Park, where organizers are helping people to grow food on city-owned land. The garden, now in its third year, was started by an activist in the local Sole Support Mothers' Group; two student coordinators were hired last summer by the Residents'

Association, and this year tomatoes, green peppers, radishes, onions, carrots, cucumbers, potatoes, cabbages, leeks and beans flourished on a lot 60 by 30 feet. Coordinator Steve Kingsley says the garden has been a boost to the self-esteem of people usually forced to rely on welfare cheques and food banks for their next meal: "It provides a way in which the community can organize and feel good about itself and do something."

Gardens of this kind point to a fact that cannot be stated often enough. While they are better than nothing, food banks still keep needy people in political limbo, as "consumers" with no money to buy food and no leverage at all in the food system.

A garden co-op can be a good antidote to this sense of power-lessness. For 200 gardeners in Cambridge, Ontario, this has proven to be the case. At the city's Community Food Co-op, gardeners work an acre of land provided by the city, and the food they grow supplements contributions to their food bank. They can also serve on committees that help with education, fund raising and garden record keeping. Each member does a specific amount of work in exchange for two food pickups a month, "earning" food as well as pride and a sense of dignity. "We're working on self-esteem," says coordinator Irene Maclean. "They're made to feel important."

Community garden organizers know that the politics of gardening allows people to address the need for food by acting on the need themselves. Levenston believes this could become even more widespread if Canada's politicians made urban food production a priority. "All land in urban areas should be catalogued and studied as rural land is, from aerial surveys," he explains. "Vacant land should be made available to people, and City Hall should have a tractor, a plough and water hookups for these sites."

Such a practical approach to poverty and helplessness should impress politicians and social activists alike. Gardens do have a part to play in a broad agenda for social change. For example, if we boycott food exports from South Africa, we leave room for locally grown produce on our tables. In this way, growing food can give us a taste of independence from the multinationals and the inhumane regimes that are the source of much of our imported food. Urban gardeners acquire new insights into the problems facing small farmers. And gardening shows us that when times are hard, we still have enough pride and skill to feed ourselves and to take care of one another.

There is a spin-off for environmentalists too: gardeners are well equipped to deal with the problem of consumer waste. Composting is a way of saying we will not allow our homes to be turned into domestic factories where we consume food and other goods and produce waste in the form of garbage and obsolescent junk. As gardeners, we can reject the idea that the home should be an extension of the marketplace, where we are passive consumers rather than responsible citizens who replace the resources we use up.

Without this basic level of knowledge and awareness, protest alone will never reconstruct the world. This is why gardening is not only political but subversive: nothing works like people who quietly assert their power to reclaim their humanness, beginning with understanding how to feed themselves well. Politics begins with a garden. No one can live, let alone protest, on a empty stomach.

Still, gardening is no panacea. It is only a beginning, the limited solution to a few limited problems. But it is a powerful antidote to the feeling of helplessness that assails so many of us so much of the time. Above all, the garden is emblematic of the new world, a society of cooperation and involvement on a human scale, a sharing of ideas, a fruitfulness, often beyond what we ever hoped for or planned. It is the classic metaphor for peace; it gives real meaning to the word. In fall, we take in our harvests, struck by the sense that the garden gives us back more than we put in or expect to receive. In part, there is the mystery of nature's bounty, but even mysteries teach political lessons: in this case, that a generous earth is one worth saving.

We do our part, gardening with little more than tools, skill and the trust that our labour can transform one place on this planet. For a moment, we hold off the threat of cataclysm and, even worse, the fear that we might give up in the face of it. Now, we think, maybe everyone can do this. Like the earth itself, hope is worth cultivating.

NAMING
FRIENDS AND
FOES

—⁓—

ELIZABETH RUSSELL
1806

From Elizabeth Russell's Diaries

—⁂—

*E*lizabeth Russell (*1754–1822*), although born in Gibraltar, lived for many years in England. In *1792*, she came to Canada with her half-brother, Peter Russell, who served in the government of Upper Canada under Lieutenant Governor John Graves Simcoe until *1799*. The Russells (neither of whom ever married) lived at York (later Toronto) on a *100*-acre park lot, in what she described as "a good House . . . in a most charming situation in the front of the Town."

Although her brother wrote that "an extensive poultry yard . . . keeps her fully amused," her own words revealed her greater interest in gardening. She wrote about what was growing (or soon to be planted) in the kitchen garden: kidney, lima, and snake beans; balm, mint, and comfrey; shallots; and an egg plum tree. She recorded the giving and receiving of flower seeds. She wrote sorrowfully that "a root of the Waxberry Plant" had not survived its trip to York. And when some pigs were uprooting grass in front of the house, she noted that she sent the dogs after them.

The events of May 31, 1806, inspired her longest garden entry. Like many gardeners, Elizabeth Russell did not suffer foolish visitors gladly.

—⁂—

Saturday May 31 1806
In the forenoon Mrs Plater came with a Mrs Lawrance (She is neice [sic] to Mrs Hill the Quaker of Young Street—her name was Crone She has been Married to Mr Lawrance between two or three Months.) They had calld on Mary who was Iorning over in her room

and she telling them I was not very well Mrs Plater wishd to see me
Mrs L— was also desirous of doing so. Mrs Plater introduced her
I have never seen her but once and that imperfectly some time ago at
Marys room window. Sent over for Mary and we walked sometime
with them in the Garden The President [Alexander Grant, president
of Upper Canada's Executive Council] came there to us Sat some-
time in the Arbour then went in. Gave them cake & wine After
Seting awhile In came Miss Cameron with Mrs Murry of Niagara
The first time she has ever been at York She has not altered much
in her looks except being fater than when I saw her at Niagara
wh[ich] will be Nine Years Next November — When they came in
Mrs Plater and her friend went away After Seting awhile went into
the Garden (The President went away soon after they came in) (Lucy
& Robert came while they were here)— I went into the House for
my Bonnet and went [sic] I returned into the Garden I saw Mrs
Murry had got some White Laylock in her hand and Miss Cameron
a Yellow Batchlors Button These I supposed they had taken of them
selves. Mary told me afterwards that Mrs Murry tore of the flower
from the Laylock & in her violence had broke an other off wh[ich]
I afterwards took Mrs M— asked if I had not the Snow Ball tree I
said I had one but I took care not to lead them to the part of the
Garden where it was Least she should it serve as she did the Laylock
and they went in without seeing it. Gave them cake & wine.

A CANADIAN FARMER
1859

"Does It Pay to Hire a Gardener," in
The Canadian Agriculturist

—⚏—

*his article, signed "A Canadian Farmer," appeared first in
Luther Tucker's* Genesee Farmer, *a highly respected agricultural journal published in Albany, New York. As was
common practice before news services and copyright enforcement, it
was soon picked up and reprinted by another journal.*

The Canadian Agriculturist, *acquired in 1858 by the semi-official
Board of Agriculture of Upper Canada, was coedited by Professor
George Buckland of the University of Toronto and William McDougall.
It carried not only the board's transactions, but also a variety of items
promoting improved methods of farming.*

*A common lament in the Canadian agricultural press at midcen-
tury was the sorry state of the rural landscape—in particular the
many unattractive farm homes and grounds. This dollars-and-cents
analysis of the benefits of hiring a gardener would have been just
what the editors were looking for.*

*The writer apparently had little trouble finding a gardener to
hire. Indeed, newspapers often carried ads placed by gardeners seeking employment. Some mentioned special skills, such as grafting,
budding, and pruning fruit trees, or laying out gardens and pleasure
grounds. For example, William Gordon advertised in Toronto in
1844 that he could attend to gentlemen's gardens and lay them out
"in the most modish style."*

—⚏—

I am a farmer with 150 acres of cleared land, with orchards, &c., as
good as my neighbors, but I was not quite satisfied with my garden.

It was, to be sure, as good as those of my neighbors, but I wished the garden better. The soil and situation were good, I had worked it, yet I was not suited. I hired a gardener in April, 1857, and in keeping a correct account of loss and gain found myself minus some $17. In looking back, I thought I could see where I had missed it, and not to be discouraged at one failure, I made a second attempt in 1858. This year I find the debt and recit pages are quite different from the former. I now find myself the gainer to the amount of $23.50 in 1858, besides the constant supply and use of many articles for the table, not taken in the estimate. Then the great enjoyment of the many delicacies my garden yields when a friend visits me, and occasionally to make a present of a dish of strawberries, gooseberries, or a few melons, as circumstances seem to justify, gives such a true relish to life that I shall pay more attention to my garden in future.

I believe my brother farmers are the losers by neglecting the garden. I know that I have lost by such neglect, and by the well-known rule, judge others by myself. The garden pays full as well as the field.

A. M. SMITH
1873

"Prize Essay on Impositions of Dishonest Tree Pedlars," in
*Annual Report of the Fruit Growers' Association of
Ontario, 1873*

—⚬—

*A*ndrew Murray Smith (1832–1910) grew up in Vermont
and western New York State, but arrived in the Niagara
Peninsula of Ontario as a young man. In Grimsby
Township he and Charles Edward Woolverton (Linus Woolverton's
father) planted the area's first large commercial peach orchard, plus
a nursery of some eight to ten thousand fruit trees. The success of the
venture convinced many mixed farmers to switch to fruit production, and after the introduction of special railway cars to carry the
tender produce to market, the area became the "Peach Garden of
Canada."

In 1859, Smith, C. E. Woolverton, D. W. Beadle, and fifteen others
formed the Fruit Growers' Association of Upper Canada (later Ontario), and began sharing their experiences in raising and marketing
fruit—first at informal meetings, and later through annual meetings,
annual reports, and The Canadian Horticulturist. The Woolverton-
Smith partnership dissolved about 1870, but Smith remained an
innovative fruit grower, an enterprising nurseryman, and an active
member of several fruit-growers' organizations.

Smith had very little formal education, but he wrote and spoke
effectively, judging by his frequent appearances in the annual-meeting
reports. In this essay on a subject that concerned many rural Canadians, he outdid himself.

—⚬—

Of all the plagues with which Canadian fruit growers are afflicted, either of beasts, birds or insects, there are none so annoying, and (at least to their peace of mind) so destructive, and so hard to exterminate, as dishonest tree pedlers. They swarm around them like caterpillars. They are harder to shake off than curculios. Their persistent boring is worse than all other tree borers combined. Their power to transform their delicious apples and pears into insipid worthless things is greater than that of the codlin moth; and if their gnawing propensities do not equal those of the mice, the gnawings of conscience at having yielded to their allurements, and the sufferings consequent therefrom, are far more vexatious; and the blighted hopes and prospects of having fine orchards and fine fruits, and the receiving of scrubby trees and scabby apples instead, is far worse than the pear blight. They not only take away our anticipated golden pippins, but they take our gold also. They not only filch from us our juicy red-cheeked Crawfords and Sweet-waters, and give us frost peaches instead, but they take away our time and care, and the red flush of youth from our cheeks, and bring the frost of old age around our heads in waiting for them to grow again. They not only substitute puckery, sour, tough, worthless pears for our sweet, melting, aromatic Bartletts, Seckles and Flemish Beauties, but they sour our tempers, and take away the sweet, melting, mellowing influence of trust in our fellow-men. They even do worse than this. They rob some of their reputation and good name, which is dearer than all. Where is the nurseryman that has not suffered more or less from them in this respect? I know of some whose reputation has been ruined in some localities by these rascals. They palm off worthless trees labelled as choice varieties, and represent them as coming from some particular nursery, when the nurseryman never saw them, or had any knowledge of the transaction whatever. They lead people to distrust, so that honest upright men, agents of responsible nurseries, are suspected, and do not meet with the success they deserve, or would have, if people had not been so much deceived by them.

Their operations are well known, and hardly need describing. They are unlike our other enemies—they come in the guise of friendship. They exhibit plates of beautiful fruits and flowers, and talk glibly of the profits of fruit culture, and recommend this and that variety. They extol the nurseries they pretend to represent, and show their catalogues, perhaps, and tell of the large orders they have got of our neighbours, and, before we are aware of it, they have our orders for a large amount of trees. They then go wherever they can get their trees the cheapest—the more unsaleable the varieties, the cheaper they get them, no matter what kinds. I have known them to get wild grape vines and berry bushes by the road-side. They then label them whatever their orders call for, and deliver them to their customers, and get their pay. Sometimes they repeat their operations the second time in the same locality. When they do this, the first time they generally deliver good trees, in size and appearance, as a bait to secure customers for the next year. But they are sure never to appear after the fruit begins to bear. Their victims wait two, three, and sometimes four or five years for their *beautiful* fruit to bear, and then find they have been *beautifully* swindled.

There is another class of these enemies a little less destructive to our fruit crops, perhaps, yet who filch, by their misstatements and representations, many a hard-earned dollar from our farmers and fruit growers. I refer to some authorized agents from the States. (There are honourable exceptions, I know, but comparatively few.) They, in order to effect sales in the neighbourhood of our own nurseries, make statements they know to be utterly false, and that repeatedly. They will show the plates of some new fruits, perhaps, and represent they cannot be got at any nursery in Canada, and sell the trees at extravagant prices, when they have been informed by Canadian nurserymen that they have them in quantity. I have known them to sell grape vines to men, by such representations, for $2 a-piece, which they could get in a home nursery, not two miles away, for 50 cents. I have known them to represent that they had been in certain nurseries, and that they had no trees to sell over a certain age and size, and that they had not got this and that variety, when they had never set foot upon their grounds, or, if they had, they knew perfectly well to the contrary. Farmers are, of course, to blame for not informing themselves, and, perhaps, deserve to be swindled, but this does not lessen the culpability of the agents. I would not depreciate American nurseries and nurserymen as a class. Far from it. Canada is indebted to them for her best fruits. Yet we can but condemn the tricks of their agents, many of which, I doubt not, are unknown to their employers, who would not stoop so low. But many of these agents sell upon commission, and think more of the almighty dollar than they do of the commands of the Almighty, and for the sake of making a few dollars extra, do not hesitate to lie a little.

Canadian nurserymen, as a class, are not slow in procuring new fruits when they know them to be really valuable, though they may be behind their neighbours in puffing every new thing that comes up for the sake of making a little money out of it, and did our fruit growers patronize home industry a little more they would be far less liable to be swindled.

Generally when men find an enemy to their fruits at work they try to exterminate it, yet what has ever been done to stop the ravages of these enemies? There are laws against swindling, yet who ever heard of these swindlers being handled by the law? There is no doubt in the mind of any sane man that thousands of dollars have been lost to the country by them, yet still they are allowed to work. It seems to me we need a little wholesome legislation on this subject. Pass a law (and enforce it) that no man should be allowed to sell trees without a license and a certificate of agency from the nursery he pretends to represent and then make the nurseryman responsible for the varieties sold, and we shall have far less vexation from these fellows, and when fruit growers can, let them go to the nurseries and select trees for themselves of men whom they know to be reliable and responsible, and then we shall have one enemy less to the fruit interests of our dominion.

ANNIE L. JACK
1911

"Doorweed for Dry Places," in *The Canadian Horticulturist*

—⚬—

*A*nnie L. Jack, née Hayr, *(1839–1912) was born in England and came to North America in her teens. She later married Robert Jack, a fruit grower, settled at "Hillside" in Chateauguay Basin, Quebec, and raised ten children.*

She must have been a woman of great energy, for she not only found time to run a lively household, but also to create and maintain what Liberty Hyde Bailey, a renowned American horticulturist, called "one of the most original gardens I know." This garden contained vegetables for the family and for sale, flower and shrub borders, a central grassy space, trees on the windward edge, and fruits on the leeward.

Jack wrote numerous newspaper and magazine articles about her garden and her many plant experiments in it. As well, she published short stories, poems, and The Canadian Garden: A Pocket Help for the Amateur *(1903, with a second edition in 1910). Her "Garden Talks" column in* The Montreal Daily Witness *had a great following.*

Her gracious, innovative nature shone out of every gardening article she wrote. "Doorweed for Dry Places," predating today's environmentally conscious xeriscaping, demonstrates her willingness to use doorweed, also known as knotweed, in an unorthodox and rather wonderful way.

—⚬—

During the past summer, so trying to lawns on account of the excessive heat and drought that caused the grass to shrivel and turn brown, a strip of ground along the north side of the house was the admiration of all comers, being vividly green, and showing the line plainly where it ended and other grasses began. It is "Polygonum aviculare," a small leaved perennial, properly named a weed, that grows along walks, and in dry hard soil where it makes a mat-like appearance, if kept regularly cut with the lawn mower.

It is a plant closely allied to the "dock" family and also to the buckwheats. So, though of humble origin, it is well connected. It proved this summer a friend in need, and has gained the name of "Doorweed." The object of bringing it into notice is that it might be useful where other plants cannot resist the dry hot weather, but it must be kept regularly and closely cut and not be allowed to straggle. Properly managed, it presents a velvety appearance that was very interesting by contrast this season.

GEORGE THOMPSON
1919

From "The Private Gardener," in *The Canadian Florist*

—ɯ—

*G*eorge Thompson learned gardening in England. He arrived in Toronto in 1911 and became resident gardener, under estate superintendent Thomas McVittie, at Sir Henry Pellatt's Casa Loma. His son Thomas W. Thompson—who would serve as Metro Toronto's first parks commissioner—was born nearby in 1913.

In a typical year at Casa Loma, George Thompson grew tens of thousands of bedding plants—cannas, geraniums, aceranthus, coleus— in greenhouses supplying the extensive grounds. He remained at Casa Loma until Pellatt's financial collapse in 1923. Shortly thereafter, he became horticulturist at Prospect Cemetery in Toronto, where he remained—living on the grounds in the original farmhouse—until his retirement in the 1960s.

Thompson had arrived in Toronto sixteen years after professional gardeners had split off from the Toronto Horticultural Society to form the Gardeners' and Florists' Society. Although World War I delayed the professionals' efforts to become a strong, independent voice, Thompson was urging them, in this 1919 paper, to look again to the future.

He remained dedicated to his profession. He served as secretary-treasurer of the Gardeners' and Florists' Association of Ontario for forty years. From its inception in 1938, he personally wrote most of The Ontario Gardeners' Chronicle *(their monthly newsletter)*, mimeographed it on his own kitchen table, and mailed it out to members.

—ɯ—

With the war brought to a successful conclusion, we may without doubt look for a decided boom in horticulture, in all its many branches. It should, therefore, be our earnest endeavor to prepare ourselves, so that we may be able to take advantage of the opportunities which are sure to come. There can be no denying the fact that in the older countries of Europe, and to a lesser degree on this continent, the private gardener has occupied a prominent place in the horticultural life of the country in which he has laboured.

In the British Isles, where, perhaps, the professional gardener, as a class, come [sic] as near perfection as anywhere, he has had a large share in the developing to the present standard of perfection, the many varieties of flowers, fruits, and vegetables with which our gardens, parks, and greenhouses are made both prolific and beautiful. All species of plants, from one end of the Horticultural Dictionary to the other, have been tried and often improved by the enterprising private gardener. What has been accomplished in other lands may be done in this, if we can prepare ourselves to take full advantage of every opportunity that presents itself, and if we can successfully overcome the difficulties with which we, as a profession, have to contend.

Perhaps the chief reason why private gardening in Canada is at present so far behind older countries is the evident fact that so far the monied people of the land have not indulged to any great extent in the country homes and large estates. Consequently, the number of good gardens is limited. With, however, the advent of good roads and better transportation facilities, we may look forward to seeing in the not distant future, country homes for the wealthy, as numerous, if not as extensive, in Canada as in older countries. A second important reason is, that, limited as the number of good gardens certainly is, the supply of good men does not exceed them.

The profession as it stands to-day has ceased almost entirely to attract the type of young man who is essential, if our particular branch of horticulture is to advance as it should. What is the reason? Has gardening become less attractive than formerly, or has the present generation no place for the professional gardener? I believe the work itself is as attractive as it ever was, and the world of to-day has as large or even a larger place for our profession; but for some reason hard to understand, gardeners are expected to work long hours for less money than any other trade or profession with which I am acquainted. I think I can honestly say that there is no work at the present time which yields so poor remuneration, when one takes into consideration what a first-class man has to be and know.

To be at the top of his profession, it is essential that the gardener be at least a fair scholar, with a knowledge of bookkeeping and proper business methods. He must be thoroughly conversant with all branches of horticulture; must be willing to take responsibility and be able to manage men to advantage; have a proper sense of the beautiful and a happy regard for colour schemes and combinations; while his work must at all times bear comparison with others perhaps more favoured than himself. Again. He should not be ignorant of botany, chemistry of the soil, greenhouse construction, steam and hot water heating. In fact, there is not a trade or profession where a man can conveniently know so much and get so little for it as the private gardener. This being the case, how can we, in this material age, hope to get the right type of men to take up gardening as their life's work? The limited number of really good places, the equally limited chance of securing one of them, and the poor wages through the years of learning may well deter these young men, horticulturally inclined, from taking hold, and making a success of themselves as private gardeners.

Is there any remedy for this, and if there is, how can we best apply it? As I have already stated, I believe that what we need most to-day is more gardens to create a greater demand for good gardeners; an increased supply of the right type of men to meet the demand; and suitable remuneration to encourage such men. While we have no direct control over the possible increase in the number of good gardens, we, as gardeners, can do much to encourage prospective employers to indulge in the joys of horticulture. It should be the object of every gardener who has the welfare of his profession at heart, to make his own particular charge such a decided acquisition to his employer that others may be encouraged to look upon a garden, not as a continual source of expense, but as something very desirable and necessary. A well kept and properly stocked garden is the profession's best advertisement, and if there were more of these, our critics would have less cause to criticise, and prospective employers would be encouraged to spend the money necessary for the upkeep of a garden.

ELLA M. HARCOURT
1930

"Garden Visitors," in *The Rose Society of Ontario*
Year Book 1930

—w—

*E*lla M. Harcourt (d. 1951) joined the Rose Society of Ontario
soon after its founding in Toronto in 1913, and remained
a member for the rest of her life. During the 1920s, she
served on the society's executive, exhibition, and publications committees—as did Lorrie Dunington-Grubb. Harcourt subsequently
became a frequent prize winner, a vice-president, a life member, and,
from 1936 on, an honorary vice-president of the society.

She edited its yearbook from 1919 through 1929, and remained
for several years afterward a frequent contributor. Her enthusiastic
reports on the society's annual shows, during the 1930s, documented
the popular roses and their successful exhibitors and provided
intriguing commentary on ordinary members, professional growers,
and wealthy patrons.

Late in her life Harcourt lived on the West Coast for several years,
before returning to her native Toronto. Although she may have enjoyed the change of climate, she had once written that even in Ontario,
"roses do rise to the occasion when the weatherman is kind."

—w—

There are certain essential qualities which should be developed in all
garden visitors, and in this age of tests and analyses there is no reason why a short examination should not be passed and a license
granted. For instance, no one should be permitted to view our gardens,—and especially mine,—who has no imagination; whose soul
is so dead that he cannot gaze ecstatically at a vast waste of earth,

dotted with wooden labels marking tiny green oases, and see beautiful visions like the pictures in the catalogues. Carefully cultivated, the imaginative visitor can become the ideal visionary who sees Roses in our piles of bone meal and Tonk's Mixture, and who loves to linger amid our Sulphur and Copper Carbonate Sprays. For it is a sad fact, recognized by all amateur gardeners, that the visitor never arrives at the right time. A much better, because sadder, motto for a sundial than "Tempus Fugit" or "Nox Venit" is "O That You Had Come Last Week!" Translated into Latin it could, perhaps, be shortened.

Another very necessary thing for the garden visitor to remember is,—let him leave his own garden at home. In fact, this should be written over the gateway,—"All other gardens abandon ye who enter here." For what is more annoying than a visitor who flits from plant to plant exclaiming— "I have that one," "What's this called?" and "So-and-So has a whole bed of these." I think the above-mentioned type is the worst because incurable,—for the ignorant and the tactless we have hope; I mean the one who wonders in midsummer, why your Perpetual Roses have no blooms, and, in autumn, why your Pernetianas have no leaves!

As we are all liable to be garden visitors at some time, let us set the standard of sympathetic imagination, interest and tact; for gardeners are sensitive people, closely akin to artists and musicians in temperament.

F. Cleveland Morgan
1936

From "Rock-Gardening in the Province of Quebec," in
*Rock Gardens and Rock Plants: Report of the Conference
Held by the Royal Horticultural Society and the Alpine
Garden Society*

—⚶—

*F*rederic Cleveland Morgan (1882–1962) was a wealthy
Montreal art collector and director of the family firm,
Henry Morgan and Company, Ltd., a famous depart-
ment store. He served in many capacities for the Montreal Museum
of Fine Arts for over forty-five years. In 1961, a special exhibition
celebrated the more than 600 items he had donated to the museum.

In addition to his philanthropic works, Morgan was an avid gardener, and often wrote and lectured about his gardening experiments.
The rock garden at his country estate, "La Sabot," on the shores of Lac
des Deux Montagnes outside Montreal, was written up in American,
Canadian, and British publications. Although Morgan called it a
"Lilliputian affair," his estate included not only the internationally
recognized rock garden, but also a bowling green, tennis court, rose
garden, shrubberies, flower borders and beds, and extensive lawn.

Morgan also dabbled in plant hybridizing, and focussed on the
iris. His 'Mount Royal,' a cultivar that he called a "surprise package,"
won the Macoun Medal for best seedling exhibited at the Ottawa
Iris Show in 1926.

—⚶—

British gardeners can scarcely realize what it means to have all outdoor work at a standstill for at least four months every winter.
Cutting wood, shovelling snow, filling ice-houses, repairing tools
and machines and such-like jobs occupy the staff during this period.

Then the warm March sun begins to take effect. Gradually the snow piles vanish. One slops through slush and water—but still nothing can be done. We get the hot-beds ready, for the seed boxes in the greenhouse are showing signs of extremely active life. We poke anxiously and hopefully at winter coverings, loosening them where their icy coats permit. But we must not be too venturesome, for blizzards are in the offing, and until April 20 is safely past strict orders are given to leave all exposed parts of the garden under part of their winter coats. It is true that in some years early comers are already in bloom. Snowdrops, Bulbocodiums, Hellebores, *Iris reticulata* and some Anemones are generally in flower by the end of April. Early pruning and spraying can now be done and digging follows as soon as the frost is out of the ground. A continuous round of the rock garden must be made watching for signs of heaving. This is particularly in the loose gravelly soil of the screes and moraines or in those sections which were rebuilt in the autumn. Plants will not have had time to establish themselves and even the rocks may need resetting and firming. By the end of April the serious cleaning-up of the winter litter commences. Already much has been removed, but now comes the careful handwork of stirring, feeding, top dressing and all those motherly attentions so necessary at this season. Even yet one must look out for trouble. How many springs have we rejoiced, as my gardener and I made our daily round, to find the fresh green mounds of some precious plant. But the hot sun was not good for such tender things, and so they withered and died under this assault. A little umbrella of Hemlock boughs might have saved them until hardened to this bitter world. Frosts may be encountered as late as the middle of May. A June sun can be too much for transplanted youngsters. Between this Scylla and Charybdis one must steer one's way and it is wise to make plans ahead of time to speed planting.

SISTER MARY ROSALINDA
1944

"Lace," in *From a Garden Enclosed: A Collection of Community Verse in tribute to Reverend Mother Mary Leopoldine, Superior General, on the occasion of her Golden Jubilee*

—⁂—

*S*ister Mary Rosalinda, S.S.A., née Agnes Nyland, (1907–1988) was born in Victoria, British Columbia. In 1947, at age 40, she entered the University of Ottawa as an undergraduate, and in 1967 received its Doctor of Philosophy in English literature for a thesis on E. J. Pratt. She taught there for sixteen years, and was also active in the Canadian Authors' Association—serving as national president from 1977 to 1979. Toward the end of her life, she returned to the Convent of the Sisters of St. Ann in Victoria.

"Prayer and poetry go often hand in hand," as the introduction to From a Garden Enclosed points out. Prayer and gardens also go hand in hand. Nuns, priests, and other religious community members have been gardening in Canada since the seventeenth century—some happily, some not. In 1653, when Sœur Marie de l'Incarnation wrote from an Ursuline convent in Quebec City to her family in France, she asked for flower seeds because there were "none here that are very rare or very beautiful. Everything is wild, flowers as well as men."

—⁂—

Dame Nature is fond of feminine frills—
The tucked and pleated excellence of the rose,
The exquisite net-work of the dills,
Stiff petal-collars 'round daisy faces

And golden frilliness of daffodils.
Everywhere she decks herself in laces—
White, delicate and ever-changing spray and froth
Of waves that ripple over rocks on beaches;
The soft fluffiness of apple-blossom foam
Or far-spreading pink carpet of the peaches;
Young leaves in spring, each crimped and curled,
Spreading their fresh green o'er winter's barren reaches;
Dew-pearled webs of finest gossamer
From Arachne's loom, dainty, and opalescent
As soap bubbles—woven just for her;
Snowflakes' airy medallions, made by enchantment,
Crocheted and joined to make, from vapour,
The earth's white coverlet, a priceless spread,
Infinitely whiter,—jewelled and more precious
Than ever has been laid on any prince's bed;
On windows, fretted patterns of finest point d'esprit
Made overnight, too delicate for touch of sun.
And, that we may hold fast the memory
Of all her dazzling beauty, when the day is done
And light is dying in one great crimson sea
She robes herself for evening and our admiring eye
In rich black lace of trees against the western sky.

GEORGE H. HAMILTON
1953

From "Ornamental Accessories," in *A Gardener's*
Source Book

—∭—

*G*eorge Harvey Hamilton (1908–1978) was an Ontario
native and a longtime science teacher in Niagara Falls,
with a Master of Science from McGill. In 1937, he initiated the academic program at the Niagara Parks Commission's School
of Horticulture, and in 1944 became the commission's botanist—a
position he held for nearly thirty years.

In 1943, Hamilton produced a major reference work, Plants of
the Niagara Parks System of Ontario, *the first comprehensive catalogue of native flora on commission lands to appear since 1896.
Already a frequent contributor to many Canadian periodicals,
including* The Family Herald and Weekly Star, *he became* The Globe
and Mail's *garden feature writer in 1948.*

His A Gardener's Source Book *was for "that vast legion of common people who are bound together by an unflagging interest in
gardening as a part-time activity." Like countless gardening books
before and since, it was organized into month-by-month discussions
of seasonal chores and related musings. Preceding the January-
through-December sections, however, was an introduction entitled
"Planned Gardening," from which we have selected these three passionate paragraphs on gilding the lily.*

—∭—

One summer, I was asked to visit a garden not far from a nearby city
in order to view an unusual display of garden ornaments. Carved
wooden figures of men and animals busily employed in watering the
lawn, drooling dwarfs, bronze leaping lizards and marble fawns so

covered the sward, that only a few timorous sprouts of green were visible.

Allowing for vast differences in taste, I must admit that I found this bizarre display repulsive and in conflict with my lifelong conviction that simplicity should always be the key-note in garden decoration. I might go even further and state that such an extravagant exhibition not only detracts from the beauty of the garden, but suggests that the person responsible is strangely lacking in refinement and knowledge of what is proper. If you have a tendency in this direction, curb it constantly. If you must have something of this sort in the garden, be content with a not too ornate bird bath, a small fireplace or a sundial, and use plants to make them as inconspicuous as possible.

A few misguided souls occasionally try to conceal their shrubbery or blot out the sun with gargantuan bird-houses. I am always thankful that the fad for erecting these monstrosities is not more common. A few moments' study will reveal that most birds are timid creatures and, like most people, prefer privacy and despise such ostentation. Certainly, make provision for the birds, and, where possible, construct shelters to encourage them to meet and stay in your garden. In doing this, however, think chiefly of the birds. If you are motivated by a desire to help your feathered friends, you will be content to hide the bird-houses in the shrubbery or other inconspicuous places. It will please both the birds and the eyes of your friends who have some artistic sense.

W. R. LESLIE
1956

From "Let Snow Be Help To Your Garden," in the
Winnipeg Free Press

—◇—

*illiam Russell ("Russ") Leslie (1891?–1985) was one
of Canada's most famous post-World War I horticulturists. He received a Bachelor of Science in agriculture in 1916 from the Manitoba Agricultural College, supervised
tree-planting along northern railways, did two years of post graduate studies at the University of Manitoba, and worked in Ontario for
several years. Then, in 1921, he became superintendent of the five-
year-old Dominion Experimental Station at Morden, Manitoba, a
position he would hold for thirty-five years.*

*At Morden, under his supervision, more than a hundred hardy
ornamental plant, fruit, and vegetable cultivars were introduced into
cultivation. As well, Leslie was the leading developer and supporter
of the Prairie Cooperative Fruit Breeding Project, which has introduced numerous fruit cultivars to the challenging rigours of the western climate.*

Leslie became the garden columnist for the Winnipeg Free Press
*on his retirement in 1956, and between then and 1971, wrote more
than 1,500 "Over the Garden Wall" columns, of which this was the
first. While many past and present garden writers have waxed poetic
about gardening, few have praised the benefits of that cold Canadian
fact of snow as Leslie did.*

—◇—

Late November sees most of the garden chores completed. The plants
have been tucked in for the winter. The one important opportunity is
to take maximum advantage of snowfall. It is the most efficient of

insulators. Piled over the flower borders, strawberry patch, base of vines, rose garden, and fruit plantation, snow brings warmth. It also conserves moisture in soil and plant roots.

Brush or other plant debris spread to windward of the garden causes air eddyings which result in trapping of the blowing snow. Slat fencing is also very practical in accumulating it.

Tender perennial plants, including strawberries, have their vigor ensured by receiving protective mulch coverings in several alternate layers. Thus, a patch already covered with brush and straw or clean hay and then by a fall of snow now receive another spread of straw, hay, evergreen boughs, or corn stalks. Later snowfall will cover this. The resulting stratified blanket will not only increase winter comfort but will extend protection later into next spring. It is in early spring that plants are particularly prone to severe injury and discomfort.

A generous snow covering is a boon to plants. It is recalled that wild raspberries from north of Lake Winnipeg are winter tender at the Minnesota State Fruit Breeding Farm south of Minneapolis. The explanation seems to be that their accustomed condition of receiving an early deep covering unmelted until well into April is lacking. In contrast, at the fruit farm the plants encounter uncertain snow covering and periodic spells of stimulating mild weather. Probably it is the winter thaws that are most responsible for the winter dieback. The northern plants are not physically prepared for being aroused into bud swelling by stretches of warm days in the middle of winter.

It is of interest to note that some plants from considerably south of us on the Great Plains are better adapted for transplanting into Manitoba prairie gardens than are those from our own northern moister evergreen woodlands. An example is the Black Hills spruce from western South Dakota as compared with the native White spruce from the Winnipeg River territory. The former withstands the long hot spells of summer and windy weather better than does our local spruce. Moreover, with its tough, thick, glossy needles, it seems less attractive to insect enemies.

Then there are two plants from away down in New Mexico which have been surprisingly thrifty in Southern Manitoba. Foestiera, a shrub to about eight feet tall, is considered to be one true olive native to North America. The fruit is only about the size of a kernel of wheat but the upright bush with small leaves adds novelty to the planting. Apache-plume, or Fallugia, a low shrub to two feet, is attractive with feathery lobed leaves and showy white flowers followed by reddish plumey fruits. Both these plant immigrants from the deep south have been doing well for a number of years at Morden on unirrigated ground.

BERNARD S. JACKSON
1977

From "How to Start a Butterfly Garden," in
Nature Canada

—ᴡᴡ—

*hen he wrote this article, Bernard S. Jackson was man-
ager of the thirty-four-hectare Oxen Pond Botanic Park
at the Memorial University of Newfoundland in St.
John's. Jackson's special interests lay in growing flowers and providing habitats for butterflies. During the 1970s and 1980s, through his
publications, talks, workshops, and tours of the park, his name
became synonymous with butterfly farming and gardening.*

*Jackson was on the crest of three waves in Canadian gardening:
the rediscovery of the naturalistic style, the rebirth of wildflower gardening, and the recognition of heritage plants. But he was modest.
"Basic butterfly gardening," he wrote to a student in 1978, "is a
reversion back to an informal garden style and the use of old-fashioned, simple, sweet-scented material, instead of all these wretched
scentless, complex modern cultivars."*

*In addition to articles on butterflies and other creatures of nature
in* Canadian Geographic *and* Nature Canada, *Jackson has written*
Butterflies of Oxen Pond Botanic Park—their Conservation and
Management *(1976) and* Growing Herbaceous Perennials in Newfoundland *(1979). He is now retired and living in Truro, Nova
Scotia, where he gardens and gives workshops and lectures on a
range of horticultural topics.*

—ᴡᴡ—

My interest in natural history, as is the case with so many nature
lovers, was initiated by the flash and colour of native birdlife. That

was many years ago and, though I still feel a healthy excitement watching warblers, hawks and sparrows, more of my interest is now absorbed by butterflies. Why this happened is difficult to say but the trigger seems to have been my passion for flower gardening.

I am a casual gardener and love the informal practices of the "old English cottage garden" style. This form of gardening is ideal for the naturalist because the variety of plants used encourages many species of small creatures to visit. I am not a lover of the modern formal garden, with its beds of scentless bloom and spray-drenched soil. Such areas are often biological barrens, and what is a garden without wildlife?

When I first tried to encourage butterflies into my garden, I looked for books that could introduce me to the techniques involved. Though dozens of books have been published on attracting birds to the garden, I soon found that there was little information on encouraging anything else.

My first discovery was the British book by Hugh Newman entitled *Create a Butterfly Garden*. This text which is available in some libraries gives the aspiring butterfly gardener an idea on how to start. But Canadian gardeners will quickly realize that not all Newman's recommended plants will grow in Canada nor are our butterflies necessarily on the wing when the recommended plants that do grow here are in flower.

What are the requirements for a butterfly garden? There are really very few: as long as you can provide a sunny, sheltered site with a profusion and variety of plant life, you have a good chance of attracting these insects. Of course, the nearer you live to their natural habitat in the country, the better your chances of success. The small garden in the city often has the disadvantage of sitting like an oasis in a concrete desert. But even here, there are usually a few butterfly species living in parks or on waste ground that can be attracted to a butterfly garden.

There is little point in trying to attract butterflies unless you can provide an open sunny site. Many species spend considerable time sunning themselves on open spots such as the stones in a rock garden, patches of bare earth, gravel driveways and the log edgings along footpaths. In my garden, species likely to appear in these situations include Red Admirals, Painted Ladies, Milbert's Tortoise-Shells and Spring Azures. Mourning Cloaks, Green Commas and White Admirals will sometimes venture into the butterfly garden, but their favourite sunning places are often high up in trees.

Wind is detrimental to butterflies as well as to the plants in the butterfly garden. The garden must therefore be sheltered. If your garden is windy, windbreaks may be the answer. These must not be solid barriers, which only deflect the wind and cause other problems, but should be made of a material which slows down and disperses the wind. Smallmeshed chicken wire is good and relatively inexpensive, and with a little imagination, you can convert it into an attractive rustic design.

The real key to a butterfly garden, however, is in seasonal progression of sweet-scented and colourful flowers. Even in years when butterflies are few, these flowers will always give more than enough pleasure to compensate for the time and effort spent growing them. Generally speaking, it is the old-fashioned type of garden plants with single flowers and an abundance of accessible nectar that are attractive to pollinating insects. Many modern varieties, though beautiful in themselves, are too complex and scentless to be of use. One only has to grow a clump of the new double Shasta Daisy alongside the old single type to show the difference.

To create the desired succession of flowers from spring through to butterfly hibernation requires the combined use of annual, perennial and biennial plants. The perennial border is essential to the garden: it should contain such plants as single Shasta Daisy, Michaelmas Daisy, Showy Sedum, Sea Holly, Scabiosa, Jacob's Ladder and *Kentranthus rubra*. Many of the perennial rock plants are useful: I have found Creeping Phlox or Moss Pink, Rock-cress or Arabis and *Sedum spurium* attractive to Mourning Cloaks, Spring Azures and Milbert's Tortoise-Shells.

While the perennial border is the backbone of the garden, the annuals are the body. Annuals that work particularly well for me are *Iberis*, *Scabiosa*, *Tagetes* (variety Naughty Marietta), *Rudbeckia* and *Ageratum*. *Alyssum*, *Verbena*, *Cosmos*, Star Phlox and annual Sweet

William should also be tried. Be sure to include cultivated *Echium*—
it is a tremendous bee flower. Finally, do not leave out such biennials as Sweet Rocket, Siberian Wallflower and Sweet William.

If you are one of those fortunate people with large tracts of land,
try leaving untouched an area of rough grass and wild flowers. Such
an area supplies valuable habitat diversity and is ideal for such butterflies as Sulphurs, Skippers and Ringlets. Incidentally, some native
wild flowers also work well in the perennial border. Of these, Oxeye
Daisies, Asters, Joe-Pye-Weed and goldenrods, especially *Solidago
graminifolia* are excellent butterfly flowers. In that rough unused
corner, plants like Yarrow, Fireweed and Black Knapweed are hard
to beat for attracting adult butterflies. I find the common dandelion
useful for Short-tailed Swallow-tails in particular.

Since a number of species such as Tiger Swallow-tails and Sulphurs
are attracted to damp ground or moist peat, it may be worth the
effort to construct a small ornamental pool and bog in your garden.
Rotting fruit is also an attractant to certain butterflies (and wasps
too). So if you have fruit trees, leave a few wind-fallen fruits.

To encourage butterflies to breed and multiply in your garden, a
collection of the necessary caterpillar host plants must be provided.
Once you are familiar with the species likely to occur in your garden, the next step is to find out what plants serve as food for their
caterpillars. This information is available in books or from members
of your local naturalist group. Although some wild plants are difficult to grow in the garden, many others can be transplanted successfully into flower beds, pots or planters (take care to avoid rare
species). Some wild flowers can even be grown from seed or cuttings.

A word of caution: the deliberate cultivation of what the non-
butterfly enthusiast calls "noxious weeds" is frowned upon and in
some areas is illegal. To avoid this, place such plants in a sunken container to inhibit the spread of roots and cut off the flower heads to
prevent seeding. European Stinging Nettle, the major host for the red
Admiral and Milbert's Tortoise-Shell, and Canadian Thistle, host for
the Painted Lady, are among the plants that can be treated in this way.

Butterflies have to face a number of natural enemies. Birds take
both caterpillars and adults. The larger dragonflies and spiders take a

toll of adult butterflies while many caterpillars are parasitized by certain types of wasps and flies and eaten by small predators such as
shrews and the large, long-legged groundbeetles. A naturalist-butterfly
gardener must take a philosophical attitude towards these forms of
life entering or inhabiting the garden.

MARJORIE PRIDIE
1980

"The Horticultural Security Blanket: Six-week-wonder compost in the Far North," in *Harrowsmith*

—ɯ—

arjorie Pridie was born in England and came to Canada as a war bride. She and her husband, Leo, moved from Alberta to Hay River, Northwest Territories, in 1953. There they began the adventure of gardening north of the sixtieth parallel, in zone zero of Canada's zero-through-nine plant-hardiness zones.

In the Northwest Territories, late-eighteenth- and early-nineteenth-century records exist of gardening on the hospitable alluvial soils at the mouth of the Athabasca and where the Liard and Mackenzie rivers meet. At Hay River, gardening had taken root in the early 1890s, with the establishment of an Anglican mission whose produce from nearly two and a half hectares had amounted by 1922 to "over 1,000 bushels of potatoes besides a good supply of cabbage, cauliflower, turnips, celery, tomatoes, cucumbers, onions, beets, peas, beans, carrots, etc."

One golden rule for every gardener—whether on the south shore of Great Slave Lake or on a north-facing roof deck in Vancouver—is to improve and sustain the quality of the soil. The Pridies' ingenious composting routine was essential to the success of their garden in the north, but it was also a model for horticultural success in any climate.

—ɯ—

Moving to the Northwest Territories in October, we were not mentally prepared to find six inches of snow on the ground, trees standing stark and leafless, the subarctic winter gathering its full forces.

After the beautiful, warm autumn day we had just left in Alberta, this land seemed unpromisingly cold and barren.

By May, the landscape began to thaw, and in June we watched great islands of ice float down the river and out into Great Slave Lake. So this was spring! Despite the lateness of the season, we felt the usual urge to plant a vegetable garden—there was a large piece of land behind our new home—and we went in search of anyone in Hay River who might have a bit of insight into gardening here.

We learned that if we made haste there was still time to plant—this was the first week of June—and so, with great hope, we dug into the virgin wild sod, turning every clump over by hand, breaking it up, shaking out the grass and roots, raking smooth a 25-by-25-foot plot of earth. Surprisingly, this seemed better soil than the hard clay we had gardened in Alberta, although there was still frost within inches of the surface; by July, we discovered, there would still be no more than 10 inches of thawed soil above the permafrost.

Ignoring the icy underpinnings of our new garden, we made neat rows and planted lettuce, peas, carrots, beets and, a week later, potatoes, along with cabbage and cauliflower transplants which had been bussed in from Edmonton. Our little garden looked prim and hopeful with the new seedlings in place and we slept well that night, thanks to the exercise, fresh air and satisfaction of having done the job well.

The next morning was clear and warm—the midnight sun had kept the garden bright all night—and when I ran outside to see how things were progressing, the shock stopped me in my innocent tracks: All our bright green plants had withered and died. All were frozen.

That was our first lesson in Far Northern horticulture: Don't blithely attempt to transplant until all danger of frost is past, and always be ready for the worst.

Since that first year, 1954, we have come to enjoy fairly predictable success, choosing the right seeds, types that grow and mature in this short season, covering our seedlings at night early in the summer, and learning to be philosophical about the odd years in which we have a killing frost in every month of the growing season.

An essential part of our weather-beating technique involves an active composting system which has added depth to our garden—raising tender roots away from the permafrost—and supplies a rich growing medium which causes plants to thrive and gives them greater strength to survive setbacks.

My husband, Leo, has gradually evolved his own system, and it has both stood the test of time and helped us produce bumper crops where none grew before. He starts the process in the spring by collecting a load of "waste" from one of the mounds of road-builders' scrapings that are so common in this country. Free for the taking, this material consists of soil and moss mixed with broken tree roots. He then collects all the lawn clippings he can garner from the neighbourhood and gathers organic kitchen scraps, wood ashes and sacks of sawdust. He may decide to augment the supplies with hay cut from roadside ditches and, in some years, may collect reject fish which can be found in certain local areas where winter fishermen discard them.

Using a motorized shredder, he grinds all of this refuse, adding a few scoops from the moss and soil mixture, and puts the shredded material into one of his four-foot-square homemade wooden composting bins, adding water if necessary, so that the mixture will be moist and degrade properly. He next covers the damp pile with a sheet of clear plastic for the first week if the weather is cool, and leaves it to decompose.

After three weeks he shovels everything into the shredder again, then moves it into the second bin, adding more water if necessary. A new mixture can now be placed in the first bin.

Three weeks later he turns the pile again, adding more water if it has dried (it should always be kept slightly damp). The heating process has peaked and stabilized by now. The pile is just comfortably warm and could be spread on the garden. It is clean-smelling and looks like black loam. We can say that the whole process takes six or seven weeks in the summertime.

After it is ready, we always leave the compost in cone-shaped piles, because Leo applies most of it in the fall. Throughout the summer he continues the process, planning to have a batch at some stage of composting in each bin until after the garden is harvested. Then, in fall, he gathers all the garden refuse, putting that through the grinder along with more moss and dirt and roots, and into the bin it goes for the winter. With the garden now clear, he spreads all the finished compost and works it in lightly with the tiller, so the garden is ready to plant as soon as the soil warms in the spring.

Over the winter, we fill at least two of the four bins with kitchen waste on top of the fall garden waste. By spring all of it is frozen solid and not rotted at all. About May 30th, however, we cover the bins with plastic garbage bags that will warm the piles and start them thawing. Soon the composting garbage begins to generate its own heat, and we are on our way again.

We now have a productive garden growing most of the root crops—potatoes, beets, turnips, carrots and onions. We have a greenhouse in which we start lettuce, onion seeds, celery and all the other green leafy vegetables. All of our tomatoes grow inside the greenhouse, as do the cucumbers and peppers. Although we use an Aladdin blue flame kerosene heater in the greenhouse every night until May while transplants and seedlings are growing, the sun does all the heating through the summer. We do not even try growing these tender crops in the garden now as they nearly always get damaged by frost at some point. The only common vegetable we do not try at all is corn. The season is just not long enough.

Generally, the ground thaws in late April or early May, and, if we have warm weather that heats the soil, then we can plant peas and other hardy seeds during the third or fourth week of May. We usually have a hot June and July, with cooling in August, and frost expected any evening from then on. September is a beautiful month when one can feel the end of summer, and in most cases local gardens are picked clean by this time.

Each year is different. We have known years when, with snow and frozen ground, September heralded winter, while at other times the snow held off until the day before Christmas. We have had temperatures of 105 degrees F in April, the heat spell lasting until June, when it ended abruptly with a snowstorm. After living here for a while one gets the feel of the country and its unpredictable weather and simply works accordingly.

We now have a 100-by-100-foot garden that supplies more food than we can use, without any commercial fertilizer. Our soil is rich and deep, and produces huge, well-formed vegetables. We are not able to reach the permafrost with the tiller any longer, although it used to lie less than a foot down. We take a great deal of pride in our garden and although we feel we've come to accept the elements as they are, thank the compost for providing a much needed horticultural security blanket.

BRIAN FAWCETT
1992

From "Some Advantages of Cramped Quarters," in
*The Compact Garden: Discovering the Pleasures
of Planting in a Small Space*

—⚭—

*B*rian Fawcett, a Vancouver poet, short-story, and, lately,
garden writer, has called himself "a writer, urban planner
and teacher." Fawcett has a number of books to his credit,
including My Career with the Leafs, and Other Stories *and* The Secret
Journals of Alexander MacKenzie.

In this excerpt from The Compact Garden, *he recounts his enriching experiences with his gardening neighbours—a theme often
found in our gardening literature. However, in the same chapter,
Fawcett mentions another cast of less benevolent characters also present in the Canadian garden: lawn-tearing dogs, roaming cats, vora-
cious insects, and tree-hating neighbours.*

—⚭—

I live in a neighbourhood that is culturally very mixed. On the lot to
the west lives a Chinese family, part of an extended family whose other
members live right across the alley. Next door on the east is a Chilean
family—not passionate gardeners, but terrific cooks. Next to them are
Archie and Phyllis, who come from around here. They are the most
meticulous gardeners I've ever met in my life. They have lived in their
house for nearly 40 years and are the unofficial historians in the neighbourhood. Beyond them are several Portuguese families. Across the
alley and down the street a little way lives Karla, who is, I think, from
one of the Balkan countries. There are several more Chinese families
on the block, as well as a couple of East Indian families.

Most of us don't have a great deal in common, occupationally or culturally. The Chinese family, for instance, is very close and insular, and the two sets of grandparents barely speak English. The Portuguese families tend to stick together, particularly during wine-making season, when they get fairly noisy about sticking together. There is, however, one thing we all have in common: we're all gardeners. It's a rare day out in the garden when I don't talk to one or more of them about something. One of my regular weekend pleasures is to take a stroll down the alley to check on what they and their gardens are up to. Almost everyone else does the same.

It's more than merely a pleasant thing to do. I've learned a great deal about gardening from talking over the fence with my neighbours—and more than a few things about life in general. One or two of my neighbours, I suspect, may even have learned from my techniques. The exchanges have taught me the most important secret of small-lot gardening: to respect and make use of the very real gardening expertise that exists around me.

All gardeners have certain plants they especially like to grow, and gardeners from different cultural backgrounds grow different kinds of plants, often by traditional methods they have adapted to local conditions. My Chinese neighbours, for instance, are superb vegetable gardeners, particularly when it comes to harvesting huge crops from a very limited space. Each year, they take three crops of bok choy from a small sunny patch next to my fence. As the summer heat comes on, they take advantage of my corn and bean crops to provide their bok choy with a little protection. And last summer, from a six- or eight-foot-long patch of carefully prepared soil, they grew an astounding number of huge exotic squashes and melons that sent vines sprawling right across their yard—and melons aren't supposed to grow well in this climate. I watch these neighbours like a hawk and have taken to using some of their methods.

A number of years ago, Karla gave me several varieties of pole beans I'd never seen before and have yet to find in any seed catalogue. In return, I gave her my extra 'Blue Lake' bean seeds. I liked these exotic pole beans so much that last year, I didn't even plant 'Blue Lake' beans. Instead, I turned them all over to Karla. She planted them very late in the season and, by wrapping the vines in plastic, was able to harvest fresh beans as late as early October.

The Portuguese families all grow wine grapes, something that the local garden centres warn not to expect too much from in this climate. But in our back alley, their grape harvests are enormous, because they have a special way of getting around the shortage of summer heat: they grow the grapes across their garage roofs. Each garage has black asphalt shingles on the roof, and the grapevines, sitting about six to nine inches above it on special frames, absorb the reflected and retained heat.

I've gotten tips about the advantages of watering with warmed water and manure tea from my Chinese neighbours. Come to think of it, I could provide an example of something particular and unusual that each one of my neighbours does. Your own neighbourhood likewise will have experts and expertise simply waiting to be tapped. Sometimes the advice will come from the old-timers who have discovered by trial and error over the years what will grow well in the local soil and microclimate. If you're lucky enough to live in a culturally mixed neighbourhood, that's another resource. The advice you get from along the back alley and around the neighbourhood is likely to be as reliable as any you'll get from your local garden shop.

There is also a more tasty and tangible bonus when you have neighbours who garden—the wonderful opportunities for trading excess vegetables and flowers. I habitually grow more tomatoes than I need and can cleverly press my advantage, as they are usually earlier than my neighbours'. In return, I get bok choy from my Chinese neighbours, bedding plants and cut flowers from Archie and Phyllis and fresh dill from outside the fence of one of my Portuguese neighbours. He has more than he needs, and he has figured out a way to keep it coming from early July into October—lots of it. When I plant dill, it's all ready at the same time.

NATIONAL CAPITAL FREENET
1994

"Invisible bug problem," in the Gardening Special Interest
Group of the National Capital FreeNet

—⏖—

*T*he explosive growth of electronic bulletin boards has opened up gardening conversations to the whole world. Want to compare notes on growing azaleas or keeping cats out of the spring bulb bed? Need a plant identified? Instead of writing to a favourite gardening magazine or calling the local horticultural society, a new breed of gardener, armed with computer and modem, is posting questions in discussion areas of what are known as SIGs (Special Interest Groups) on electronic bulletin boards—in this case, the National Capital FreeNet in Ottawa.

Freenets are exciting experiments in providing communities with a centre of electronically accessible information on government, social services, educational institutions, as well as on-line library catalogues and forums for discussion on topics ranging from classical music to travel destinations.

This summer 1994 exchange between three enthusiastic Ottawa-area gardeners—Alfred K. Neilson, Sandra P. Hoffman, and John Foulds—is a typical "thread" (linked postings on one subject) exhibiting the humour and knowledge tempered by a genuine spirit of helpfulness that characterizes many of these exchanges.

—⏖—

From: Alfred K. Neilson
Date: Thu Jul 28 13:57:18 1994
This year, it seems, I have bugs that I cannot see or find on close inspection, so I appeal to those of you with more knowledge than I, to try to solve this mystery.

I have a healthy, vibrant, and naturally fertilized garden with—carrots, parsnips, radishes, wax beans, tomatoes (cherry and beefsteak), and a patch of watermelon. Around the garden is a planting of sunflowers on the south and west side (almost ready to flower).

The problem is this—The sunflowers, radishes, and beans are being eaten by some invisible bug——I have inspected, until I am green in the face, for the culprit, but cannot find one. I do notice that the sunflowers are full of ants but, I do not think ants eat leaf vegetation—or am I wrong??

I have dusted occasionally with Rotenone, but the problem still exists!! All of the other vegetation is bug-hole free!

I did notice that I have a large patch of Nightshade (I think) behind the garden that is eaten full of holes in the leaves!! This plant is full of little purple cluster flowers with green fruit pods——Is this the carrier of my invisible bug??

The sunflowers that I have next to the house foundation are less eaten by bugs, but they still have the ant coverage problem.

If you have a solution to this please let me know—it's driving me wacky!!

From: Sandra P. Hoffman
Date: Fri Jul 29 19:10:31 1994
My guess would be earwigs. Go out at dusk or early in the morning to see if any are around. A soap and water solution sprayed right on them kills them in seconds.

From: John Foulds
Date: Fri Jul 29 21:59:35 1994
Hmmm. This is an interesting problem. I have had earwig problems before, but never in my radishes or beans. And the ones in my sunflowers never appeared until the heads were fully developed and they crept inside the canes to the flowerheads invisibly without damage.

But then earwigs would make sense as they work at night and you wouldn't see them. If you're up late one night, try a midnight trip with a flashlight. And when you figure it out, please post the conclusion to this great ongoing mystery.

From: Alfred K. Neilson
Date: Sat Jul 30 21:28:24 1994

It's SLUGS!!!!——aaaaaccckkkkk——It's like a superhighway of SLUGS!

The mystery is solved, thanks to some good advice from Sandra Hoffman and John Foulds (many thanks). I donned the Mosquito balm and took the flashlight out to the garden about an hour after sundown, and the slugs were all over the place—mostly going up the long poplar stakes that I put in to support the sunflowers!! No slugs were to be seen on the stalks of the sunflowers as I guess the surface was too picky and coarse for them to travel over! Live and learn!

I hurried off to Ritchies today and got some great advice from the resident manager about Diatomaceous Earth and crushed eggshells, and two sided carpet tape!!

The Manager told me that not only will the crushed shells and Diatomic material kill the slugs but the tomato plants just thrive on calcium, which these two materials are rich with!

Forgive my naivete, but I am a good gardener, and only started doing the green thumb bit in my late 40's (4 years ago), so although late in starting, I am new in learning the ropes!!

I can't wait for the cherry tomatoes to ripen—they look so full I am sure they will be better than last year, and they were great then!

I swear that watermelon vine has a mind of it's own!!

Cheers!

MARJORIE HARRIS
1994

"How to garden defensively," in *The Globe and Mail*

—∿—

arjorie Harris, a Toronto writer, has written many garden books, including The Canadian Gardener, Ecological Gardening *and* Marjorie Harris's Favourite Garden Tips. *This selection appeared in her regular* Globe and Mail *column.*

We all have our favourite noise makers we love to hate: those booming tape players, roaring leaf blowers, and droning air-conditioner compressors. Noise has become such a polluting presence in our large urban areas that the traditional idea of the garden as a place of contemplation has all but disappeared there.

Let's elect Harris national spokesperson for the "Silent Sundays" campaign!

—∿—

To me, the garden should be a sanctuary, a serene place to observe nature at work. My neighbours think this is dopey—I should move to the country if I want quiet. My neighbourhood is a place of whining machinery. Seven days a week the renovators are out there with hammers and saws making a din. Any foray into the back yard becomes an act of courage.

I have taken to practicing defensive gardening. I wear a radio called The Wanderer, shaped like huge earmuffs with a built-in FM radio, and meander about the garden looking like a jet pilot, listening to Bruckner or Bach. I have no idea what awful things this is doing to my hearing, but at least it keeps the buzz of machinery and barking dogs at bay.

Another machine I've tried will definitely cut through the noise of leaf blowers and gas motors. It's called the Noisebuster, and what it does is fill the ears with white sound that masks the outside noises, reducing the decibel level by half.

Defensive gardening doesn't just stop with noise. A few years ago, a friend came upon a group of children plucking her superb crop of spring flowers. She ducked into the house, blackened two teeth, donned an old black raincoat and in her most quavering old-lady voice threatened to dissolve them into puddles if they continued. They haven't been back since.

My favourite way to keep dogs out of the front garden is to tell careless owners that it's been sprinkled with a vile poison—the kind that will give dogs sick stomachs. I would love to get this message across to all the cats that use the garden as a litter box. Cayenne pepper works on open areas, but it must be sprinkled every day. Now I'm mulching with wood chips to make it uncomfortable for the local tabbies.

The worst assault, however, happened to a fellow gardener who returned home from work one evening to find that the splendid centrepiece of his front garden, a Japanese maple two metres tall, had completely disappeared. Neighbours said they saw three young men in a big van roll up that afternoon and dig it out, but they didn't think to call the cops. The nursery said a replacement would cost $700. The saddest thing is that the plantnappers did a terrible job of tearing out this tree while it was in full leaf, and it probably died.

The only way to defend yourself against this kind of felony is to put up a security gate. My creative neighbour to the south designed and built such a gate in the alley between our houses. It's only slightly larger than those on medieval castles, and it's gorgeous. We haven't had unwanted intruders since.

Then there is the personal danger. While turning the compost a few weeks ago, I inadvertently stirred up a bunch of feeding wasps. One flew up and bit me right under the eye, another on the leg. My husband said I looked like Jake LaMotta on a bad day. A visit to an emergency room told me that the poison hadn't gone into the eye, but I should take antihistamines. This was my first bite in 27 years of gardening, and it's left me a bit skittish.

The wasps left after I dumped masses of leaf mould, soil mixed with manure and garden cuttings on the compost to cover up whatever was attracting them.

One small triumph is that we've finally found a way to defend ourselves against the thoughtless people who play their music outside or start their lawn mowers at dinner time. We now have a little fountain on the deck. It's a simple rig: a lion with a spout in his mouth spits water into an old-fashioned tub. A small circulating pump keeps the water going around. A few plants, some pretty rocks and—*voilà*—an inexpensive way to surround yourself with a pleasant, consistent sound of your own choosing.

Still, I miss the sound of birds and, especially at this time of the year, the buzz of bees. I've often thought how wonderful it would be to have just one day when everyone would agree to stop—perhaps Silent Sundays.

PRAISING
FAVOURITE
PLANTS

CATHARINE PARR TRAILL
1833

From "Letter IX," in *Backwoods of Canada: Being Letters from the Wife of an Emigrant Officer, Illustrative of the Domestic Economy of British America*

—⚮—

*C*atharine Parr Traill, née Strickland, (1802–1899) the youngest of "the literary Stricklands," emigrated from England to the Rice Lake area of Upper Canada in 1832 with her husband, Lieutenant Thomas Traill. She already had nine books to her credit. Backwoods of Canada, her first of eight books from Canada, consisted of letters to her mother and friends in England, written in 1832 and 1833 and not originally intended for publication. An instant success, it appeared in several further editions, all in quick succession. With a McClelland and Stewart reprint in 1929, it became a Canadian classic.

These passages from a letter written in April 1833 reveal the optimistic and adaptive personality, the immense practicality, and the keen interest in botany that were to characterize much of Traill's Canadian writing.

—⚮—

Lake House,
April 18, 1833.

We have now got quite comfortably settled, and I shall give you a description of our little dwelling. What is finished is only a part of the original plan; the rest must be added next spring, or fall, as circumstances may suit. . . . When the house is completed, we shall have a verandah in front; and at the south side, which forms an agreeable addition in the summer, being used as a sort of outer room, in which we can dine, and have the advantage of cool air, protected from the glare of the sunbeams. The Canadians call these verandahs "stoups." Few houses, either log or frame, are without them. The pillars look extremely pretty, wreathed with the luxuriant hop-vine, mixed with the scarlet creeper and "morning glory," the American name for the most splendid of major convolvuluses. These stoups are really a considerable ornament, as they conceal in a great measure the rough logs, and break the barn-like form of the building. . . .

I am anxiously looking forward to the spring, that I may get a garden laid out in front of the house; as I mean to cultivate some of the native fruits and flowers, which, I am sure, will improve greatly by culture. The strawberries that grow wild in our pastures, woods, and clearings, are several varieties, and bear abundantly. They make excellent preserves, and I mean to introduce beds of them into my garden. There is a pretty little wooded islet on our lake, that is called Strawberry island, another Raspberry island; they abound in a variety of fruits—wild grapes, raspberries, strawberries, black and red currants, a wild gooseberry, and a beautiful little trailing plant that bears white flowers like the raspberry, and a darkish purple fruit consisting of a few grains of a pleasant brisk acid, somewhat like in flavour to our dewberry, only not quite so sweet. . . . I have called it the "trailing raspberry." . . .

Among our wild fruits we have plums, which, in some townships, are very fine and abundant; these make admirable preserves, especially when boiled in maple molasses, as is done by the American housewives. Wild cherries, also a sort called choke cherries, from their peculiar astringent qualities, high and low-bush cranberries, blackberries, which are brought by the Squaws in birch baskets,—all these are found on the plains and beaver meadows. The low-bush cranberries are brought in great quantities by the Indians to the towns and villages. They form a standing preserve in the tea-tables in most of the settlers' houses; but for richness of flavour, and for beauty of appearance, I admire the high-bush cranberries . . . The bush on which this cranberry grows resembles the guelder rose. . . .

The first time you send a parcel or box, do not forget to enclose flower-seeds, and the stones of plums, damsons, bullace, pips of the best kinds of apples, in the orchard and garden, as apples may be raised here from seed, which will bear very good fruit without being grafted; the latter, however, are finer in size and flavour. I should be grateful for a few nuts from our beautiful old stock-nut trees. . . .

I am very desirous of having the seeds of our wild primrose and sweet violet preserved for me; I long to introduce them in our meadows and gardens. Pray let the cottage children collect some. My husband requests a small quantity of lucerne-seed, which he seems inclined to think may be cultivated to advantage.

JULIANA HORATIA EWING
1869

Letter 76, in *Canada Home: Juliana Horatia Ewing's Fredericton Letters, 1867–1869*

—⚉—

*I*n the two years that Juliana Horatia Ewing, née Gatty, *(1841–1885) spent in Canada—while her husband, Captain Alexander Ewing, was stationed at Fredericton, New Brunswick—she wrote frequent letters to family and friends back in England. She was by then already a published short-story writer of several years' standing. The verve and optimism of her letters, which were often accompanied by sketches, would not have surprised those who knew her or her narrative and artistic abilities.*

Soon after their arrival in Fredericton in July, she began sketching flowers and writing of her plans to "grub" in the garden of the house they would occupy. By September, she was thinking of house plants for the winter months and requesting seeds and bulbs for the coming spring. "My mind is quite absorbed with the thought of my garden," she wrote early in 1868. She continued to report her pleasure in flowers and vegetables throughout the year, despite a mid-season move to another house.

As we see in this letter of February 23, 1869, she rose to the extra challenges of gardening in winter with energy and good humour.

—⚉—

Fredericton. New Brunswick. Canada.
Feb. 23. 1869.

My dear Miss Thompson.

I know you will sympathize with me in the joys & sorrows of my window garden during this long & severe winter. Not that it has been anything like so cold as the last year's was, but I mean that the length of Canadian winters & the intensity of the frost make indoor gardening very different to what it is at Home. On the other hand anything green—growing—& sweet is doubly & trebly welcome when every trace of one's garden is buried 4 or 5 feet deep in snow— & the ground is frozen *so* hard that you know that there is no getting at anything that you did not take up in the Autumn (or even a bit of garden mould) till May!—*I* have been much more successful this year than last. 1st—Our little house will keep out the extreme frost—& the other one we lived in last year—would not. (we used to carry the hyacinth pots up to bed with us—put them round the stove—& bury them in dressing gowns &c. but the poor things were frozen & thawed—over & over again!! 2dly—Last year I bought my bulbs here, & they were not first rate I think. This year (the Bishop was kind enough to bring them &) I got them from *Carter & Sons* at Home. They were not kept dry enough—& when I got them mould had begun. I lost *all* the aconites—& anemones—& almost all the snowdrops & crocuses—but my hyacinths & narcissi—& tulips were none the worse—& have been most successful. I only lost *one* bulb—(a hyacinth) by a sharp frost. I planted them in leafmould & sand just as I used to do at home —kept them in my dress closet in my room for their *dark* month, & brought them out by degrees into my "forcing house."!!!! This is the tiny "landing" at the top of the stairs. It has a window—& what is called a "dumb stove"—i.e. a "drum" or box of iron through which the pipe of the hall stove runs—& which thus warms the upper part of the house. The window is very near it, & on the window sill I *force* my bulbs! But every night—I have to move them from the glass (though we have double windows)—as if a "snap" of increased frost came, I might lose them one & all. Our house is very warm, & they would probably be safe 6 nights in 7—but if one doesn't do it always one is apt to forget on the cold nights—& I have lost one hyacinth—my only rose—& some other things already, besides my poor Calla Ethiopica which was just looking grand!! 3dly Mrs. Medley is such an admirable gardener that I get many hints from her. I do wish you *could* see *her* window gardens! She has long narrow boxes (I think I shall try them next year) just painted green. Two iron supports (wood of course wld do, but you can buy the iron ones for screwing on, & they are prettier) are just screwed on to the woodwork of the windows—& a shelf or ledge of wood (also green) laid on them. On to this the box is put—& lifted backwards & forwards as is needful. The pots are just sunk in the box with saucers beneath & moss round them. She has variegated sweet geraniums—kept *very dwarf* in pots & lycopods (like the "stag's horn moss" on the moors) which was got in the autumn & which is not growing, but still looks wonderfully green—(& will freshen up by soaking a night in a pail of water) The *flowers* this year have been hyacinths, tulips, narcissi, crocuses, scillas, lachenalias, & cyclamens, with little bunches of *lichen*, & some red "highbush cranberry" berries dotted about (*not* growing) The boxes are quite narrow—only holding one pot in width, & just the length of the window sill. She has no greenhouse—pit—or *anything* that you & I had not at Home—& she doesn't line her boxes with zinc—or buy "forcing cases" or do anything expensive or out of *my* reach—which makes her hints more valuable to *me* than book receipts. She rears, & coddles all her bulbs, seeds, cuttings &c. in the windows of her bedroom, the Bishop's study, & the landing; & has not even a gardener or any garden but a very narrow strip in front of the house shaded by trees, & facing east. When you look at *my* illustrations—I fear you will think of Barr and Sugden's Catalogues, & how easy it is to *draw* "Zinnia Elegans Flore-pleno" the size of a prize dahlia & correspondingly rounded in outline & full in quill; & how far from easy we found it to produce similar specimens in the garden!! So I will give you one or two statistics. I only treated myself to 3 polyanthus narcissi (all "soleil d'or") & put the 3 bulbs in one pot— They sent up 4 stems—& I have counted 29 blossoms. I had one *exquisite* blush single hyacinth (name lost) which sent up a stem with 18 very large bells: the same bulb has now sent up a second stem with 9 bells quite as large as the others. I have pressed one of the 2d lot against my penholder—& from point to point the spread petals are as wide as the line I have drawn. In the same pot was a single white *faintly* tinged with yellow (*Rousseau*) Also very fine. The first stalk bore 18 bells—& the 2d seems to have 30—but I can hardly be *certain* yet—they are so closely packed. That makes 75 bells from the 2 bulbs in one pot. I only had 9 hyacinths—they have

certainly *fully* repaid me. *I* never had such blooms as some of them,
I think. I lost one—gave one away—& the other 7 have been a great
enjoyment to me. Now that we have given notice to leave our house
in May—I have no *garden* to consider—so I brought everything I
have to the windows, & commenced Spring forcing as soon as I
heard the news; for I may as well enjoy them as *pot* plants. Our
house is taken already but I hope the next tenant will be civil, & let
me take the wild flowers & ferns &c. &c. that I stored in my little
flower patch last summer. I have a large patch of Sweet Williams
from Ecclesfield seed too—in the kitchen garden! It is one of the
inconveniences of military life—that one may be moved *just* as one
begins to settle down—& get a home about one. This is a small cross
however!— And we have so many comforts & blessings, that I do
not complain. We know nothing whatever of our movements except
that if we remain *here*, we shall probably go into quarters. There I
should probably have a sunny aspect & a verandah before my windows—which I mean to hang with flowerbaskets & fill with plants.
In summer it wld be really pretty. For it looks upon the green where
the bands play—& on the river—& the big willows where tree fire-
flies float about like sparks of fire—after sunset. I am now forcing on
my few things—that I may make cuttings from them in good time,
& increase my stock: for plants &c. are very dear here: & as we do
not know *when* we may move (nor where) I spend as little ready
cash as *possible* just now—since we might want it all at a few weeks'
notice to pay my journey expenses, & furnish our *3d move*! I fear
there is no chance of our coming Home—but we know nothing.

I had a lovely major convolvulus last year, & yesterday—walking on snowshoes in my garden (The snow is nearly up to the top of
the palings, & I walked over my latest sowing of *peas* —across the
top of the peasticks!!!)—I saw some of the seed vessels still hanging
from the house. I wonder if the frost has killed it—or whether the
seeds wld grow. I shall put one or two in this & you shall try, &
when you write—you shall put one or two seeds from your own
stock of seeds into your letter, if you will, & we will make one link
between Grenoside & New Brunswick!

I am proud of my bulbs—but am perverse enough to be more
proud of an English primrose that is coming into bloom—& of 2

cuttings struck in a *bottle*, because I broke them off a beautiful fuschia[sic]at a time not orthodox for "gardener's cuttings"— I have had such comfort & beauty from the store of moss I laid up before the winter. It is wonderful how it *revives* in water—& adorns my flowerpots. If we have a box out in Spring—I will have some from Home—& I should like a contribution from Greno Wood!

Your always & affat [JHE]

Rex's best regards to you, & mine to Hannah & her husband please. Alas! I fear the seeds *are* spoilt.

A. HOOD
1879

From "Tomatoes," in *The Canadian Horticulturist*

—◊—

A. Hood of Barrie, Ontario, was writing at a time when maintaining a home vegetable garden in large eastern Canadian cities and some towns was no longer necessary for survival. Householders were beginning to rely more and more on farmers' markets, fruit and vegetable pedlars, market gardens, and general stores for fresh produce.

As well, many urban lots were too small to include a vegetable garden in addition to the space needed for the family's stables, priv-ies, and clotheslines. In working-class areas, vacant space that could be cultivated was almost nonexistent.

But at the same time, the home gardener of the 1870s and 1880s had easier access than ever before to tools, other garden supplies, and seeds. Already in 1872, D. W. Beadle was writing that the tomato "is grown by every one who makes any pretensions to keeping a garden."

More than a century later, modern gardeners can easily identify with many of Hood's enthusiasms about tomato cultivation. Yet wherever they live, they certainly still share Hood's delight in eating a sun-warmed tomato right off the vine.

—◊—

If you wish to enjoy this fruit in its greatest perfection eat it fresh off the vines. Take a sweet cake or soda biscuit in your hand, about an hour after dinner, and visit the tomato patch, select one that is not too ripe, and if the eating of it does not give you an appetite for another you have not got the right kind of tomatoes. I have only very recently discovered the right kind myself. Years ago we thought of nothing but the Large Red and the Large Yellow, but as earliness with me was always a desideratum, I cultivated the Early Red French, which I think must be identical with Hubbard's Curled Leaf, and have found it to be the very earliest kind I could procure, and I think it has that distinction still. Its flavor is good, very much superior to the Large Red, but it grows so wrinkled and uneven in shape that it is generally rejected for kitchen use, and it does not sell well. It is also very watery, having scarcely any pulp adhering to the skin; but with all its faults, it is so much superior in flavor to the Large Red, that while I enjoy eating it raw like a plum, I should never make use of the latter unless cooked.

This year I have had a surprise, and an agreeable one too. I have cultivated two kinds of tomatoes that I had never before tried, viz: the Trophy and Hathaway's Excelsior. These are of a more regular shape, have both a thicker pulp, and a thick fleshy lining adhering to the skin something like that of a musk-melon, which gives them that firmness which is called in the catalogues "very solid." The flavor of the Trophy is good, but that of the Excelsior is better; yes, superior beyond all expectation. It is as much superior to the common Large Red as a Lombard is superior to a wild plum. It is not so large or productive as the Trophy, nor have I found it any earlier. I obtained the seed of Jas. Vick, of Rochester [New York], who describes it in his catalogue as "of excellent quality every way—the best tomato I have ever grown," and it quite justifies the description. This fruit is evidently improving, plums will have to get out of the way or it will catch up to them.

I dare say some of my readers will think that if tomatoes are good they are not deserving of all this eulogy. Well, judging by the same rules as other fruits, perhaps not, but they must take into consideration the comfort they feel after partaking of a liberal allowance; what a delightful sense of fulness and internal satisfaction they experience; and then how flattering it is to one's hopes of longevity to know that you are day by day adding a little flesh to your none-too-corpulent figure; to feel that your vest is getting too small, and that the waistband of your pants will certainly have to be loosened out. What a relish too you have for your food during the next six months. How glorious a thing it is to be able, like Macbeth, to say, "Throw physic to the dogs," and rejoice in the diminution of your doctor's bills. What a pity it is that we cannot have two crops in the year, so that our shadows might never grow less.

MRS. SYMMES
1879

From "Flower Culture," in *Report of the Montreal Horticultural Society and Fruit Growers' Association for the year of 1879*

—⚏—

Mrs. Symmes of Aylmer, Quebec, has one of those authentic voices in the Canadian garden that we immediately trust. It is the voice of experience enlivened by a ready wit and a cheerful way of giving advice. She seems to have been an adventurous indoor gardener who travelled well beyond the ferns and geraniums of some of her contemporaries.

Although she is speaking to us over a nearly 120-year divide, her lively voice bridges this gap. We can easily visualize scenes of the indoor gardening life of the late 1870s. As well, the gentle mockery toward her gardening friends is still fresh and amusing today.

—⚏—

The Verbena is the most difficult house-plant I have ever grown, because it is essentially an out-of-door plant. It is difficult under the best conditions—impossible with any other. Verbenas must be placed close to the glass, monopolizing, in a small green-house, all the best places. In the houses of the *habitant* they often make the best growth, as they are kept upon the window, where the fresh air filters through the sash and they have the whole light of the winter-day. It is quite useless to put anything but a basket plant or a bulb in a north window. This question of light is one of the troubles of growing Verbenas; they are never dormant; the loss of all their leaves is certain death to them. The full sunshine of summer days brings them to perfection; winter days are so much shorter, they are so much of the time in absolute darkness, the only wonder is that any survive. Verbenas prefer a dry atmosphere; in summer, when well started, they bloom persistently through some weeks of drought. Owing to the dampness of the climate, they are not successful as bedding-plants in England; they mildew, and present a very different appearance from the gorgeous masses of bloom we are so proud of here. I am generally able to keep from twenty to thirty plants through the winter, but I start in the fall an unlimited number, and spend some rather solemn hours in removing the empty pots from the shelves, one, two, three, sometimes a dozen at each watering. This dreary work is nearly finished at New Year's, and unless plants are actually dying before the days begin to lengthen, the sun brings them forward at once. Someone may ask why I take this trouble, when Verbenas are raised readily from seed. Seedling Verbenas come in dull colors; sometimes there are thirty pale purples or magentas in one lot. In a collection of one hundred seedlings I have sometimes propagated only three for winter. . . .

Verbenas are as likely to do well in the window as in a green-house; but those ladies who place their Verbenas, Heliotropes and other soft-wooded plants behind a curtain in the "dim religious light" of a conventionally darkened room, can have little idea of the natural conditions of plant life, or, indeed, of human life. The disposition must be hopeful which would expect health and bloom without light. People who cannot endure the sunlight, and raise their curtains at least two-thirds the height of the windows, should give up window gardening. I have seen quite a number of plants behind a green shutter, white blind and a muslin curtain; they were not pretty plants, and their owner complained sadly that they did not blossom. The Oleander, Calla, Fuchsia, common Geraniums and bulbous plants will exist in semi-darkness, probably because they are scantily watered and have stored up some vitality out of doors in summer; but mere existence is hardly an object to those who take the trouble to start and pot plants for the house. Verbenas grow best of all hanging up either in some of the numerous hanging devices, or suspended by wires in pots (strings decay). Anything hanging up loses its moisture more rapidly and must be carefully watched and watered.

One invariable rule I wish to give: Plants growing *well* and evidently requiring nourishment should be well watered; those dormant, sickly and making no demand upon their roots should be left comparatively dry. We all know that the sick stomach will not assimilate food, and it must be equally plain that a root which is appropriating very little moisture needs no soaking.

VELMA PETERSON
1939

From "Our Garden: A horticultural achievement in
Alberta's driest corner," in *The Country Guide*

—◊◊—

*V*elma Peterson, a native Albertan, lived on land her parents had homesteaded nearly thirty years earlier. She
was one of hundreds of country women who, in the
years before telephones in every home and modems on many desks,
contributed advice and shared their experiences in the many
Canadian agricultural magazines and weekly newspapers. Although
some women did write in to give advice on crops or animal hus-
bandry, it was mainly in the "homemaker" sections that their successful treatments for baby's croup, new ways to "turn" a collar for
one last use, poems, recipes for beef stew, easy-to-use farm account-
ing systems, and gardening advice could be found. Before the term
"sisterhood" was in common use, these farm women were busily creating support networks.

In the community of gardeners, Peterson was not unique. However, she forms another link in the chain of those gardeners, past,
present, and future, who enjoy sharing their plants, seeds, and warm,
encouraging advice with friends, neighbours, and unseen readers.

One wishes she had contributed more to these magazines. Her
written voice is so immediate you can almost hear her talking.

—◊◊—

We live in the semi-desert of southeastern Alberta, 75 miles from the
nearest city. To most of its inhabitants this is a "next year" country,
but as we watch our crops dry up, next year is rather a sorry conso-
lation. However, as far as our garden is concerned, we can plan with
a good deal of confidence on "this year's" results. . . .

Our vegetable garden is the work of the whole family, but my special interest is in my flowers. I am not sure just how my hobby began, but one of my earliest recollections is of trotting behind my mother's heels up the garden path through the trees to pick the fragrant sweet peas. When I was about eight an old gentleman gave me a few clumps of pinks, which formed the nucleus of my perennials.

A few years later I exhibited flowers at the local fairs. I began to save seeds from each variety and every year since I have bought or been given a few new kinds. By this means I grew 66 varieties last summer. The majority were annuals but I am finding a few perennials that can cope with the long dry season. I do not spend more than 50 cents a year on seeds, and the pleasure I get out of growing them nets me a fortune.

When I clean my seeds in the winter I begin to plan a diagram. I always have to change or modify it when planting time comes, but try to stick to the general outline. Summer cypress always predominates in the scheme, as I have never found its equal in setting off flowers. Besides, its beautiful verdure is so welcome in this land of sombre browns. I try to make my plan like a miniature park, a different scheme each year. In the centre of my little park the men erect a structure from poles and wire. I never knew what to call this contraption, but have decided it could pass as a pergola. Around it I plant the morning glories, scarlet runners and other vines. It is a continual surprise to me how fast the pergola is covered.

The birds and bees and butterflies seem to find my flowers an oasis in the desert. I became fond of three tame butterflies, but they left as soon as the Sweet William went to seed. The bluebirds saved my cypress bushes when the worms marched in. The meadowlarks made my pergola their choir loft. But my mother never feels at ease among the swarms of bumblebees.

My flowers are pressed into service at dinners, weddings, funerals.

Gathering seeds used to be my most tedious garden task, until people began asking for them. Now, my seeds are scattered in gardens all over this community, and visitors have taken them to other parts of our province, to British Columbia, Saskatchewan, and to three of the United States.

So now I see a vision of scattered gardens gay with flowers which are the result of my hobby out on the bald open spaces.

ELSIE REFORD
1944

From "Gentiana Macaulayi, variety Wellsii, at Estevan
Lodge, Grand Metis, P.Q. Canada"

—∿—

*E*lsie Stephen Reford, née Meighen, (1872–1967) inherited a
fishing camp, Estevan Lodge, near Rimouski on the lower
St. Lawrence River, and turned it into a summer estate
whose gardens, renamed "Les Jardins de Métis," have been open to
the public since 1961. Reford began planting perennials into her
"wild meadows and Spruce woodland" when she was in her fifties,
and gardened actively into her eighties.

The location was normally blessed with deep snow in winter, a
late spring, and a warm summer moderated by mists from the river.
Reford often said that these conditions enabled her to grow plants
from all over the world, and including the lilies of Canadian breeders Alwyn Buckley, J. W. Crow, Beatrice Palmer, Isabella Preston, and
F. L. Skinner.

Her husband, Robert, photographed the gardens, and she kept
written records—describing particularly the plantings as she found
them in May and as she left them in September or October. She also
wrote in the Royal Horticultural Society Lily Year-Book for 1939 and
in The Lily Yearbook of The North American Lily Society for 1949.
In 1944, apparently for submission to an American journal, she prepared this article—whose final sentence expressed the thoughts of
many like herself who had family members overseas in World War II.

—∿—

It is a half revealed truth that gardeners, for the most part, differ
from many of their fellow men in that when success has at length
crowned their efforts, whatever may have gone before, toil, trial and

error, disappointment after disappointment, failures, all are swept completely from memory—obliterated in the ecstasy of pure joy at the sight of the plants yielding up their loveliest rewards. For this reason, unless the amateur gardener is unusually persevering in keeping accurate records, he or she has little to offer by way of assistance to others when it comes to passing on more or less scientific information regarding the elements and conditions which have contributed to their particular achievements. The present writer is no exception to this regrettable generality. However, as the cultivation of Gentiana Macaulayi, variety Wellsii, in the garden at Estevan has been comparatively simple it is possible that what there is to tell may be sufficient for some small degree of helpfulness to members of the companionage of gardening who may wish to experiment in growing this matchless gem among Alpine hybrids. . . .

The growing of G. Wellsii began at Estevan in 1935 when some two dozen plants were purchased in England and the following year another fifty were imported. Prior to that other species of Gentians had been grown with sufficiently encouraging results to stimulate a deeper interest in the whole family. Gentian lore was sought out wherever it could be found and carefully perused; the Bulletins of the Alpine Garden Society of England and the Journals of the Royal Horticultural Society proved veritable gold mines in which to quarry for the desired information. For five years Gentiana Wellsii were planted in various parts of the garden; they were even grown in the Scree, where indeed they did extremely well. Nowhere did they fail to thrive but in positions most favourable to them the increase was phenomenal, so much so that by 1940 the problem of providing them with greatly extended space had to be given consideration if their cultivation was to be continued. By that time through the experience gained in having grown the Gentians under varying conditions and in association with various flowers, it had become clear that to obtain the full effect of their exquisite beauty G. Wellsii should not be grown together with any other plant and not even in too close proximity with others of the same race. There is a certain quality about these entrancing flowers, something that is perhaps best described as an aloofness in character which renders their combination with other plants not only difficult but which is apt to produce an effect of a sin committed against horticultural good taste. To abandon growing G. Wellsii could not be contemplated. The alternative was to break new ground for them and this was done. The ground prepared has since been named the Gentian Walk and is in the form of a curving path of one hundred and forty feet in length running between two borders of four to four and a half feet in width . . . During the latter part of August, through September and well into October there is to be seen, along that path, a miracle of beauty, for there, stretching out in long sweeps are tens of thousands upon tens of thousands of the glorious blue trumpets of G. Wellsii at the height of its flowering. Truly a breath-taking spectacle.

It may be asked, how comes it that these plants of asiatic parentage have adapted themselves so unreservedly to our Canadian climate and to a locality where winter temperatures frequently range down well below zero while in summer the thermometer rises to over eighty degrees? The first answer to the question is, as already indicated, to be found in the ever present atmospheric moisture and the purity of the air, without which no Gentian will flower, however well it may grow. The second is that their requirements have been met in regard to soil and their dislikes have been respected. Opinions differ as to their tolerance of lime but my own experience is that they most certainly do not require it for there is not the slightest trace of it in the soil where they are grown at Estevan. All are agreed that G. Wellsii will not endure a sticky or clogging sort of ground, that they must be given impeccable drainage, that the soil for them must be rich in humus and porous in texture. To accomplish this for the Gentian Walk at Estevan the natural soil, which is chiefly of a forbidding sort of clay, was excavated to a depth of two feet and the first four inches filled in with beach stones about the size of an egg; after that six inches of gravelly grit and the remaining fourteen inches were given a mixture of two parts finely cut leaves, one part of peat and one part of a gritty sand. Into this the Gentians were planted and the whole strewn over with fine gravel. This gravel is, of course, not seen except in the spring when the plants are still in the rosette stage for the long shoots very quickly cover the ground completely. The borders are made with a very slight slope and this, together with the ample amount of grit incorporated into the soil makes for the indispensable perfection of drainage. The measure of care which G. Wellsii demands is more or less determined by the rainfall during the summer months for the plants must never be allowed to become dry at the roots. If hot dry spells occur during midsummer the Gentians at Estevan are thoroughly drenched every second day with a sprinkler playing over them for hours for even the atmospheric moisture is not sufficient to keep them in good health without water to the roots. In a cool climate, such as we have on the Lower St. Lawrence, Gentians do best in full sun. Given their dearest desires of moisture and soil ingredients G. Wellsii will respond with such richness of increase that it may even become an embarrassment for when that transpires lifting and division become imperative. The prescribed time for this to be done is every three years and if neglected the penalty is paid in general deterioration of the plants. In this year 1944 the time had come at Estevan for the Wellsii Gentians to be divided and though one absolutely quailed before the prospect of the labour it would entail it was undertaken immediately after flowering in October. Here perhaps there ought to be given a word of caution. All authorities on Gentian growing, without exception, stoutly maintain that these and other autumn flowering Gentians should only be divided in early spring when they begin to show above the ground, but as circumstances make it impossible for it to be done at that season at Estevan, greatly daring, division has always been made in the autumn and in no instance have the plants suffered any harm. When they were lifted this autumn they were so full with splendidly healthy strong roots that with a view to their future well being each plant had to be divided into four as an absolute minimum for replanting while into eight or ten would have been better—but where was the prepared ground for them? Many of these Gentians had produced from one hundred and fifty to two hundred blooms per plant and naturally this wealth of flowering had exhausted much of the original nourishment put into the soil, so it was thoroughly re-worked and finely cut leaves and peat added in a two to one proportion. Directly after the snow will have melted in the spring and the ground is clear the Gentians will be given a top dressing of leaves finely powdered in a grist mill. Into the borders of the Gentian Walk there were replanted in October three thousand three hundred and fifty four G. Wellsii, many were sent to other gardens while over two thousand were put into reserve to await the day when more time and labour will become available for the pursuit of the ancient craft of gardening—when the heavy war clouds will cease to cast their long, dark shadows of sorrow and peace will return to men's lives over the face of the earth.

PERCY H. WRIGHT
1950

Letter to Isabella Preston, March 17, 1950

—⚬—

*P*ercy H. Wright (1898–1989) was one of the pioneer Prairie plant breeders determined to make the west bloom. He became interested in plant breeding during a bout of measles when he was seventeen, and to pass the time, he read horticultural magazines. He founded a nursery in 1925, completed a degree in arts and sciences at the University of Saskatchewan in 1929, and founded a second nursery in 1938—all by age forty. However, along the way, his aspirations were tested and temporarily destroyed by debilitating sickness, drought, fire, and flood.

After each setback, the affable Wright would rebuild the nursery and breeding program that he continued to support with a number of jobs, including that of garden columnist (1956–1966) for the Saskatoon Star Phoenix. When he retired in 1966, however, he turned full-time to plant hybridizing.

Although he worked with lilies, daylilies, ornamental crabapples, honeysuckles, and plums, he conducted his favourite plant breeding experiments with roses. His most famous introduction was the remarkably hardy 'Hazeldean' shrubrose—which survived temperatures well below minus 40 degrees Celsius.

Wright's letter to a fellow hybridist—in this case, the esteemed Isabella Preston in Ontario—is typical of the handwritten and hand-typed communications that joined Canadian horticulturists throughout the preelectronic age.

—⚬—

Box 106, Sutherland, Sask.,
March 17, 1950

Dear Miss Preston,

Thank you for yours of March 15, which reached me next day. Thank you for your good wishes. As a matter of fact, I am a little proud of my work in roses, not because the results are themselves so remarkable, but because I have done it all without any financial assistance, and in spite of extreme lack of funds. Somehow, it just seemed as though there were nothing else worth while to do.

Yes, I got the plant you sent. Ross rose x (rugosa x sweetbrier), and it did well for a few months. Then it developed severe chlorosis. I doctored it with iron sulphate, but the treatment was only partially successful. At last I got tired of nursing it, and dug it out. Your example, however, has encouraged me to use Ross rose (and *R. beggeriana*) in my own pollinations. It was not everblooming in my district—a fact which astonished me.

I shall be delighted to mention your book on lilies, not once, but every opportunity I get. I wish I were living nearer you, so that I could encourage you to write further books. Books on lilies necessarily get out of date rather rapidly, and you have done lots of good work apart from that on lilies, and deserve to have something more than that to be remembered by. I am sending for a copy of your book tomorrow, and when I get it, will, if you are willing, send it to you to be autographed. You are one of my heroes, not only because you have been successful in a line which I should like to be successful in, but because of your long record of helpfulness and human sympathy.

In regard to the "questionnaire" you suggest, the information I mostly want is on how you acquired the early bent that gave you the impulse to devote your life to gardening, and how you first got a "toe-hold" in your line of effort. These first beginnings reveal the human side of things. Later progress is more natural, for enthusiasm feeds on its early successes. I am sure your interest began long before you came to Canada. What drew you to Canada, if I may ask?

By the way, the seedling rose from Betty Bland that you sent me has done well for me. I call it "Presto" because it comes into bloom while such a young plant. I have now over a dozen plants from the one, and will soon be able to test it. It is really fairly close to Betty Bland in all respects, but has a slight handicap (from the nursery-man's point of view) in that it does not layer as readily as Betty Bland.

Best wishes,

Percy H. Wright

ISABELLA PRESTON
1956

From "Note sent to Mr. Charles H. Curtis for the R.H.S. [Royal Horticultural Society] Lily YearBook, 1956"

—〰—

*I*sabella Preston (1881–1965) was an unusual woman for her time. After emigrating from England in 1912 at age thirty-one, she enrolled in the Ontario Agricultural College at Guelph, but soon gave up her studies to conduct practical work under the supervision of Professor J. W. Crow, a well-known plant breeder. She obviously found her life's calling. By 1916 she had become the first professional woman plant hybridist in Canada, and was part of a select circle of renowned Canadian plant hybridists. This amazing transformation was due to her meticulous crossbreeding of international-award-winning lilies.

In 1920 she joined W. T. Macoun at the Central Experimental Farm in Ottawa, embarked on 26 years of intense plant breeding activity, and originated nearly 200 hybrids (roses, lilacs, Siberian iris, Roseybloom crabapples, and always her beloved lilies).

Preston wrote numerous articles, as well as the first Canadian book on lily cultivation. During her lifetime, she, as well as her hybrids, gained many prestigious awards and honours. By 1940, her colleagues were calling her the "dean of hybridists."

—〰—

I was born in Lancaster, England, in 1881 and was educated at a private school in Liverpool. My father and mother were very fond of gardening and as long as I can remember I had a small flower bed of my own. I attended a short course at the Swanley Horticultural College in 1906 but for some years after that I had no garden. In 1912 my sister accepted a position as music teacher in a College for girls in Ontario and persuaded me to come out to Canada at the same time. For a few weeks I worked on a fruit farm picking raspberries, plumbs and peaches. In the autumn I attended some lectures on horticulture at the Ontario Agricultural College at Guelph and occasionally worked in the greenhouses. The following spring the late Professor J. W. Crow arranged for me to look after an experimental planting of strawberries and also to look after some plants in one of the greenhouses. Amongst these there were a few pots of small seedling lilies which he had crossed. Unfortunately they died. In this same greenhouse Prof. Crow had some dwarf pear trees which I cared for. Watching him emasculate and pollinate the flowers. This was my first introduction to practical plant breeding.

When it was arranged for me to continue working at the College Prof. Crow ordered some Lilium bulbs which I grew in the greenhouse. The idea was to grow seeds so that we could increase our stock and also to make as many crosses between species as possible. In the Lily Year Book for 1933 these efforts are listed. Unfortunately the young bulbs had to be planted out in an unsuitable place and most of them died during the winter. The cross between L. Sargentiae (female) and L. regale was too precious to be put out doors and was kept in the greenhouse until the bulbs were large enough to be put into a cold frame. In "Lilies of the World" of Woodcock and Stearn the cross is named "Imperiale". Two clones have been named. The well known George C. Creelman is an ancestor of most of the white tubular lilies that are so popular now. "Crow's Triumph" is the other and was more popular with florists.

In 1920 the late Dr. W. T. Macoun, Dominion Horticulturist, wanted someone to do plant breeding work with ornamental plants and I applied for the position. I wanted to discontinue working with vegetables which I had to do during the war. Dr. Macoun gave me a list of plants and told me to see what I could do with them.

The first plant to receive an Award of Merit was the lily shown at the Chelsea Flower Show in 1931 by Viscountess Byng and later named L. Davidi var. Lady Byng. The lilies now generally called the "Stenographer Series" originated from a cross made in 1929 between L. Davidi var. Willmoltiae [sic] (female) and an unknown dauricum seedling. I got the idea of trying this cross when I saw several natural hybrids among a collection of open pollinated seedlings of L. Davidi. I knew where this had been grown and was able to find in our records that an upright-facing lily, growing in the same bed, was flowering at the same time. Seven of the "Stenographer Series" were named from almost forty seedlings. They set seed freely and a number of seeds were sown. "Hurricane" and "Spitfire" were two of the seedlings named. Later controlled crosses were made.

To go back to 1921—Tigrimax was a cross between L. tigrinum (female) and Maximowiezii (male). Dr. Stout of the New York Botanical Garden made the same cross about the same time but I believe mine flowered a year earlier than his.

I might mention that several of the well known lily specialists in the United States and Canada have used varieties of the Stenographer Series in their breeding work.

Perhaps the Syringa (Lilacs) hybrids are more important to Canada than the lilies as not many shrubs are hardy enough to do well in the really cold districts. By crossing S. villosa (female) with S. reflexa (male) a number of seedlings were obtained which are quite distinct from the parents and are more floriferous. They flourish in the northern districts as well as in warmer climates. Crosses were made between other species including Josikaea and reflexa. Only one seedling, Guinevere, grew from this cross but it was the parent of Bellicent which received a first class Certificate a few years ago at the Royal Horticultural Society Show.

Few roses are hardy on the Canadian Prairies so I crossed several hardy species with less hardy ones and a few shrubs have been introduced.

The Roseybloom crabapples are described in the Journal of the New York Botanical Garden, August 1944, which I am sending under separate cover. They have become very popular and are being featured in the Driveways and Parks in Ottawa and other cities.

Siberian Iris have always interested me so I crossed a tall dark siberian with orientalis Snow Queen. Gatineau is one of the seedlings and it is still popular.

John H. Tobe
1958

"Tobe's Folly," in *Romance in the Garden*

—⚬—

*J*ohn H. Tobe (1904?–1979) arrived in Canada as an *infant and later became a nurseryman—and much more. His love of words shone in the very name of the nursery he established about 1937 at Niagara-on-the-Lake, Ontario: Tobe's Treery. He was a friendly man, a great talker and listener, and the energetic writer of some eighty to a hundred letters a day.*

At the invitation of Robert Rodale, Sr., Tobe wrote a monthly column for Organic Gardening and Farming. *He also wrote hundreds of wise, witty, and delightful essays for "Growing Flowers," his nursery's five-times-a-year newsletter. These essays became the stuff of two gardening books—*Growing Flowers *(1956) and* Romance in the Garden *(1958). In addition, he wrote books about health issues, herbal remedies, and survival on five acres of land.*

Tobe's Treery had no agents, and shipped its high-grade stock directly to customers—100,000 of them, in the 1950s—all across the country. Its slogan was "Canada's lowest priced nursery." But however low the price, as Tobe confided in "Tobe's Folly," his favourite plants were never out of stock.

—⚬—

To begin with, let me emphasize that I'm not talking about "follies". I was trying to explain to some of my girls of foreign birth what folly meant and, believe me, I had quite a time of it.

I cited the episode of Seward's Folly and then of Fulton's Folly—although both of these boomeranged and the years have shown them to be wise. But those were due to fortunate turns of events—which I can't count upon.

But now out here at the nursery the girls call a certain group of plants Tobe's Folly and I will admit there are grounds and justification for this name calling.

I go to great ends, a lot of trouble and through many difficulties to procure seeds, plants and trees of various special, new or sensational items but all of which wind up leaving me in the red.

But I say to my crew, "Look, these are sterling, splendid, unusual, wonderful and rare horticultural items and I must try to make them known and offer them to my customers."

So this year when I go to list them, I get into a hassel [sic] with my left and right bowers. "What's the sense of growing and listing these items?" they said, "They don't pay their way."

"But think", purrs I, "of the beauty, the grandeur and the loveliness of the Dawn Tree, the Metasequoia glyptostroboides . . . Just fathom—this tree was first discovered only a few short years ago and it's considered to be the oldest living tree on the face of the globe. Why it's like having a museum piece in your garden! Shouldn't I be able to offer this to my friends and customers?"

"Yes", pipes up Gerda, "You should—but last year we sold two of them."

"Now think", says I, of the Acer ginnala—that beautiful low growing Maple that has the finest color of all Maples with graceful habit and unusually handsome foliage that turns bright red in the autumn—a really much better tree than the Japanese Dwarf Maple and much hardier, although its leaves are not red during the summer."

Then Pearl tells, "I didn't see one order come through for that item last season."

"Well", I continued, "Think of those beautiful Deodara Cedars. That's the genuine Cedar. It was undoubtedly the handsomest, gayest and most interesting item that we had in our evergreen fields this year and everybody who saw them admired them and asked its name and its history and origin."

"But how many did we sell?" asks Pearl.

"Two of them," says Gerda, "And four hundred asked questions about them and kept me from my work."

But stoicly [sic] I went on, "Think of those beautiful Cedar of Lebanon that I had. They are the first that I've known to be grown in this area. They do make a beautiful specimen and think—it's a tree that was described in the Bible and is still growing throughout that hallowed land."

Gerda jumped in, "Yes, and all of the specimens that you started with are still out in the fields."

I had to ignore this uncouth type of interruption so I smilingly pursued my course. "Just think—we have these lovely Hollies growing in our fields . . . the real, genuine English Holly with the sharp prickles and those luxuriant, thick leaves."

"Yes", said Pearl, "And you haven't sold one in two years."

"Come, follow me," I held forth, brushing aside that hurdle. "Let me show you these beautiful Pieris japonica. You remember how striking they were in the early spring with those grand blossoms hanging down by the million from each plant. It was like a little tree covered with Lily-of-the-Valley flowers and they were nicely perfumed too. Look at them now. They are changing color. They really have a different tone or shade for every month of the year and they retain their leaves through the winter too. What a wonderful shrub it is!"

"I haven't been asked for nor have I sold one during the entire summer or fall", chirped Gerda.

Disregarding the interlopation, I walked over to the Koster Dwarf Globe Spruce. "There", I said, "Is something that the horticultural world has been looking for many, many years—a dwarf specimen of a genuine Blue Spruce and here it is and I am one of the few people in the North American continent who has it."

"We sold the first two the other day for a cemetery planting", says Pearl, "It seems clearly obvious that people are just dying for it."

"Look at those Cotoneasters", I went on, blithely undisturbed by the hindrance. "They are one of the finest of all shrubs that I know and I'm trying to educate people to appreciate them."

"I think we've sold three of them in four years", admitted Gerda, "I don't remember which variety it was. But most people who come to the nursery don't know how to pronounce the name—and I can't even help them."

Hanging on like a bull-dog, I pointed and said, "Now aren't these Espaliers a grand sight and we've been eating delicious pears and apples from these trees since early August."

"Yes", Gerda effused, "And think of the work, the effort and the years it takes to grow one of them. You sell them as cheap as borscht and even then nobody buys them. When somebody does send in an order once in a blue moon, two girls have to spend a day to pack up one tree because they're so difficult to handle."

"Hmm", it was not possible to ignore the outburst any longer and clearing my throat, I orated, "A man has to have a little latitude. Grant me a sliver or two of foolishness, won't you?"

"But you've listed innumerable unusual, new, rare types of bulbs, seeds, plants and trees for the past 25 years and most of them haven't paid off. Why continue to list these crazy items? Why not let the other fellow do the experimenting and you stay with the sound, popular and in-demand items where there is an element of profit?" the girls chorused.

"But", wails I, "A man can't live on bread alone."

"Nor can we women", they sang out again, "We'd like some raisin bread, cake or pie, too. But if we keep up at the rate we've been going, we won't even have bread. Why not face it? You like handling these unusual items. So why not call it your hobby and let it go at that? Some men drink, others play the horses or gamble and there are some who hunt and others who fish or go boating or collect stamps. You like searching or locating strange and unusual plants and convincing other folk that they have genuine merit."

Says I, "That's a little different angle . . . one well worth thinking over."

So that's it, folks. It's my hobby. I think they're the finest and most unusual items in the world. They're yours at a very reasonable rate—far less than they would cost if you tried to buy one individually from somewhere else.

I can't plant the seed of the love of the rare, the meritorious or unusual in your soul but I can try to tell you about it anyway.

LOIS WILSON
1970

From "Winter Beauty in Your Garden," in
Chatelaine's Gardening Book

—∞—

*L*ois Girvan Wilson (1908–1993) was one of Canada's few
nationally known garden journalists in the centennial
year of 1967. She was therefore a clear choice as author
of Chatelaine's Gardening Book, *published in 1970 after at least
three years of nationwide networking and research. It was welcomed
as a garden book for all of Canada, and it remained a steady seller
for almost two decades.*

*Wilson, a graduate of Victoria College, University of Toronto,
became an active member of the Garden Club of Toronto in 1947,
just one year after its founding, and served as its president in 1965
to 1967. An award-winning floral arranger, Wilson also wrote two
books about flower arranging, in 1963 and 1967.*

She began writing about gardening for Canadian Homes *in the
early 1950s, and then served as gardening editor of* Chatelaine *for
nine years. She lectured widely and appeared on CBC's "Radio
Noon." She was always active on many boards and committees.*

*Wilson often urged readers to try unusual plants and plant com-
binations, and to plan gardens they could enjoy from a window seat
or a lawn chair. She opened Chatelaine's Gardening Book* with an
essay on "A Garden of All-Year Beauty" *—and began that essay with
winter.*

—∞—

Winter's main delight isn't flowers, although a few lucky gardeners
in the more temperate parts of the country can coax a Christmas or
Lenten rose into bloom and the Pacific coast gardener does have, in

what he calls a "normal" winter, his ice pansies, his camellias, the glistening lively green of rain-wet mosses and ferns.

But for most of us in this country, winter's delight is bare, muscled strength in tree trunks, the leafless black tracery of their twigged branches against a late-day turquoise sky. It's the surprising brightness of bark on many trees and shrubs—gold in the willow, red in shrubby dogwood, shiny bronze-purple in cherry, grey in beech, and dozens of others. Where they're hardy, it's the glossy green of broad-leafed plants—the rhododendrons, mahonias, firethorn, wintercreeper and ivy on a wall. It's a high bush-cranberry hung with puckered, ruby-jewelled fruit. And of course, everywhere, it's evergreens, feathery and deceptively soft—and in dozens of shapes and shades of green.

As well, and especially in winter, it's being aware of those fast-fingered apprentices of the garden—the sun that casts bright blue shadows on sparkling white snow; the rain that, freezing, turns every tree, every twig, every needle, into a magical glitter of glass; the great bowl of the sky; the birds that visit your garden. To me, it's always a miracle that something as tiny a bundle of feathers as a chickadee can survive our winter cold, sometimes, birders in the Yukon report, 60° below.

Planning for this liveliness in your garden precedes delight. If you haven't already one large tree to act the flexing wrestler in winter, plant one and experience the pleasure of watching it grow. If you haven't already used evergreens as a major part of your garden design, rethink your planning, because just about every kind of evergreen grows well and looks well in these northern airs of ours. Well placed, their fine shape and texture in winter is more clearly seen when it is not blurred by trees and bushes in leaf around them.

Consider a Christmas-tree-shaped one where its mature conical height will be cleanly outlined against the winter sky. Use groups and clumps of bushy ones near a feeder where their friendly shelter will comfort wild birds. Feather a bank with horizontal juniper or yew to catch a frosting of snow. Think of an evergreen hedge as an all-year faithful blocker of an unattractive view.

When you come to choose leafy bushes and trees, check their winter effect not only of shape and bark but for bright fruit. While you are installing services in your garden, plan for the dramatic effect of night lighting. There is nothing, absolutely nothing, so thrilling as a storm of crystal snowflakes teetering down in the floodlit black of night. Put up feeders and connect a warmed drinking pan to draw in the birds.

If you live where sweeping wind is a familiar part of winter—in the Midwest, by any of our great lakes or wide rivers, by the sea— plant a shelterbelt of both deciduous and evergreen trees to break the thrust of the wind. And if you live on that ocean-warmed part of our favored Pacific coast where everything grows with such abandon, choose some of your plants from those with special winter beauty of foliage and flower.

HELEN SKINNER
1984

From "Heirloom Gardens: Where are the plants that
grandmother grew?" in *CenturyHome*

—⚬—

*H**elen Skinner, a native of Toronto, is a former teacher,
a knowledgeable gardener, an accredited horticulture
judge, and a popular speaker. She edited* Plants of
Pioneer and Early Days in Ontario *(1970) for the Garden Club of
Toronto, and wrote the text of* The Canadian Flower Arranger *for the
Garden Clubs of Ontario when that organization hosted the Fourth
World Flower Show in 1993.*

*Skinner has made a special study of early landscaping and pioneer
gardens in Canada. Her articles on gardening—often with nineteenth-
century voices complementing current wisdom—have appeared regularly since 1983 in* CenturyHome, *of which she is gardens editor.*

*When she wrote "Heirloom Gardens" in 1984, the Canadian
Organic Growers had recently held a conference on the decrease of
genetic diversity in food crops. Shortly afterward, the Heritage Seed
Program—as Skinner mentioned in her article—was born. It became
independent in 1987, and established its own publication and seed-
exchange schedules in 1988. Under the guidance of Heather Apple
of Uxbridge, Ontario, the program has been flourishing ever since.*

—⚬—

Many of us have sunny recollections of the colour and fragrance and
the luscious eating in our grandparents' gardens. I remember being
led by the hand by a frighteningly tall grandfather to admire his
roses; almost burying my face in what seemed like soup plates of
scented silk petals. In our own gardens today some of us still cherish
Granny's Peony or Aunt Ruth's Artimesia ponticum, whether it's for

their charm, beautiful form and fragrance, or for their sentimental reminder of things past.

For some, seeking out plantings and plants to grow old varieties has become a fascinating hobby, while for others it is a way to protect varieties from extinction. Either way, it's a real challenge to collectors, since it's estimated that less than 20% of the original plant varieties can be found today. When you read old catalogues and seed lists, you begin to realize why old plant seeds have become such collectibles. The names of bush bean varieties, for instance, covered more than a full page in an old catalogue, while today's seed houses list a mere dozen. Scientific plant breeding has eliminated disease-prone plants and encouraged the culture of those that mature early, those best adapted to machine harvesting, and those firm and flexible enough to withstand modern marketing methods. There is a growing feeling among gardeners and the scientific community that too many old varieties have been lost too quickly and easily, and that there is a real danger in limiting our food crops to just a few highly successful producers.

After all, variety is the spice of life, and a multitude of choices should be available in the foods we grow and eat. While one person may want a variety of corn that matures early, another will choose one for flavour and colour, while still others will need varieties that grow best under certain conditions. By preserving many varieties, these and other choices are always open to growers and consumers.

But more important than choice is the preservation of a cultivar as a genetic bank. More than 10,000 genes combine to make each variety unique and when one variety disappears, so too do those same 10,000 genes. Many old varieties died out because they did not meet modern standards. Some had little flavour, others spoiled early or were susceptible to disease. Yet perhaps they were worth preserving just as a bundle of genes. It's possible old varieties might contain characteristics needed in the future. As our environment changes, food crops may face new stresses. Plants may have to be tolerant of acid rain, increased carbon monoxide or as yet undiscovered dangers. But when plants disappear, the gene pool is considerably depleted for experimentation.

From the beginning of time the best food plants were sought by nomads, then cultivated as humans settled in one place. Seeds from plants that grew well were saved, while others were discarded. Selection eventually produced better grains, larger fruits and vegetables, and rice that matured quickly enough to permit three crops a year. Growers preserved seeds of plants that flourished for their specific requirements and weather conditions, and as a result specialized seeds appeared—for hillside terraces, for valleys, for shade, for sun, for particular tastes. Seeds were passed from family to family, and eventually sold locally. Until well into the 20th century, seed houses would carry a wide selection of fruit and vegetable seeds unique to their particular area.

In this century, new methods in plant breeding and hybridization produced uniform crops with better yields and growers were quick to change. Economics alone reduced the number of varieties to the few that produced the most. But one of the chief dangers of uniformity is the possibility of one disease wiping out an entire crop. The Irish potato famine was an extreme example—concentration on one variety with the same genes, resulted in the whole country's crop succumbing to the same blight.

This brings into focus the major concern many growers have at the disappearance each year of more domestic foodcrop varieties. Yet only recently has there been much concern over the conservation of older domestic seed varieties which are the storehouses of vast numbers of genetic possibilities for the future.

This concern has prompted the formation of a *Canadian Heritage Seed Program* by the Canadian Organic Growers Association. It's a relatively new program, but already many volunteers are involved. Some act as curators and grow one or two older varieties and save the seed. Other enthusiasts have become Heritage Growers and close to a dozen from across the country maintain anywhere from 40 to 400 heirloom vegetable varieties each. For example, one grower north of Edmonton grows more than 300 varieties of heirloom vegetables while, near Aurora, Ont., Alex Kierans has a heritage garden with 65 varieties of potatoes, over 50 different varieties of beans and tomatoes and several incidentals like garlic, onions and turnips. Kierans grows the 'Refugee' bean which he obtained from a woman in the U.S. whose family has passed the seeds down from mother to daughter since 1834.

Governments too are saving seeds. More than a thousand cereal, vegetable and tree seed varieties are in atmosphere-controlled storage at the Federal Plant Gene Research Centre in Ottawa. The Horticulture Research Institute of Ontario is revamping its Centennial Museum Orchard and soon its 90 varieties of early apple trees including the Seek-No-Further and the Fameuse will be accessible to the public at Vineland, Ontario. Many architectural museums and pioneer villages have heritage gardens, including the Agricultural Museum in Milton, Ont., and King's Landing Pioneer Village in Fredericton, N.B. Botanical gardens save seeds, and the Royal Botanical Gardens in Hamilton, Ont., grows both early Indian food plants and heritage vegetables in its demonstration gardens.

JO ANN GARDNER
1989

From "Black Currants," in *The Old-Fashioned Fruit
Garden: The Best Way to Grow, Preserve and
Bake with Small Fruit*

—✳—

*J*o Ann Gardner, with her husband, Jigs, moved from
northern Vermont to Orangedale, on Cape Breton Island,
Nova Scotia, in 1971. There, through old-fashioned hard
work, they have supported themselves by gardening, small-scale
farming, selling at farmers' markets, taking in guests, and writing.
Jo Ann Gardner's articles have appeared in Atlantic Insight, Country
Journal, Harrowsmith, Horticulture, *and* Rural Delivery.

The Gardners have been selling their homemade jams and jellies
to satisfied customers since the early 1960s. In this book, Jo Ann
Gardner shared with readers her years of experience in growing, pre-
serving, and cooking with the small fruits that once grew in many
kitchen gardens: rhubarb, strawberries, raspberries, red and black
currants, gooseberries, elderberries, and the citron melon.

Her chapter on the much-maligned black currant ends with a
recipe for wine that concludes, "You can make a lot of wine from a
small amount of currants." This reminds us of Thomas Dalton of
Toronto, who wrote in 1834 that he had made "nearly 200 Gallons
of excellent Currant wine, from the produce of a Garden." We won-
der what amount of currants he used.

—✳—

I may as well tell you straight away that I am a black-currant fancier,
one of a small but growing number of people in North America (the
number is higher in Canada than in the United States) who think that
the black currant has been unfairly neglected. The black currant shrub's

hardiness, immunity to disease, and ability to produce great crops with little or no attention are hard to match. Given suitable growing conditions, the shrubs grow and produce fruit with more vigor than either gooseberry or red currant bushes. Black currant bushes are also beautiful, with their curved branches dipping down to the ground. In early summer, they are crammed with clusters of small greenish-white flowers and then with clusters of ripe black berries.

So why doesn't everyone have a black currant bush in his or her fruit garden? The case against black currants has gained a large following over the years. The charges are as follows: black currants are host to white-pine blister rust, black currants have an undesirable flavor, black currants are not worth growing.

Let's look at those accusations. Yes, black currants do carry white-pine blister rust, but so do other members of the *Ribes* group (gooseberries and red currants). This fact has not prevented gardening writers from promoting gooseberries and red currants, however, and as a result, those fruits are enjoying a modest comeback in the trade. On the other hand, the black currant suffers from bad publicity, often being singled out as the sole culprit of white-pine blister rust, without any further explanation. Therefore I think the following account is in order.

White-pine blister rust was inadvertently brought to North America around the turn of the century, the same time that the white pine was enjoying considerable commercial popularity. In the first stage of its development, the fungus lives on the *Ribes* species, and it does little harm. But in the second stage, it lives inside the stem of the white pine, causing severe damage or death to the tree. By 1918, millions of acres of pine forests were infected by the fungus. At that time, the United States government took steps to prohibit the growth and sale of currants and gooseberries. Eventually, the white pine's commercial value declined, and in 1968 the government revoked the quarantine and eased the restrictions against *Ribes* species. Each state then set up its own regulations.

By contrast, Canada, according to some horticulturists, has had a more enlightened policy toward *Ribes*. Though there is no shortage of white pines in Canada, there are no restrictions against currants and gooseberries. Instead, authorities have worked to combat the problem through breeding programs. Perhaps this attitude stems in part from the fact that there is a stronger British tradition here. Indeed, the British are avid fans of *Ribes*, of black currants in particular.

When I was researching this book, I decided to investigate state prohibitions against black currants. After all, if Americans were not allowed to grow black currants, what would be the use in telling them how wonderful they are? I was also interested in finding out if United States horticultural officials knew why black currants were pinpointed as the worst offenders against white pines. The more I looked into the matter, the more confused the situation appeared to be. My first inquiries, sent to plant associations and horticultural authorities, drew a blank. Nothing, it seemed, was known about black currants. No one knew if the plants were for sale anywhere in the United States; no one knew if the plants were allowed to be grown. In short, I got the definite feeling that black currants were regarded as pariahs of no horticultural interest.

Then I sent out inquiries to 16 state agricultural research stations and departments of conservation and to the United States Department of Agriculture. I asked about the status of black currants in their areas, whether or not they were thought to be more susceptible to white-pine blister rust that other *Ribes* species and, finally, whether black currants had a future, and if so, what was it? In no time, I accumulated a rather bulky folder of information. The answers I received, although direct and to the point, were sometimes conflicting.

Maine and New Hampshire, where the white pine is still a viable commercial crop, outlaw black currants, with some restrictions on red currants and gooseberries. Rhode Island and Michigan prohibit the growth and sale of black currants but admittedly do not enforce the laws. (For example, a nursery in Ypsilanti, Michigan, received permission to sell black currant plants because there are not any white pines in that area.) It was generally felt, except in a few instances, that the question of enforcing prohibitions is academic, anyway: wild *Ribes* species grow vigorously and cannot be controlled. Some officials in Alaska noted as well that even though there was no ban in their state, white-pine forests were unaffected. Some officials were adamant that black currants were more susceptible to white-pine blister rust than gooseberries and red currants, while others were just as adamant that all *Ribes* are equally guilty. Many of my respondents, pointing to the inefficacy of past bans and the decline of the white-pine industry, said it was time to revise and review old, outdated laws. Some held out promise for a more lenient attitude toward black currants because of the availability of more effective controls, such as fungicides and disease-resistant varieties.

At the same time that these plant officials voiced differing views, scientists in Canada and individuals in the United States were continuing work to breed varieties resistant to white-pine blister rust, as well as types with bigger fruit and higher yields. The three cultivars most resistant to white-pine blister rust (Consort, Crusader, and Cornet) have all been developed in Canada, at the Horticultural Research Institute of Ontario, at Vineland Station. Of these, Consort is considered the most resistant. It is also the most popular and the most widely available in Canada, as well as the United States. In addition, two new cultivars from Europe are currently being tested in Canada; the Josta, also disease resistant, was developed in Germany. With the continued and growing interest in many "old-fashioned" fruits, there is no doubt that government-run experimental fruit stations in the United States will be moved to conduct similar research.

As for the charge that black currants have an undesirable flavor, I am convinced that most gardening writers in the United States have never tasted black currants in any form. Those few people who do go out of their way to try black currants are well rewarded. The noted American gardening writer Lewis Hill once said that he and his wife were "converted to the taste when we bought a jar of 'confiture de cassis,' black-currant jam, in Canada." When I sent Hill a sample of our dried black currants, he was more than enthusiastic: "We are certainly going to expand our production. They are great!"

What exactly is the flavor of black currants? In 1944, the great American horticulturist U. P. Hedrick said that the black currant has an "assertive flavor and aroma . . . it is most pleasant to eat out of hand or in culinary dishes." Others have called its taste "musky." It is assertive, but I'm not sure about musky. The word *musky* usually carries negative overtones, yet it also describes the appealing scent of many flavors.

To be honest, however, I think that black currants must be processed to be properly appreciated. Gardeners and commercial growers in Europe understand this well, although the British do enjoy a dish of fresh black currants and cream for breakfast. In any case, British children are as familiar with morning glasses of black currant juice as American children are with orange juice. (Black currant juice is high in vitamin C, too.) In Europe, black currant is a highly prized flavoring for cordials, liqueurs, wines, desserts, and candies; rum with a shot of black currant syrup, I'm told, makes an incomparable drink.

Finally, are black currants worth growing? If you know nothing about a fruit except that it is a carrier of a dread disease (like Typhoid Mary) and tastes funny, you may well conclude that it is not. But if you have ever tasted black currant jam, jelly, wine, juice, or dried berries, if you have ever seen a bush drooping under the weight of its fruit, you will search from one end of the country to the other to find just one rootstock to plant in your garden. If you can find the *real* thing, in whatever form, on the shelves of a specialty shop or in the pages of a British mail-order catalog, you can make up your own mind about the flavor of black currants. And from there, you can decide whether to grow them.

ELSPETH BRADBURY
1994

"Little gods of the garden," in *The Vancouver Sun*

—⚉—

*E*lspeth Bradbury is a Vancouver landscape architect who specializes in residential garden design. Besides The Vancouver Sun, *her articles have appeared in* Atlantic Advocate, Boulevard, Fine Gardening, Garden Design, Gardens West, *and* Harrowsmith. *Fiddlehead Press published a collection of her poetry in 1982. The Harrowsmith Gardener's Guide on* Spring Flowers *(1989) included her chapter on "Thoughts of Spring." Polestar published her* Garden Letters: A Growing Correspondence, *coauthored by a New Brunswick friend, Judy Maddocks, in 1995.*

Bradbury grew up in Britain, moved to New Brunswick in 1968, and from there to British Columbia a few years ago. After each of these uprootings, she has written, her garden has helped her to settle in, put down new roots, and renew her sense of belonging to a place.

She still lives on the zealously planted suburban lot she has described in several articles, including this one. Her depiction of the profusion she inherited from previous owners fits the image gardeners in the rest of Canada have of those in the favoured climate of coastal British Columbia: Everything they plant not only grows, but grows big.

—⚉—

How can I describe the garden I inherited when we moved to Vancouver? A jungle, a joke, a joy? It must have contained one of every plant known to B.C. horticulture, and a few beside.

In a space no bigger than my kitchen, I counted one fir, two deodar cedars, several wild cherries and a tame plum (I knew it was a plum because it still wore a faded nursery tag). A couple of large rhododendrons and other assorted shrubs crowded in underneath and, at the bottom of the heap, were yuccas, sword ferns and a promising mat of sprouting leaves that turned into the horribly invasive variegated ground elder.

Somebody had obviously loved the place at some time—somebody with oddly eclectic tastes and a collector's passion.

I have a picture of her in my mind. She is pushing her way through the tangled undergrowth with a few seedlings balanced on the tip of a trowel. She is searching for something. Ah—there—a tiny patch of bare earth!

Tenderly she plants a baby horse chestnut, and goes on her way well pleased, her eyes glued to the ground. If she looked up, she might see that her darling is directly under the branches of an apple, which is under a pine, which stands a few feet from a hemlock.

Her partner meanwhile, is trying to cram a walnut between a magnolia and an aralia. "It's no good," he calls to her. "There's no more room." That's why they left; I'm sure of it.

Whenever I went outside, I discovered four or five new plants: sometimes a treasure, a rooted cutting of an evergreen azalea, sometimes a demon, *convolvulus* or horsetails.

I also discovered the West Coast slug. The first one I saw was oozing across a path, and I nearly stepped on it. Ooooff! The thing was longer than my hand and thicker than my thumb and a sickly yellow blotched with brown. I've come across plenty since then, ranging in colour from putty to jet black, but they still stop me dead in my tracks.

Everything was growing like crazy and it was a scrum out there, a free-for-all but, in a way, splendid. The whole thing had reached that stimulating stage of disarray that comes before the outbreak of total anarchy. It was depressing to know that whatever I did would make things look a lot worse before they looked better.

We think of plant communities as peaceful. They're not of course: they're battlefields that seem calm only because the skirmishes are fought in silence and slow motion, often underground. A garden is just a lull in the warfare, and it exists only as long as the gardener's authority lasts. We're the arbiters, the little gods. It's a tough job.

My ignorance was laughable. Living in the Maritimes for 20 years, my palette of plants had shrunk to a precious few: the iron-clad hardies that survive the onslaught of freezing rains and a five month winter. Now I found myself lost in the wonderful world of the broadleafed evergreen: the laurels and hollies, camellias and (heaven help me) the vast tribe of rhododendrons.

It hardly seemed right that a rhodo-illiterate like me should be entrusted with a collection of these minuscule mounds and hefty giants, domes of purple, pink, yellow and red. On one of my early explorations I made a mental note of the rhododendrons I considered junk: a few scraggy cuttings, a few leggy runts, one with sickly looking variegated foliage (*President Roosevelt*, as it turned out) and two great spindly things with scruffy yellow leaves dangling down.

But what was this? These two had strange trunks, smooth and cinnamon coloured. The *Arbutus menziesii* is the only broadleaf evergreen tree native to Canada, and hereabouts it's the tree that everyone knows and loves. It's fondly called the madrona. You can curse a cedar if you care to, you can despise a dogwood, but you don't dare mock a madrona.

I've seen symmetrical, free-standing specimens but, for the most part, they are weirdly eccentric, leaning and wandering as the spirit moves them. In dry situations they bulge at the base as if they have melted.

They hate to be transplanted and resent any attempt to pamper them with good food or a decent supply of water. Lucky the gardener with established trees.

A certain status goes with them, comparable to that of antique family furniture and old money. I didn't think much of them at first, but it didn't take me long to learn that the funny looking non-rhododendrons with the touchable skin were two of my most precious possessions.

At that point, I had decided to wait a full six months and take a plant identification course before I did any drastic culling.

LOOKING
BACK

—ᵐ—

MICHAEL GONDER SCHERCK
1905

"The Old-Time Garden," in *Pen Pictures of Early Pioneer Life in Upper Canada*

—⁂—

ichael Gonder Scherck's (1862–1927) maternal ancestors were United Empire Loyalists from Pennsylvania who settled in the Niagara Peninsula of Ontario. His paternal great-grandfather was a Mennonite who emigrated from Pennsylvania in 1799 and settled near Preston in what is now Waterloo County. His childhood memories were rich with details of visits to his grandparents.

Although Scherck became a retail druggist in Toronto's east end, he remained interested in his rural roots. In Pen Pictures of Early Pioneer Life in Upper Canada, *he described social customs, routine chores, tools and materials, even tastes and smells.*

However, he did not pursue the connections between religion, culture, and the garden, especially in the case of his Mennonite great-grandfather. Nancy-Lou Patterson, Professor Emerita of Fine Arts at the University of Waterloo, Ontario, has done truly groundbreaking work on this subject in her article "Mennonite Gardens," in Canadian Antiques and Art Review *[vol. 1 (June 1980), pp. 36–39].*

Scherck later adopted a simpler spelling of his surname. As M. G. Sherk, he completed "Reminiscences of the Upper Part of the Old Niagara River Road" for the Ontario Historical Society just two days before his sudden death at age sixty-six.

—⁂—

The gardens of our forefathers were models of neatness and order as well as pictures of beauty. Among the Pennsylvania Dutch settled in Canada, the garden plot stood close by the house and was surrounded by a picket or board fence to keep out the poultry, pigs and other animals that would soon make havoc of the flower and vegetable beds, if accidentally allowed to enter. A path ran round the sides of the garden and one or two paths through the centre. The bed enclosed by the centre-walks was usually devoted to flowers and the rest of the garden to vegetables, herbs, etc. One could not help wondering how our busy grandmothers found time to devote to such work, but their gardens were apparently their pride, and they spent a good deal of time working in them. It was the custom always to take visitors out and shew them through the garden before leaving. We can see the women now, with perhaps a white handkerchief or an apron tied over their heads, strolling through the garden and yard, interested in looking at the flowers. In the spring of the year our grandmothers would bring out the boxes in which were stored the seeds collected the previous fall, each kind of seed being wrapped up in a separate parcel, some in folds of newspaper, some in pieces of brown paper, some in cloth, some in paper bags, all carefully marked and pinned up or tied with a piece of string or tape. Together with the flower seeds there were also all the common vegetable seeds, as lettuce, cabbage, onions, beets, beans and cucumbers. In the flower-beds plants were to be seen blooming the whole summer through, commencing early in the spring with the crocuses, tulips and daffodils, and ending in the fall with the dahlias, phlox and asters. There was generally a border of daisies and amaranthus (called in German Schissel Blume, because the shape of a dish, or rather cup and saucer) and in the centre hyacinths, marigolds, Caesar's crowns, bachelor's buttons, carnations (called pinks in the early days), primroses, sweet Williams, four o'clocks, pansies, sweet peas, mignonette, a choice rose bush here and there, peony, white-scented and red (called Gichter rose by the Germans, because its roots were supposed to be a cure for fits), and a tomato stalk with its red fruit, called love apples sixty years ago, and cultivated only as an ornament, as its fruit was not thought to be fit to eat. In a corner of the garden was to be found a bush of "Old Man" and one of live-for-ever, used in bouquets. A grape arbor or trellis was to be seen in the garden or yard and a hop-pole or two in one of the corners. Then there were beds for vegetables of all kinds and a bed for the herbs used for medicinal and culinary purposes, such as rue, thyme, sage (Ger., *solvein*), sweet savory, fennel, carraway, loveage (Ger., *lieb-steckley*), wormwood, pennyroyal and catnip. In the fall of the year these herbs were collected and dried for winter use. Along the garden fence, on the inside, were to be seen holly hocks and gooseberry and currant bushes, and on the outside, in the yard or lawn, a few beds of daffodils (smoke pipes), always yellow and white, peony and fleur-de-lis. Scattered through the yard were to be found a variety of shrubbery, such as rose bushes, lilacs, syringias and snow balls; against a lattice near the house a honeysuckle vine, and around the back door the familiar sunflower.

L. M. Montgomery
1910

From "A Garden of Old Delights," in
The Canadian Magazine

—᠁—

*L*ucy Maud Montgomery (1874–1942) was born in Prince
Edward Island—a setting she used for much of her
writing, including her world-famous "Anne" novels. As
she showed by Anne's interest, as a young adult, in the Avonlea
Village Improvement Society, Montgomery herself was aware of the
early-twentieth-century City Beautiful movement. But she was also
interested in everyday gardening. As early as 1901, she explored in
her journals the essential qualities of "old-timey" or "old-fashioned"
gardens—their gradual development, secluded corners, trim walks,
and perennial flowers "planted there by grandmotherly hands when
the [nineteenth] century was young."

By 1902, Montgomery was personally caring for the garden of
her own maternal grandmother, Lucy Ann Woolner Macneill, who
was by then nearing eighty, and in whose house and garden at
Cavendish Montgomery had been raised. In this evocative article—an
earlier version of which appeared in National Magazine in 1907—
she described what was almost certainly her Grandmother Macneill's
garden.

—᠁—

What wonder that wise old Eden story placed the beginning of life in
a garden? A garden fitly belongs to the youth of the world and the
youth of the race, for it never grows old. The years, which steal so
much from everything else, bring added loveliness and sweetness to
it, enriching it with memories beautiful and tender, but never blight-
ing its immortal freshness. It is foolishness to speak as we do of "old"

gardens: gardens are perennially young, the haunt of flowers and children. And Grandmother's garden was always full of both.

Some of her many grandchildren always came to the old homestead for their summer holidays. One summer there were a half-dozen there as guests; and, counting the other ten who lived near her and spent more time at grandmother's than at their own homes, we were the merriest little crew in the world. The garden was our favourite haunt, and we passed most of our waking moments there. It was to us an enchanted pleasure-ground, and there is nothing in all our store of remembrance so sweet and witching as our recollections of it. Places visited in later years have grown dim and indistinct, but every nook and corner of grandmother's garden is as vivid in memory as on the day I saw it last. That was many years ago; but I could go straight with shut eyes at this very moment to the bed beside the snowball tree where the first violets grew.

The door of the big living-room opened directly into the garden. You went down four wide shallow steps, formed of natural slabs of red sandstone which great-grandfather had brought up from the shore. The lower one was quite sunk into the earth, and mint grew thickly about its edges. Often crushed by so many little feet, it gave out its essence freely and the spicy odour always hung around that door like an invisible benediction.

The garden was long and narrow and sloped slightly to the west. On two sides it was surrounded by a high stone wall; at least, we thought it high; but I have a mature suspicion that I might not think so now. Things have such an unwholesome habit of dwindling as we grow older; but then we could barely see over it by standing on tiptoe, and we had to climb to its top by the little ladder fastened against the western end if we wanted to get a good view of the wide, sloping green fields beyond, and the sea calling so softly on its silvery, glistening sand shore.

The third side was shut in by the house itself, a long, quaint, white-washed building, lavishly festooned with Virginia creeper and climbing roses. Something about the five square windows in the second storey gave it an appearance of winking at us in a friendly fashion through its vines; at least, so the story-girl said; and, indeed, we could always see it for ourselves after she had once pointed it out to us.

At one corner of the house a little gate opened into the kitchen garden, where the vegetables grew; but we never felt much interest in that—perhaps because grandmother's old servant Jean looked upon it as her special domain and discouraged intruders.

"Get awa' wi' ye into the floor garden—that's the proper place for bairns," she would say, with an instinctive perception of the fitness of things.

The fourth side was rimmed in by a grove of fir trees, a dim, cool place where the winds were fond of purring, and where there was always a resinous, woodsy odour. On the farther side of the firs was a thick plantation of slender silver birches and whispering poplars; and just beyond it what we called the "wild garden"—a sunny triangle shut in by the meadow fences and as full of wild flowers as it could hold: blue and white violets, dandelions, Junebells, wild-roses, daisies, buttercups, asters, and goldenrod, all lavish in their season.

The garden was intersected by right-angled paths, bordered by the big white clam-shells which were always found in abundance by the bay, and laid with gravel from the shore—coloured pebbles and little white shells well ground into the soil. In the beds between the paths and around the wall grew all the flowers in the world, or so, at least, we used to think. The same things were always found in the same place; we always looked for the clove pinks, sown in grandmother's bridal days, behind the big waxberry bush, and the shadowy corner behind the sumacs was always sweet in spring with white narcissus.

There were many roses, of course, roses that grew without any trouble and flung a year's horded sweetness into luxuriant bloom every summer. One never heard of mildew or slugs or aphis there, and nothing was ever done to the rose-bushes beyond a bit of occasional pruning. There was a row of big double pink ones at one side of the front door, and the red and white ones grew in the middle plot. There was one yellow rose-tree to the left of the steps; but the ones we loved best were the dear little "Scotch roses"—oh, how fragrant and dainty and thorny were those wee semi-double roses with their waxen outer petals and the faint shell-pink of their hearts! Jean had brought the rose-bush with her all the way from an old Scottish garden when she was a "slip of a lassie," so that in our eyes there was a touch of romance about them that the other roses lacked.

Grandmother's bed of lavender and caraway and sweet clover was very dear to her heart. The caraway and sweet clover had a tendency to spread wildly, and it was one of our duties to keep them in proper bounds, rooting up every stray bit that straggled from the allotted space. We picked and dried the lavender for grandmother's linen closet; and she made us delicious caraway cookies such as I have never eaten anywhere else. I am afraid such cookies are not made nowadays.

All the beds were edged with ribbon grass. The big red peonies grew along the edge of the fir grove, splendid against its darkness, and the hollyhocks stood up in stiff ranks by the kitchen garden gate. The bed next to them was a sight to see when the yellow daffodils and tulips came out. There was a clump of tiger-lilies before the door and a row of madonna-lilies farther down. One big pine tree grew in the garden, and underneath it was a stone bench, made, like the steps, of flat shore stones worn smooth by the long polish of wind and wave. Just behind this bench grew pale, sweet flowers which had no name that we could ever find out. Nobody seemed to know anything about them. They had been there when grandfather's father bought the place. I have never seen them elsewhere or found them described in any catalogue. We called them the White Ladies—the Story Girl gave them the name. She said they looked like the souls of good women. They were very aerial and wonderfully dainty, with a strange, haunting perfume that was only to be detected at a little distance and vanished if you bent over them. They faded whenever they were plucked, and although strangers, greatly admiring them, often carried away roots and seeds they could never be coaxed to grow elsewhere.

There was one very old-fashioned bed full of bleeding hearts, Sweet William, bride's bouquet, butter-and-eggs, Adam-and-Eve, columbines, pink and white daisies, and Bouncing Bets. We liked this bed best, because we might always pluck the flowers in it whenever we pleased. For the others, we had to ask permission which, however, was seldom refused.

Poppies were the only things in the garden with a license to ramble. They sprang up everywhere; but the bed of them was in the northwest corner, and there they shook out their fringed silken skirts against a low coppice of young firs. Asparagus, permitted because of the feathery grace of its later development, grew behind the well-house, near the lilies-of-the-valley; the middle path was spanned at regular intervals by three arches, and these were garlanded with honeysuckle.

The well-house was a quaint, lichened old structure built over the well at the bottom of the garden. Four posts supported an odd peaked little roof like the roof of a Chinese pagoda, and it was almost covered with vines that hung from it in long swinging festoons nearly to the ground. The well was very deep and dark, and the water, drawn up by a windlass and chain in a mossy old bucket shaped like a little barrel and bound with icy hoops, was icy cold. As far down as we could see, the walls of the well were grown over with the most beautiful ferns.

The garden was full of birds; some of them we regarded as old friends, for they nested in the same place every year and never seemed afraid of us. A pair of bluebirds had an odd liking for a nook in the stonework of the well; two yellowhammers had preempted an old hollow poplar in the south-western corner. Wild canaries set up housekeeping in the big lilac bush before the parlour windows. One exciting summer a pair of hummingbirds built a nest in the central honeysuckle arch. A wild August gale and rainstorm tore it from its frail hold and dashed it to the ground, where we found it the next morning. We girls cried over it; and then we cast lots to decide who should have the wonderful thing, fashioned of down and lichen, and no bigger than a walnut. The hummingbirds never came back, though we looked wistfully for them every summer. Robins were numerous, especially in early spring, great, sleek, saucy fellows, strutting along the paths. In the summer evenings after sunset they would whistle among the firs, making sweet, half melancholy music. . . .

Early morning was an exquisite time in the garden. Delicate dews glistened everywhere, and the shadows were black and long and clear-cut. Pale, peach-tinted mists hung over the bay, and little winds crisped across the fields and rustled in the poplar leaves in the wild corner. But the evening was more beautiful still, when the sunset sky was all aglow with delicate shadings and a young moon swung above the sea in the west. The robins whistled in the firs, and over the fields sometimes came lingering music from the boats in the bay. We used to sit on the old stone wall and watch the light fading out on the water and the stars coming out over the sea. And at last grandmother would come down the honeysuckle path and tell us it was time that birds and buds and babies should be in bed. Then we would troop off to our nests in the house, and the fragrant gloom of a summer night would settle down over the Garden of Old Delights.

ADA L. POTTS
1929

"Early Canadian Gardens," in *The Chatelaine*

—◊—

*da L. Potts, née Pascoe, (1869–1950s?) had a keen
eye for well-developed grounds. During the teens, her
by-line (Mrs. R. B. Potts, Hamilton) appeared several
times in* The Canadian Horticulturist *series on "Canadian Gardens"
in southern Ontario.*

*As the wife of a physician and the daughter of a long-serving
Methodist minister, she must also have had a keen sense of civic
duty. In 1920 she attracted the attention of* The (Hamilton) Herald
*by blowing the whistle on a Scoutmaster who had allowed his boys
to become "spendthrifty" by operating a canteen.*

*By 1925, Potts was a widow, and living in Toronto. Between 1928
and 1932, as Ada L. Potts, she wrote at least a dozen gardening articles for a new periodical,* The Chatelaine. *Her writing then disappeared from mass circulation.*

*Potts was a discriminating reader of garden literature. Her "Early
Canadian Gardens" was a pioneering effort to put together, from
many sources, a history of gardening in Canada. Those familiar with
the sources will recognize some errors and inaccuracies, but these
hardly diminish her accomplishment.*

—◊—

Since it is claimed that "a history of a people's gardens is very nearly
a history of the people themselves," one may find a very interesting
record in Canada's early horticultural and agricultural history. In justice to "the first Canadians," mention must be made of the gardens
of the Indians, for they had developed a successful agriculture before
the white man arrived. This is proved from the writings of Champlain

and others who tell of the fields of corn, beans, pumpkins, tobacco and sunflowers which were found near the fortified towns, each Indian having an allotment to cultivate and later sharing in common the harvested crops. Today, professional growers recognize the work done by the Indians on the corn and the sunflower especially, and refer to the unknown workers as "Aboriginal Burbanks." Champlain took the sunflower back to France with him, and from there it reached Italy, India, Turkey, Russia, China, and other parts of the world.

When the early adventurers from France decided upon making a New France on this side of the ocean, it was Champlain who declared that he had found no place so beautiful as the land he chose for the site of his first town, and, when building "The Habitation" on the right of the landing-place, had the grounds laid out as a garden.

These newcomers from France brought with them a knowledge of the gardening carried on in their native land for many centuries, and we find that much of our native flora had specimens sent back to France and planted in the "Jardin des Plantes," Paris. Those coming from other lands found our wealth of flowers appealing and gave eulogistic descriptions of them in their writings.

Prior to Champlain's arrival in Lower Canada, there were gardens laid out in the Maritimes, for here Louis Hébert dwelt for a time at Port Royal, in that lovely inlet now known as Annapolis Basin. Here he "sowed corn, planted vines, and cultivated the soil."

When the Héberts arrived in Lower Canada, Louis Hébert cleared ten acres of land on the heights of Quebec, built a stone house and planted seeds from France. He included rose bushes as well as apple-trees in his plantings, though his only tool was a spade. He is said to have worked and re-worked the soil until it was ready to receive the seeds he planned to sow, and he lived to see not only golden ears of corn but the flowers and the fruits of his motherland growing around his home.

During these first days of Quebec's growth, we learn that a number of handsome private houses, with "laid out" grounds, had been built by the noblemen who had come to settle in New France. These new Canadians had an eye for landscape beauty which Champlain openly admired as a background, and the tidy farms, with the homes

of the Héberts, the Martins, the Couillards and others, added the finishing touch to the beauty of the picture.

It is but natural to expect that the first gardens planted were of
a useful rather than ornamental type, though it is evident that the
influence of the latter can be traced throughout the story. Some faded
pictures of the early homes and gardens have fortunately been preserved as treasured possessions, while others appear occasionally
from unexpected sources thus enabling us to catch some glimpses of
home gardens when Canada was in her infancy.

Somewhat more distinct in detail, at least, are the pictures of the
periods which followed as Canada grew up and reached the day of
her coming of age. Mrs. Simcoe, wife of the first Governor of Upper
Canada, enters during one of the earliest of these periods, and mentions "evidence of progress," beginning with the transition from the
first log-cabin home to "the neat frame houses" built two or three
years later. With better houses came improved surroundings, for the
U.E. Loyalists, who were among the very early arrivals, we are told,
had left luxurious homes, were cultured people of the professional as
well as artisan class, and naturally in their new settlements, sought
to maintain their previous standard of living.

Mrs. Simcoe, in her "Diary," mentions first the homes in Lower
Canada which she visited prior to reaching Upper Canada where she
was to take up residence. She writes of the elegant mansion and
richly laid-out estate of Judge Mabane; the country villa on the side
of the mountain as well as the town residence of Mr. Frobisher, where
Mrs. Frobisher "has an excellent garden," and the island home on
St. Helen's of La Baronne de Longueil, where Mrs. Simcoe saw "the
only hot house" since her arrival.

After arrival at Navy Hall, numerous homes visited in the Niagara
district are referred to, and we find mention of "yards and courts"
neatly fenced, enclosing "fine gardens and pleasant."

Just prior to this arrival of the Simcoes at Navy Hall, Niagara,
Count de Puisaye, a refugee from his native France, had purchased
land in this district and "sought to build again a home for himself in
this new land similar to that which he had been accustomed to."

A period followed known as "the Great Immigration" time, and
during this period, we find from old records that a landscapist from

Holland, one Andre Parmentier, who had established himself in Brooklyn, N.Y., had visited Lower Canada, surveyed and laid out two hundred and three [two or three] gardens in the vicinity of Montreal. He planted these with material grown in his own nurseries at Brooklyn. There are even earlier records, however, from which we glean the fact that Mr. James McGill had purchased Burnside Manor, "a beautiful estate of forty-six acres lying on the slope between Mount Royal and the river," and had "built a handsome home and laid out fine gardens."

When the Strickland sisters arrived in Canada about 1832, Mrs. Traill, though unable to inspect the town of Montreal to any extent, because of an outbreak of cholera, writes: "The houses are interspersed with gardens and pleasant walks which look very agreeable from the windows of the ball-room of the Nelson Hotel."

Later Mrs. Traill mentions the verandahs, or "stoups" as these were then called, adding: "Few houses, either log or frame, are without them. The pillars look extremely pretty, wreathed with the luxuriant hop-vine, mixed with scarlet creeper and 'morning glory,' the American name for the most splendid of major convolvuluses."

It would be unfair to omit Mrs. Traill's delightful description of her own home surroundings. In 1835 she wrote: "We are having the garden, which hitherto has been nothing but a square enclosure for vegetables, laid out in a prettier form; two half circular wings sweep from the entrance to each side of the house; the fence is of rude-basket or hurdle-work, such as you see at home, called by the country-folk wattled fence. This fence is much more picturesque than those usually put up of split timber. Along this enclosure I have been planting a sort of flowery hedge with some of the native shrubs that abound in our woods and lake-shore. Among those already introduced are two species of shrubby honeysuckles, white- and rose-blossomed."

Mention is also made of the spireas, roses, leather-wood, fragrant daphne, wild gooseberry, red and black currants, and "two bearing shoots of the purple wild grapes from the island near us, which I long to see in fruit."

Another writer of this period, Mrs. Jameson, in a letter to her sister, says: "The house is very pretty and compact, and the garden will be beautiful, but I take no pleasure in anything," and, although personal trouble prevented her from being happy in her husband's Toronto home, she was able to enjoy the homes and gardens which she saw en route from Niagara, through Brantford and Woodstock, in order to visit Colonel Talbot at Talbotville. Here she writes of the gardens and orchards planted with European fruits, and adds: "What delighted me beyond anything else was a garden of more than two acres, very neatly laid out and enclosed. . . It abounds in roses of different kinds, cuttings of which he brought himself from England in the few visits he made there."

Mrs. Jameson, however, saw a number of rose-gardens and orchards which pleased her as she journeyed through Chatham and the district to Detroit. Possibly she touched a Canadian note more nearly than she imagined. When writing of "Stamford Park" she said it combined "the old world ideas of an elegant, well-furnished English villa and ornamented grounds, with some of the grandest and wildest features of the forest," adding: "It enchanted me altogether."

In this same district of Niagara we learn, through the biography of Hon. W. H. Merritt (1851), that he "employed a young Englishman by the name of Edward James, a gardener by profession, who had lately arrived from England, where he had been employed in the royal gardens, under H.R.H. the Duchess of Kent. This gardener was to lay out the improvements around his (Mr. Merritt's) residence on Yate Street, and what is now known as 'side hill.' The whole resulted in the beautiful esplanade, which cost our subject several thousand dollars, as well as affording a sightly street-walk."

According to an old volume at hand, there was a nursery established at St. Catharines prior to this, and, also one advertised as located "one and a half miles from the market-place, on the Kingston Road, Toronto," where seeds and plants not only of the useful but ornamental varieties were offered for sale—flowering shrubs, roses, herbaceous plants, such as home-gardeners, making beautiful their surroundings, would require. That there were such home-gardeners is evidenced by the fact that horticultural societies existed and flower shows were held, and the Botanical Society, which was organized in 1860, sought, as do live horticulturists today, to have botanical and experimental gardens established.

One of the early day writers speaking of the home surroundings of those bygone times wrote as follows: "Our forefathers set their homes a very short distance off the main roads; they planted flower gardens in front and vegetables in the rear. In the pioneers' gardens, stocks and pinks and lilies-of-the-valley grew beside sweet-william, foxglove, asters, and blue bachelor's buttons. Mignonette and southernwood perfumed the air. Mistresses cherished cabbage and blush rose-bushes; purple lilacs and acacia grew beside the porch and beneath the window."

It must be freely admitted that into the first picture at least, the log fence loomed large; yet, as Isabel Skelton in "The Backwoods Woman" says: "they were a rather picturesque addition to the vista, particularly after they settled a little into the soil, and goldenrod, hop-vines and summer weeds and flowers grew along or over them at random."

Despite the fact that log fences did prevail pretty generally, E. A. Talbot in "Five years residence in the Canadas" writes: "Between Fort George and Queenston is the most alluring portion of the Province, the neighborhood of Sandwich and Amerstburg [sic] excepted. Fine farms, flourishing orchards, and comfortable cottages, give it the air of an European Landscape, and if it were not for the rail fences, it might fairly stand in competition with some of the most beautiful districts of the British Isles."

As Byron once said: "the best of prophets of the future is the past," and these early day efforts to create and bequeath beauty should prove a great incentive to those making gardens here today. The pioneers sowed, often amid hardships and discouragement, but as the years pass the harvest of their efforts becomes more and more apparent. The call is to us all to continue the good work which we know was started when Canada was very young, that succeeding generations may in turn be benefitted, for . . . "in today already walks tomorrow."

J. Russell Harper
1955

From "Loyalist Gardens," in *The Maritime Advocate
and Busy East*

—⟋⟍—

*J**Russell Harper (1914–1983), an Ontario native, was a
pioneering author, curator, and professor of Canadian art
history. He wrote a number of landmark books, including*
Painting in Canada *(1966),* A People's Art: Naïve Art in Canada *(1974),
and* Krieghoff *(1979). He was appointed curator of Canadian art at
the National Gallery in Ottawa in 1958, and taught at Concordia
University in Montreal from 1967 through 1979. Through his writing,
museum work, and teaching he not only inspired another generation of
Canadian art historians, but also helped ordinary Canadians recognize
their country's visual-arts heritage.*

*During the 1950s he lived in New Brunswick, where he was asso-
ciated with the New Brunswick Museum and the Lord Beaverbrook
Art Collection. Just prior to his move to the National Gallery, Harper
—whose degree from the University of Toronto had been in art and
archaeology—was in charge of excavations at Fortress Louisbourg in
Nova Scotia.*

*Referring to Harper's painstaking research in Canadian art his-
tory, the artist Carl Schaefer once called him "a good digger." This
excerpt shows Harper's fine ability to dig, sift, sort, and examine
some disparate fragments in another field: Canadian garden history.*

—⟋⟍—

New Brunswick Loyalists like the Honourable Ward Chipman of
Saint John, George Leonard of Sussex, and Edward Winslow of
Kingsclear, were more than a little proud of their gardens. A garden
for them was not just a plot of ground surrounding the house in a

new land, but stood as an outward symbol of two things: it was that something which made a house into a home, and the mark which spelled quality. The flower and vegetable garden together with the orchard was a part of every English gentleman's estate. There were magnificent early gardens in New England, and the Loyalists brought with them a deep-seated love of gardens and gardening. Descriptions of early New Brunswick gardens are scattered and vague, but surviving fragments tell something of their story.

Apple trees were a first demand of Chipman, Winslow and others when they established themselves in New Brunswick. This was for a very good reason—rum and spruce beer were cheap and plentiful, but in gentlemen's houses tastes ran to the more costly and scarcer wine and cider. A prodigious amount of cider was consumed in some establishments. One Loyalist bewailed the fact that only a hundred gallons were available for his winter's supply since an additional forty gallons on which he had counted had been lost in transit. The importation of cider in such quantity from the established orchards of Nova Scotia and New England was expensive. Accordingly Ward Chipman sent to Windsor, Nova Scotia, for apple cuttings to plant around his house on the site of the Saint John Public Library. A certain Mr. Joseph Gray supplied them, and sent with the cuttings detailed instructions for planting them in a nursery at intervals of one yard for the first three years and then transplanting them into the orchard proper with thirty-three feet between the trees. He included gratuitously several twigs of honeysuckle "that blows all summer" for planting around the house and for distribution amongst his friends.

Ward Chipman engaged Robert Logan as first gardener for his new house in the spring of 1788. Logan wrote out a list of vegetable and herb seeds which he felt to be suitable for the garden and added a footnote suggesting in addition "as many flower seeds as your honour may please". His Honour found that the only seeds to be bought in Saint John were at General Benedict Arnold's store. Not only did Arnold demand a "monstrous" price, but he had imported his stock from England and it was then so old as to be utterly unreliable. Accordingly Chipman sent to Newburyport, Massachusetts, for £2 4-worth of seeds getting several varieties of peas, kidney and Windsor beans, asparagus, parsley, cucumbers, turnips, lettuce and other things. Balm, summer savory, sage and sweet marjoram came for the herb garden. He promised half his supply, although late in the season, to his old friend Winslow. A month before he had sent up the river to him with John Hazen a supply of early charter cucumber seeds bought from Arnold which he thought were still fertile, and some other seeds that "General" (actually Colonel) Bruce, Commandant at Fort Howe, had given him in the previous year. He remarked: "I think you can depend on them".

Certainly this same Edward Winslow seems to have been the most avid gardener of all the New Brunswick Loyalists. He had taken his wife first from New York to Annapolis where for two years they worked hard at their garden which "produced the most desirable vegetables and fruits," and which they stored in a root house of their own making. They had there such a "prodigious fine greenhouse" that they mentioned it along with their goose house, pig house and other houses as desirable features to attract prospective purchasers when they went to sell the establishment in 1785. He moved to a new estate at Kingsclear and four years later sent to a Boston relative for a new gardener. Isaac Winslow of Boston wrote to him the whole sad story of his experience up to the time when the boat departed for New Brunswick on which the man should have sailed. He says:

> "I thought I had engaged you a gardener to go by this vessel, but as I did not choose to advance him money lest he would be off, he came last night rather in liquor which was no recommendation. He still talks of going in the vessel and another man with him, whose appearance I had a better opinion of. I had produced a box of garden seeds put up of various kinds by a gardener. They cost 20 shillings. I have added some scarlet beans convolvus [sic]. Next year if we live and you desire it, I'll lay myself out to purchase for you some curious flowers. It is much the diversion here and there are various sorts which were unknown before the Revolution, at least to me.
>
> Your affectionate friend and kinsman,
> ISAAC WINSLOW.

P.S. Capt Howard sails in an hour and I do not see either of my chaps who intend going. I am sorry at not sending, having taken considerable pains about it. There is a vessel sails next week, and if I can meet with an undergardener such as you describe on low wages, I will venture to send him. I was to have given the fellow I engaged eight dollars a month and been answerable for his passage. He has been employed at Tracy's, Deane's and some of our first Gardens, but I suppose Drink has put him out of employ and I am glad I discovered it before you were troubled with him."

Winslow called on friends from many places for assistance. Mr. Finlay, the Postmaster-General at Quebec, sent him a parcel of hardwood cuttings for graftings in March, 1790, and another bundle was with them for Governor Carleton's garden in Fredericton. Some accompanying packets of seeds Mr. Joseph Chew of Montreal had collected from various gentlemen in England on a trip the previous year. As an afterthought, Finlay included a few grains of Indian corn which had come all of the way from Alexandria, Egypt, and some of the finest watermelon seeds from New York.

Gardening was not easy during the Napoleonic War year of 1794. Scarcity of help, isolation and lack of seeds are all described in a letter from Ward Chipman to Edward Winslow written in May of that year which reads:

"How are you in the midst of all these wars and rumours of wars? How has the freshet behaved to you this season, and how does your garden get on without seeds—I have been hoping in some way or other to get a supply from N. England, that I might have contributed to your wants, but our intercourse with that country seems to be completely closed, and I have at last been obliged to write to Sproule for seeds, which he has supplied me with abundantly, and I hope you have been assisted from the same source—here there have not been any to be had for a whole season—Wanton has cursed his Garden & quitted it. Murray is cultivating it with his soldiers, for except them there is not a Laborer to be had—as I don't employ Logan this season, I don't expect to have my Garden dug this month—one half of it I am laying down to Grass."

The men to whom Chipman refers can be identified readily. Sproule is the Honourable George Sproule, first Surveyor-General and Deputy Auditor of New Brunswick. Wanton is William Wanton who held the lucrative post of Collector of Customs in Saint John for over thirty years and was buried in the Loyalist Cemetery. Colonel John Murray who used soldiers from the Fort Howe Garrison to cultivate his garden, was a Loyalist from Rutland, Massachusetts, and who, like Winslow, went first to Nova Scotia and then came to New Brunswick at the conclusion of peace. He was an impressive man, six foot three tall, a veritable giant for those days. Like Chipman, Winslow and Leonard, these men were all numbered among the so-called élite of the community.

Troubles brought on by the war soon passed, but the exchange continued. Mary Odell, the Honourable Jonathan's wife, sent "Chip" some spinach and asparagus seed as well as some melon seed intended for the Honourable E. Botsford. David Owen of Campobello brought them down river under his coat to keep them dry. He forgot to deliver Mrs. Odell's packages until some days later. Owen's apologetic letter carried an implied but unexpressed "damn" at the humbug of having to carry such trivialities just to please the ladies.

Ward Chipman's sister sent him at one time some new and exotic flowers from the Cape of Good Hope, but these were the extraneous and elaborate decorative fringes of his vegetable garden which he considered basically to be a good business proposition. He exported potatoes to Boston from it, and when he took over the Presidency of New Brunswick in 1823, one of his first acts was to have the Government House gardener in Fredericton supply him with a list of the vegetables which had been put down in the root cellar for the Governor's use. Here is the list:

"Seven bushels of onions, 9 of carrot, 10 of parsnip, 3 of salsify, 2 of beets, 2 of 'Harty Chokes', 12 of turnip, and a very good supply of cabbage, cauliflower and pot herbs."

WILLIAM DOUGLAS
1959

From "Winnipeg Parks," in *Transactions of the Historical and Scientific Society of Manitoba*

—◊—

*W*illiam Douglas (1878–1963) was a public-spirited man who made major contributions to Manitoba and Masonic history. This prominent Winnipeg businessman was a Grand Master of the Manitoba Masonic Lodge, a president of the Manitoba Historical Society, and a city alderman—one of those individuals usually called "a pillar of society."

In this article, Douglas touches on one of the most popular urban improvement projects in our history—park building. The first public park in Canada was the Halifax Public Gardens, opened in 1834. Before public parks were common, city and town dwellers strolled and picnicked in attractive natural areas, in privately run entertainment grounds, and in new, nondenominational, landscaped cemeteries. During the City Beautiful movement, many parks were created by efforts of concerned citizens who were usually members of a horticultural or improvement society. Others, in larger centres, were created and maintained by official Parks Boards.

Winnipeg was especially active. Between 1893 and 1897, eight parks were built. Assiniboine Park, where William Douglas delivered this paper, was begun in 1903, officially opened in 1909, and developed along the plan drawn up by Frederick G. Todd of Montreal. The 152-hectare park included at least one of everything: pond, enclosed pavilion, formal gardens, wooded sections, walks, a small zoo, rolling lawns, and playing fields.

—◊—

The creation of Manitoba as a Province in 1870 brought great changes and settlers began to fill many vacant acres. Dr. George M. Grant tells of a visit he paid in 1872; "a walk in the garden at Silver Heights was sufficient to prove to us the richness of the soil of the Assiniboine Valley. The wealth of vegetation and the size of the root crops astonished us, especially when informed that no fertilizer had been used."

We can search the early records without much success to find any reference to the growing of flowers in the early Red River days. The pioneer doubtless was too busy raising crops to bother himself or herself with flowers.

One of the earliest references I have found was written by a settler from England who, with evident nostalgic longing, had this to say: "The well-known flower seeds, mignonette and sweet peas do well, indeed all annuals will here grow luxuriantly; but perennials, as a rule perish in the severe winter frosts, though if covered over with manure, they might withstand it." He continues his comment; "One sadly misses the sweet smelling flowers and glorious roses of Old England, the climbing ivy and many hued creepers, but if the nostrils are not regaled, vision is abundantly favored by the bewildering beauty of the woods and prairie."

Perhaps we have here a hint that in the early days of Manitoba the profusion of wild flowers growing all over the prairie were in themselves sufficient to satisfy the personal desire. When I arrived in Winnipeg in 1904, I actually believed that only sweet peas could be grown here, and there was good reason for such an idea. Many of you, no doubt, will recall these beautiful blooms were the crowning glory round the verandah throughout the City. So prominent was the sweet pea that someone, in all seriousness, suggested its adoption as the Provincial flower of Manitoba.

With many negative attitudes and a not very pronounced favourable opinion it required more than average optimism to write into the Statutes of the Province, in 1892, The Public Parks Act. During the consideration of this Bill, the provision of a fund "not exceeding a half mill on the dollar" was a stumbling block. One member of the House, a representative from Winnipeg, expressed the opinion that the amount ought to be "one mill" while another member, from a rural point, heatedly insisted that one quarter mill would be ample. The politician of yesteryear seems to have been quite as adept as is his successor of today.

With the passing of the Public Parks Act by the Manitoba Legislature, the way was paved for action by the Winnipeg City Council. The father of our Public Parks System, Alderman Carruthers, lost no time in preparing for the future. Less than ten months after the enactment of the Bill, the City Council passed the necessary by-law and forthwith appointed the first Parks Board in January, 1893. During the first year of operation, the newly-created Parks Board, in addition to organizing its work and routine of operation, purchased four parks; i.e., Victoria Park, Fort Rouge Park, Central Park; and St. John's Park. All four, with the exception of Victoria Park, still give increasing pleasure and enjoyment to thousands of our citizens each year.

Speaking from a personal standpoint, I have never forgiven the City Council for selling Victoria Park to the City Hydro. Where once existed, in the very heart of Winnipeg, a real beauty spot, on the bank of the Red River, we now find a gigantic commercial building, smoke stacks, coal dump, smoke and soot. And why should I feel grieved? Well, this particular bit of land was a part of the first piece of cultivated soil in the Canadian West. Originally it stood just outside the picket stockade of Fort Douglas. It was known as the Colony Farm and produced sustenance for our old originals. It was deeded to Alexander Ross in 1825 and through the years was known as "Colony Gardens." Perhaps the utilitarian instincts of the City Fathers far outweighs their perspective when it comes to offset dollars against an historic link connecting the present with the yesterdays of our community. So we lost Colony Gardens, renamed by the Parks Board, Victoria Park in honour of the revered Queen.

I have a sentimental attachment toward St. John's Park. Here was the starting line of the survey made by Peter Fidler in 1814 and the original settlers plowed their lands and raised their crops right there.

As we look around the greatly expanded City today and visit the many parks now operated on behalf of the citizens, it is difficult to fully realize that development of this important segment of our community life was slow—indeed the patience of the working staff has been marvellous. From a bald, almost forbidding stretch of prairie, there has emerged the miracle, not of three or four parks with gardens, but a group of real show-places which are second to none on this continent. Yes, they have cost money—a lot of money, over the years—but it has been on the investment side of the ledger, and cannot by any stretch of imagination be debited as an expense. The citizens get so much for so little. Without checking closely with the authorities, I understand that the per capita cost of our park system is about $1.50. At times it cost more than this to remove snow from the City streets. Modest is too modest a word for what we get for our park dollar.

One could further enlarge the glorious success story which followed the institution of the Parks Board sixty-five years ago. We have indeed entered into a heritage and it should be our constant purpose to give full encouragement to the men who carry on and improve what has been done.

The citizens of Winnipeg have been well served and still receive devoted service from the aldermen and citizens who comprise the Parks Board. We remember many of the big-hearted souls who, over the years, occupied the responsibility of being chairman. This is no sinecure. It takes time, energy, and above all administrative ability to fulfil the duties of the office. I could particularize by naming those I have known, but in doing so I would do a disfavour to other chairmen equally great. They have given great service to their fellow citizens.

It is not appropriate that I take time to recapitulate in statistical form figures as to area, cost, tenure etc., of our park system. Tonight, we are seated in a typical Winnipeg park and it consists of some three-hundred acres. Who among us is really concerned about the cost or the annual upkeep expense? To me the mystery is, how so much can be put at our disposal for so moderate a cost.

All my life I have loved a garden. The love of a garden, like charity, never fails. The joy is ever present from the time a baby tries to grab the artificial flower from its mother's coat until the snow is on its head. Or, to quote the old gardener, "until we reach the octo-geranium stage." Regardless of age, the man who loves a garden always has summer in his heart.

The wisdom of the men who first created the Parks Board and the success which has followed their modest first beginnings is reflected in all parts of the City. Not only is this the case in the public parks but it is found to a lesser degree in the home grounds of our citizens and these seem to increase in beauty with every passing year.

BARRY BROADFOOT
1977

"His Garden Was a Marvel," in *Years of Sorrow,*
Years of Shame

—⚏—

*I*n one of the sorriest chapters in recent Canadian history, over 20,000 Japanese-Canadians living within 160 kilometres of Canada's Pacific coast in 1942 were interned in camps in the interior of British Columbia and on sugar-beet farms in Alberta and Manitoba. In some cases families were split up; in many cases lives were shattered. The Canadian government sold off all their property, including their homes, businesses, and personal belongings.

The government, under William Lyon Mackenzie King, said that this community had to be moved for national security reasons. However, not one Japanese-Canadian was ever charged with treason. It is only recently that the Canadian government apologized to Japanese-Canadians for the wrongs inflicted on them and offered financial redress.

Barry Broadfoot interviewed a number of survivors of this internment as well as the non-Japanese who lived near them, hired them, or supervised them in the residential and work camps. The description of this anonymous man's garden in the midst of hardship and tragedy says much about the indomitable human spirit and the urge to garden.

—⚏—

There was an old man at Roseberry Camp and he had been a gardener somewhere near the South Dyke near Ladner there, and when he set out to create a garden he really did a good job. He did more than that, for I'd say that he created the best garden in all of British Columbia in those years.

The man was a wonder. I can't think of his name and I wish I had taken a picture of this garden and the flowers and the paths and the little structures he made out of peeled pine to make it look very Japanesy, but it was a marvel. He spent a great deal of time at it and the vegetables he produced, they were just out of this world.

When people used to come visiting or they came to the office on business, we'd take them down to see this garden and the flowers, and the old man we'd see him working in the garden and when he'd see us a distance away, quick as a flash he'd be in his house. We'd get there and start looking and then he'd come out, all dressed in white, white shirt, white pants, and highly polished black shoes and then he was ready to show us around his garden. He was an exception. He was so proud.

A lot of people put in a garden the first year after the year they arrived but most gave it up. Too much work. Too easy to buy from the stores and by this time a lot more of them were just too apathetic. There just wasn't enough to keep them busy, their minds occupied. Not in a place like Roseberry.

But the old man. He was proud as punch when we brought visitors.

ANNE O'NEILL
1985

From "Discipline and Beauty: The orderly gardens of 18th century Louisbourg," in *Canadian Collector*

—⚭—

*A*nne O'Neill, born in Nova Scotia, has worked at the reconstructed Fortress of Louisbourg, a Parks Canada site, since 1974. She was curator of the gardens there for eleven years, and participated in much of the research that went into the careful recreations of these gardens. Today, when O'Neill isn't enjoying gardening on her own home lot, she is manager of Visitor Activities at the fortress.

The recreated gardens in the fortress range from the grandly designed mix of ornamentals and edibles in the chief engineer's garden to the smaller, more rudimentary gardens of lower-ranked residents. Visitors feel as if they have stepped back in time as they watch authentically costumed interpreters tend the gardens using reproduction period tools.

When we think of the European gardening influences on eighteenth- and early nineteenth-century Canadian gardens, we sometimes visualize the naturalistic landscape style that came into vogue in Britain in the 1700s. However, we often forget the more structured styles that held sway even longer. The formal gardens at Louisbourg are a living example of the French garden culture, and a fine example of the importance of research into Canada's landscape history.

—⚭—

As Louisbourg was dependent on outside sources (France, Québec, Acadia and New England) for the bulk of its food supplies, any food that could be produced in the town was welcome. In 1744, with the declaration of war between France and Great Britain, enemy privateering and a crop failure in Québec combined to encourage Louisbourg residents to pay particular attention to their backyard gardens.

Town plans of the period indicate that there were more than 100 gardens within the walls of 18th century Louisbourg. It is obvious from these plans that the gardens retained some basic elements of the French style. Square and rectangular shapes sectioned by walking paths are much in evidence. Inventories and court cases involving property disputes can also provide information concerning dimensions and locations. Armed with these documents and knowledge of French gardening, Fortress researchers and gardeners have designed and built five period gardens.

The formal garden of Louisbourg chief engineer Etienne Verrier, reflects his important position in colonial society. His social status and artistic background are expressed by wide-gravelled walking paths and careful symmetrical arrangements of planting surfaces, with a sun dial as a central focus. At the same time the concentration on vegetables, herbs and medicinal plants emphasize the need for practicality. The garden designed for military officer Michel DeGannes is much simpler than the engineer's. DeGannes, colonial-born and the father of six children, has a garden designed more for function than for beauty, although it adheres to basic French gardening principles. However, its paths are narrower and the raised beds are retained by rough boards.

When the design of the gardens was complete, researchers returned to the 18th century sources to determine a range of appropriate plants. A list of the most popular *potager* plants was contained in *La Nouvelle Maison Rustique*, and it is reasonably sure that seeds for such plants could have been brought from the mother country. Another important reference was a 1752 census of Ile Royale that mentioned "cabbages, turnips, beans, peas, pumpkins and all sorts of roots" growing in various parts of the island. Cookbooks of the period also give a good idea of what vegetables and herbs were in common use. We know, for instance, that potatoes did not form a common part of the diet in 18th century France and that tomatoes were not considered edible until well after our period.

Plant lists from New England were deemed acceptable because of the connection through trade between Louisbourg and the American colonies. Similarly, archaeological seed analysis has revealed that certain types of foodstuffs were available, although whether they were grown locally or imported cannot be ascertained. During the 18th century royal officials encouraged experimentation with indigenous species, so it is reasonable to assume that some New World plants would have been transported into gardens and tested for useful qualities.

A large variety of herbs and medicinal plants are cultivated and used as they would have been in Louisbourg households 250 years ago. Some herbs are those used in preparations for medicines, others for dyes, cosmetics, religious ceremonies and, of course, culinary purposes. Many of these herbs were in fact brought by the colonists to the New World in the form of seeds, cuttings and roots. Today, a number of them grow wild in Cape Breton, such as chives, elecampane, caraway, chicory, wild parsnips, and angelica.

D. WAYNE MOODIE
1987

"Historical Indian Gardens," in *The Prairie Garden*

—⚹—

ong before European contact, Native people had been practising sophisticated gardening techniques and medicinal plant use. Charlotte Erichsen-Brown in her monumental pioneering study, Use of Plants for the Past 500 Years *(Aurora, Ont.: Breezy Creeks Press, 1979), documented these practices and many others as well. For example, they planted edible nut trees near their fields for ease of harvesting, and they practised selective cultivation of native apples by always choosing the largest and sweetest to plant near their fields. Some bands sprouted pumpkin seeds near their fires and grew them indoors until the danger of frost had past. Native peoples were boiling down maple sap as early as A.D. 400, and raspberries, strawberries, grapes, and the May apple were semicultivated from early on.*

In this article, D. Wayne Moodie, who was then a professor in the Department of Geography at the University of Manitoba, pays homage to the often ignored contributions of Native people to our gardening history. Canadian geographers are still active in the study of the wider issues of cultural landscapes.

—⚹—

When the first Europeans explored the lands to the west of Lake Superior, they found the Indian inhabitants of this vast region subsisted entirely from hunting, fishing and gathering. In the early years of the 19th century, however, some of the Indians living in the Manitoba Lowlands and the mixed forests of adjacent northwestern Ontario and northern Minnesota began to cultivate gardens. Although none of these Indians became dominantly agricultural, the products of their gardens supplemented their traditional food supplies in a period when the game resource was in decline. Some of the more enterprising of these Indian gardeners also raised surplus produce, which they frequently sold to the fur traders of the region.

One of the most significant aspects of this native cultivation was that it was based upon the traditional corn-beans-squash complex of North American Indian agriculture. These crops were first domesticated by the Indians of Mexico several thousand years ago. They subsequently spread northward and were eventually adopted by most of the Indians of the eastern United States and by some of the tribes of southeastern Canada. At the time of the arrival of the whiteman, the northern limit of Indian agriculture in the interior of North America lay at the Missouri River villages of the Mandan and Hidatsa Indians in present North Dakota. The first European to describe the agriculture of these northernmost Indian cultivators on the plains was the French explorer, La Vérendrye who noted that these Indians grew corn, beans, squash, pumpkins, sunflowers and tobacco. With the exception of the sunflower, which was domesticated by North American Indians, all of these crops were of tropical origin. In the process of diffusing north of Mexico, however, they were slowly but significantly altered through natural selection, and adapted to a wide array of environmental conditions. Corn was the most adaptable of the Indian cultigens, and was by far the most important food crop in their economy. Thus, the flint corn raised by the Mandan Indians had been selected for generations for rapid growth in the short summers of the northern plains. In the process, it became a hardy, dwarf corn that had some resistance to frost and drought. When agriculture later appeared among the Ottawa and Ojibwa Indians of Manitoba and northwestern Ontario, the Indian crops raised were corn, beans and squash derived from the Mandan and Hidatsa Indians in North Dakota. That such a northward extension of Indian agriculture was possible was largely owing to the seed varieties developed by the Missouri Indians and their ancestors.

In addition to Indian crops, the Ottawa and Ojibwa also planted crops of European origin which they obtained from the fur traders. At times, these included barley, onions, turnips and carrots, but the most important of these was the potato. Just as the fur traders planted

Indian crops in their gardens at the trading posts, so the Indians were quick to perceive the advantages of certain European plants. As a result, corn and potatoes became the staple food crops of the Indian gardeners in Manitoba and Ontario. In time, Indian gardening spread north beyond the limits to which even Mandan corn could be raised to maturity, and potatoes became the staple crop raised by the Indians in these regions.

The earliest historical occurrence of Indian agriculture north of the Missouri River was at the Indian village of Netley Creek, located near the mouth of the Red River. The Ottawa first began to plant at this site in 1805 and from there, agriculture subsequently spread among neighbouring bands of Ojibwa Indians. Neither the Ottawa nor the Ojibwa were living in the Red River valley when the fur traders first arrived but, beginning in the 1780's they began to replace the Cree and Assiniboine Indians to whom this country had formerly belonged. The Ojibwa who migrated into the Red River valley were part of a general westward expansion of Ojibwa peoples from the forests to the east. The Ottawa, in contrast, were more recent arrivals, who had come to the west from their tribal territories in the Upper Great Lakes. According to the fur trader Alexander Henry the Younger, they first appeared in the Red River valley in 1792, "when the prospects of great beaver hunts lured them from their country".

It was the Red River Ottawa who first began to cultivate north of the Missouri and who played the crucial role in disseminating agriculture among the more populous, neighbouring Ojibwa. According to Lord Selkirk, who founded the Red River Colony in 1812:

> The Indians who inhabit the country from Lake Superior to Red River are mostly of the Chippeway (Ojibwa) Nation, who have never been in the habit (of) cultivating the ground. The Ottawas, who speak the same language and reside near Lakes Huron and Michigan have long been accustomed to plant Indian Corn, and some other vegetables tho' on a small scale. A band of these Indians, prompted by the growing scarcity of game in their own country, determined to migrate to Red River where they continued the practice of cultivating the ground.

John Tanner, a whiteman who had been adopted by the Ottawa as a boy, and who was living with them at Netley Creek at this time, further observed that it was the Ottawa who taught the Ojibwa to plant corn. In Tanner's words, "We went down to Dead River (Netley Creek), planted corn and spent the summer there. Sha-gwaw-koo-sink, an Ottawwaw, a friend of mine and an old man, first introduced the cultivation of corn among the Ojibbeways of Red River."

By the 1820's, agriculture had diffused over wide areas from Netley Creek. To the east, one of the most important sites to emerge was at Garden Island in Lake of the Woods. One of the first descriptions of this complex was written by a Hudson's Bay Company officer in 1819, who wrote: "I visited their tents which were pitched alongside of the piece of ground which they had under cultivation which from the regular manner in which it was laid out would have done credit to many . . . farmers; excellent Potatoes, Indian Corn, Pumpkins, Onions and Carrots." Indian gardening subsequently developed in many parts of Lake of the Woods, but Garden Island remained the main centre of agricultural activity and its people frequently sold their corn to the fur traders of the region. One of the best descriptions of the island was written by a member of the Canadian Exploring Expedition during the 1850's, when as many as 500 Indians congregated on the island during the summer.

> Garden Island is about a mile and a half long at its widest part. Its western half is thickly wooded, the greater portion of the eastern half cleared and cultivated. A field containing about 5 acres was planted with Indian corn, then nearly ripe. The corn was cultivated in hills, and kept very free from weeds . . . Near the space devoted to Indian corn, were several small patches of potatoes, pumpkins, and squashes. An air of great neatness prevailed over the whole of the cultivated portion of the Island.

As early as 1815, gardening had developed to the north of Lake of the Woods and, in that year, several Indian families living around Escabitchewan House on Tide Lake were cultivating Indian corn, beans and potatoes. In 1823, it was reported that the Indians at Eagle

Lake had "good gardens" that were "very productive of Indian corn". Beyond these locations, gardening developed later and was essentially confined to potato culture. The most northerly development of Indian agriculture occurred in the Manitoba Lowlands. By the 1820's, the Ojibwa were cultivating corn, pumpkins and potatoes on the southern shores of Lake Manitoba, and large quantities of potatoes were being raised on some of the islands in the Narrows of the Lake. Later, the Canadian Exploring Expedition observed several places along the Mossy River "where the Indians grow potatoes, Indian corn and melons". This observation is particularly noteworthy for it appears to have been the northernmost instance of Indian corn cultivation on the continent.

The spread of Indian crops into such northerly latitudes in Manitoba and Ontario was made possible in part by the hardy, quick growing varieties derived from the Missouri Indians. However, it was also owing to the gardening strategies of the Ottawa and Ojibwa Indians, who generally planted their gardens on sandy or coarse textured soils on islands or around the shores of lakes. These warm, well-drained soils prompted quicker growth, while the thermostat effect of adjacent water bodies reduced the likelihood of frosts during the short growing season.

At its northernmost limits, this gardening was a small-scale and often uncertain activity. Nonetheless, it was most distinctive in that it led to the most northerly development of Indian agriculture in North America, bringing to a conclusion the lengthy process of agricultural diffusion that had begun in Mexico several millenia ago.

TIM BALL
1987

From "Fur Trade Gardens," in *The Prairie Garden*

—⚍—

*T*he thought of Hudson's Bay posts, established in the
north in the late 1600s, conjures up romantic images of
voyageurs and Indian scouts — not of sweating gardeners
*labouring over patches of turnips. However, the Hudson's Bay
Company played not only a major role in our early economic life,
but also a role in our garden history. There were many many horticultural failures, due to company directors sitting in the warmer climate of England and sending out English seeds that they thought
could be grown successfully at similar latitudes in Canada. Even so,
the brave New World gardeners made an impressive effort to expand
the borders of gardening.*

*And this continued into the 1940s, when the company began
supplying its posts with manuals instructing gardeners on the best
ways to cultivate northern gardens. Although the manuals concentrated on vegetable growing, they also included tips for flower growing. A report on a 1942 competition open to all post gardeners noted
that "in the case of flower gardens, only wives and other female relatives of the post staff are eligible for prizes."*

*When Tim Ball wrote this article, he was teaching in the Depart-
ment of Geography at the University of Winnipeg.*

—⚍—

The first references to gardening in the Prairie region appear to occur
in the daily journals of the Hudson's Bay Company maintained at
York Factory and Churchill Factory. In the journal for May the 5th,
1715, James Knight notes, "sow'd some seeds in the garden". . . .
There was not much of a yield that first year. An entry for the 14th

of September gives the bare details. "Turnips—we have had very cold weather and frosts for the time of the year".

Today it is hard to imagine why any attempt would be made to grow vegetables in such harsh climatic conditions, especially when you consider that the climate was much more severe in that time that is now known as the Little Ice Age. . . . The answer is economics, a familiar one to many Prairie gardeners, although later the nutritional and anti-scurvy qualities were also recognized.

The Hudson's Bay Company made a very clear distinction between what they called 'Country provisions' and 'English provisions'. The former were things obtained in the region where the Post was located, the latter were supplies brought in from England on the annual re-supply ship. Anyone who has seen the ship Nonsuch in the Manitoba Museum of Man and Nature can understand why space was at a premium and supplies brought from England were restricted to those things that could not be obtained locally. Self-sufficiency meant monetary savings but it also meant a more diversified diet and a chance to savour food that brought memories of home that was so far away.

The gardens were usually prepared and seeded in the first two weeks of May, although there were years in which this was severely hampered by extreme weather conditions. The usual practice was to fence off a portion of ground to protect it from animals and people then to ensure that the area was kept free from snow from about the first of April onward. The objective was to expose the ground to the warming rays of the spring sun so that the ground would thaw out much earlier than normal, especially in a region of permafrost. This did not always work as an entry for the 2nd of June, 1732 attests; "digging part of the garden rest still frozen", or the 5th of June, 1734, "sowed seed rest of ground so wet and ice so in ground that we cannot sow any more seed as yet we have had hitherto a very cold and uncomfortable spring and summer".

The turnip has already been mentioned and certainly was the major vegetable both in terms of quantity and quality at Posts on the west side of the Bay, probably because it was capable of withstanding some degrees of frost. There were years however when the turnip crop was lost or had to be recovered early as in 1761 when an entry by Ferdinand Jacobs for September 30th states, "Dug up turnips green from garden."

The most common vegetables grown, after turnips, were radishes, lettuce, peas and an early form of cabbage called coleworts. The latter were transplanted although the date varied considerably apparently as a result of the weather. For example in 1779, it occurred on the 4th of August while in 1780, it was done on the 14th of July. Despite this, the crop seems to have been fairly bountiful, relatively consistent and certainly was recognized for its value.

CATHERINE HENNESSEY AND EDWARD MACDONALD
1990

From "Arthur Newbery and the Greening of Queen Square," in *The Island Magazine*

—⅏—

*E*dward MacDonald *is curator of history with the Prince Edward Island Museum and Heritage Foundation, and editor of* The Island Magazine. *Catherine Hennessey, one of the island's leading heritage advocates, is urban beautification coordinator for the Charlottetown Area Development Corporation.*

In listing sources, the authors mention the earlier research on the Queen Square Gardens by Mary K. Cullen of Parks Canada; family memorabilia and memories shared with them by two of Newbery's descendants; and period photographs of Queen Square, at the Provincial Archives and Record Office. Indeed, a search of government documents, private sources, and newspaper accounts reveals at least a little about the evolution of many of Canada's nineteenth-century public-building landscapes.

All too often—just as at Charlottetown—the greening of these landscapes was very low on a government's list of priorities. If a landscape design was commissioned at all, the funding for its implementation was short-term, and for its later upkeep, generally inadequate. Nevertheless, the elements of Newbery's Queen Square—a system of paths, a canopy of trees, a floral display, and a central feature such as a fountain—complemented many public buildings in post-Confederation Canada.

—⅏—

"Is it not disgraceful," the Charlottetown Islander asked in April 1860, "that the Public Square, which should be an ornament to the city, should present . . . the appearance of a farmer's pig pen or cow yard?" The editor was referring to Queen Square, the centrepiece of one of North America's most orderly town grids. Here, in the official heart of the Island's capital, the Colonial Building rose majestically from a muddle of foot paths and ragged grass plots. Clots of manure radiated out from the adjacent market hall, creating a minefield for unwary legislators. There were no trees, no flowers, no fences. Save for its public buildings, Queen Square was a bald pasture.

It stayed that way until 1884. Until then, there were sporadic calls for the beautification of Queen Square. The most serious attempt, in 1856–67, ended in dismal failure when cows from the market uprooted the seedlings that had been planted on the north side of the square.

A conjunction of trends and events changed matters by the mid-1880s. Two decades of steady growth had brought substantial new buildings to both Charlottetown generally and Queen Square in particular. The federal government's Dominion Building and a new brick courthouse now flanked Province House (the Colonial Building). As Charlottetown's architecture grew more impressive, Charlottetonians' taste grew more refined. When that flamboyant apostle of the aesthetic, Oscar Wilde, lectured on the decorative arts in the city's Market Hall in October 1882, he seemed more a curiosity than a prophet. Yet by mid-decade, some of Wilde's ideas had taken root; in more colourful paint schemes and a new attention to decoration, Charlottetown's home owners seemed to be expressing their agreement with Wilde that even the most ordinary objects need not be ugly.

More beautiful buildings seemed to require more beautiful settings, but there were also practical reasons behind the call for greenery. In 1883, a major fire destroyed many of the buildings along Richmond Street on the south side of Queen Square. A year later, the newly-constructed Dominion Building burned down. Trees, the local newspapers subsequently claimed, would act as barriers to the spread of fire. The papers set a spur to civic pride by promoting tree-planting along the dusty, bare streets and on the unkempt squares. The vehicle for this greening of Charlottetown was to be Arbor Day.

Ceremonial tree-planting had a lengthy tradition in European culture, but it was the State of Nebraska that first institutionalized the practice by proclaiming an "Arbor Day" in 1872. In time, a group of Charlottetown's leading citizens followed Nebraska's lead, establishing the Charlottetown Arbor Society in May 1884. With City Council's approval, it named 24 May as the first Arbor Day.

The inaugural Arbor Day concentrated on planting Charlottetown's five public squares with judiciously selected trees. The Society appointed a committee for each square under the guidance of a planner. Among the 18 members of the Queen Square Committee were Premier W. W. Sullivan, Members of Parliament Louis H. Davies and Donald Ferguson, and Mayor Hooper. But the driving force behind the committee was one of the province's few civil servants. For Arthur Newbery, the Assistant Provincial Secretary, Queen Square would become a life's work.

By Island standards, Newbery's origins were somewhat exotic. He was born in the Tuscan town of Sienna, Italy, in 1850, the son of an expatriate Englishman and his Italian wife. John Fenton Newbery was the scion of a distinguished English publishing family. His great-grandfather was John Newbery, after whom the Newbery Medal for children's literature is named. John Fenton did a degree at Oxford before moving to Italy because of ill-health. He was a gentleman, and he married a lady, Adele Travaglini. Of their 15 children, the sons were reared as Anglicans, the daughters (out of deference to their mother) as Roman Catholics.

In 1856 Newbery took his family to North America. He arrived on Prince Edward Island around 1860 after stays in New York and Halifax, where his wife died. The family settled at Ringwood, a fine estate in Rocky Point across the harbour from Charlottetown. A few years later, the family moved across to the colonial capital.

Arthur was raised in a home where art and beauty were highly prized. His mother was an amateur watercolourist of some skill, while his father, according to family tradition, gave Arthur's playmate, Robert Harris, his first painting lesson. In contrast to his cosmopolitan upbringing, Arthur's career was rather prosaic; after completing his education at Prince of Wales College, he spent over 50 years as Assistant Provincial Secretary-Treasurer. Instead, Arthur's finely developed sense of the aesthetic found expression in one of his hobbies, gardening. Although he had no training as a landscape architect, he was an inspired amateur, imaginative, eclectic, and thorough. Walking to work each day and gazing from the window of his office at Province House, he could see the potential—and the sad reality—of the grounds on Queen Square.

Newbery was secretary of the Queen Square committee and planner for the plantings there on the first Arbor Day. On a damp, showery day, a crowd of volunteers planted 135 trees of 11 different varieties. The locations were selected in advance by Newbery and marked with numbered stakes. Each of the trees was paid for by local citizens.

Arbor Day, inaugurated with such enthusiasm in 1884, quickly became a tradition in Charlottetown. By 1885, Arthur Newbery had been named secretary of the Charlottetown Arbor Society, a far more onerous position than the largely honourary presidency. The following year, the city schools were officially enlisted as key participants in the celebration of Arbor Day. As the decades passed, Arbor Day gradually developed into a school festival centred on ceremonial tree-plantings.

But the greening of Queen Square became something more than an Arbor Day project. Four days after the first celebration, on 28 May 1884, the Queen Square Committee met to consider ways to finance further beautification of the square. The committee members had more than tree-planting in mind. They wanted grounds that would rival the Public Gardens in Halifax. Newbery was put in charge.

In Halifax, Newbery recruited a landscape gardener named George Fletcher to lay off Queen Square's walks, flower beds, and grass plots. But Newbery drew up the plans and supervised the work, and it was Newbery that met with federal officials to persuade them to landscape the area around its new edifice, the Cabot Building. When architects David Stirling and W. C. Harris laid out the federal portion of the square in 1887, they integrated their design into Newbery's.

In designing the Queen Square Gardens, Newbery may not have worked from any "master plan"—at least, none survive. The grounds were laid out employing the fashionable eclecticism of the picturesque mode. A double belt of trees shaded avenues along the Grafton and Richmond Street edges of the Square, paralleling its three major buildings, and marched in diagonals towards the north face of Province House. A single line of trees fringed the western perimeter. Other trees were scattered or clumped for effect within the square. The gardens dominated the design. Amid elaborate flowerbeds and shrubberies, footpaths curved or slanted in patterns that were elegantly balanced without being strictly geometric. The whole effect was one of studied informality.

The basic layout for Queen Square was complete by 1887, but there were modifications and additions over the years. A beautiful, Newbery-designed fountain was added to the south side of the square between the Cabot Building and Province House in 1889. Six years later, a hexagonal wooden bandstand was erected on the opposite side of the square. Other changes included electric lighting, concrete footpaths, an ornate drinking fountain, improved fencing, cannons, and monuments.

If creating the gardens entailed much hard work, paying for them took nearly as much energy. Until the 1890s, the Charlottetown Arbor Society supplemented small government grants with privately raised funds to finance maintenance of the Queen Square Gardens. Eventually, financial responsibility for the gardens was entrusted to an intergovernmental committee.

CHARLES R. SAUNDERS AND
MANY OTHERS
1992

From "A Visit to Africville," in *The Spirit of Africville*

—⚬—

*C*harles R. Saunders, an author and newspaper columnist, *and others collaborated on this illustrated book about Africville, a black community with roots in the 1840s, on Bedford Basin, Halifax, Nova Scotia. Between 1964 and 1970, following a series of ill-considered decisions, the city relocated all the residents of this settlement—by coercion or force. The homes were destroyed, as was a way of life forged by ties of family, church, and friendship, by racial and economic segregation, and by physical separation from the city and its most basic services.*

The destruction of Africville has been reexamined many times: in a study entitled Africville: The Life and Death of a Canadian Black Community; *in an inquiry held in Halifax in 1989; in a photographic exhibition; and in a thirty-five-minute documentary,* Remember Africville, *produced by the National Film Board with the CBC.*

Another form of reexamination and healing is the annual reunion, held on the site by The Africville Genealogical Society, composed of former residents and their descendants. From them, Saunders has created a piece that, although set in Africville in the summer of 1959, is representative of the way many of us remember landscapes.

—⚬—

Summer, 1959
Next door to Aunt Tibby's is Deacon Ralph Jones' house. His son's house is right beside it. A lot of people build their houses on their parents' property. Keeps the land in the family, deed or no deed.

You can't miss the end of Deacon Jones' lot. That huge tree we're passing is about the biggest property marker you'll ever see. We call it the Caterpillar Tree. That's the only kind of fruit it grows—caterpillars. There's a story behind that tree. A long time ago, Deacon Jones went out and got a post to mark off his land. Next thing he knew, that post was sproutin' leaves, and over the years, it grew—and grew. Nobody knows why the caterpillars like it so much.

ASTA ANTOFT
1972

"Afterthoughts," in *Thoughts from my Gardens*

—⁂—

*A*sta Antoft *(1896–1992) emigrated from Denmark to Canada in 1930 with her husband. After three years in Winnipeg, they settled in Nova Scotia, where they began farming and gardening. In time her gardens, nestled in the Annapolis Valley, became an internationally known "beauty spot."*

After her husband's death in 1954, she decided to start up a commercial nursery. Despite being turned down for bank loans because she was "just a woman," she persevered, and her Acadia Nurseries became a large and profitable enterprise.

Antoft was entirely self-taught. She said she had learned from her parents, who had a large garden, as well as from her mistakes—but never, she wrote, from "the same one more than once." She also learned from one of her best friends, Roscoe Fillmore, who taught her how to graft plant material.

In Thoughts from my Gardens, *a sixty-six-page booklet distributed throughout the Atlantic provinces, Antoft answered the questions asked most often by her many thousands of garden and nursery visitors. In "Afterthoughts," she reflects on the many pleasures of gardening—not the least of which is sharing one's successes with others. We like Antoft's words so much that we chose her to be the last voice in this anthology.*

—⁂—

As I look back over the years, I see in my mind the annual miracle of spring as all living things stir from the sleep of winter. I see the bursting forth of the wondrous symphony of colour that comes to the garden as the days grow longer and warmer.

I see, and almost feel, the oppressive heat of high summer, when all plant life in my garden with almost audible gratitude accepts the monotonous swish of the fine spray from the sprinkler system. And I see the autumn, as shadows turn longer and lend depth to the colour of dying leaves and the extravagant hues of late-flowering 'mums.

But in winter, with my few houseplants to remind me that the miracle of life goes on, the most precious memory of all is that of the thousands of people who over the years came to visit and to enjoy my gardens. These are among the most precious flowers in my memory garden. To these friends I dedicate this little book.

Sources and Permissions

—៣—

CALLING ALL GARDENERS

Bond, William. "To be given away." Advertisement in *Upper Canada Gazette* or *American Oracle* (York), 5 September through 10 October 1801.

G., W. T. "Gardening in Canada." *The Canada Farmer*, 1 March 1864: 60–61.

Beadle, D. W. "Conclusion." In *Canadian Fruit, Flower, and Kitchen Gardener* (Toronto: James Campbell & Son, 1872): [389].

Rutherford, Edith Stevenson. "Peace, Springtime and a Garden." *The Canadian Horticulturist*, 42 (April 1919): 93–95.

Wilson, Mrs. J. A. "Women and Gardening." In *Report of the Horticultural Societies of Ontario for 1933* (Toronto: Horticultural Societies of Ontario, 1934): 37–39. Reprinted by permission of the estate of J. Tuzo Wilson.

McKinley, Jean. "What Makes the Canadian Garden Canadian?" *Canadian Homes and Gardens*, 29 (February 1952): 9, 37.

Herbert, H. F. "Why Does Your Garden Grow?: Warnings by our Anguished Indoor Man." *Canadian Commentator*, 4 (May 1960): 18–20. Reprinted by permission of W. H. Baxter, Baxter Publishing Company, publisher of *Canadian Commentator*.

Fillmore, Roscoe A. "Introduction." In *The Perennial Border and Rock Garden* (Toronto: The Ryerson Press, 1961): v–viii. Used by permission of McGraw-Hill Ryerson Limited, Whitby, Ontario.

Guy, Ray. "Plunge into Pineapple Plantation, Maude." In *Ray Guy's Best* (Halifax: Formac Publishing Company, Limited, 1987): 29–32. Reprinted by permission of James Lorimer and Company Limited.

BREAKING NEW GROUND

Simcoe, Elizabeth. Diaries. Archives of Ontario, Simcoe Family Papers, F 47, Series 8–17; and Innis, Mary Quayle, ed. *Mrs. Simcoe's Diary* (Toronto: Macmillan of Canada, 1965): 73.

[Aylmer, L. A.] "Some Notes on Architecture, Interiors, and Gardens in Quebec 1831: 'Recollections of Canada 1831' by L. A. Aylmer in the *Rapport de l'Archiviste de la Province de Québec*, 1834–35, pp. 279–318." *APT Bulletin*, 7 (No. 2, 1975): 2–7. Reprinted by permission of The Association for Preservation Technology International.

Lloyd, Rev. F. E. J. *Two Years in the Region of Icebergs and What I Saw There* (London: Society for Promoting Christian Knowledge, 1886): 11–12.

Bullock-Webster, Julia. Diaries, 1894–1896. British Columbia Archives and Record Service, Victoria. Transcription courtesy of The Grist Mill at Keremeos, British Columbia.

Bealby, J. T. "Our New Ranch." In *Fruit Ranching in British Columbia* (London: Adam and Charles Black, 1909): 84–93.

Parlby, Mrs. Walter. "The Woman's Garden." *The Grain Growers' Guide*, 8 (7 April 1920): 16, 80–81. Reprinted by permission of Gerald Parlby and *The Country Guide*.

Dunington-Grubb, H. B. "The Landscape Architect in Canada." *Landscape and Garden*, 2 (Autumn 1935): 106–107. Reprinted by permission of The [British] Landscape Institute.

Cox, Holland. "Prince Rupert Gardens." *Canadian Homes and Gardens*, 17 (January–February 1940): 62–64.

Sanders, Frances Steinhoff. "Oasis on the Roof." *Canadian Homes and Gardens*, 25 (June 1948): 29, 108.

Berton, Laura Beatrice. *I Married the Klondike* (Boston and Toronto: Little, Brown and Company, 1954): 232–233. Reprinted by permission of Pierre Berton.

Skinner, Frank Leith. "Problems and Objectives." In *Horticultural Horizons: Plant Breeding and Introduction at Dropmore, Manitoba* (Winnipeg: Manitoba Department of Agriculture and Conservation, 1967): 9–10. Reprinted by permission of Mrs. F. L. Skinner and Hugh Skinner.

Stairs, Carol. "Uptown Radichetta." *Harrowsmith*, 3 (July 1979): 32–34.

Janes, Percy. "A Newfoundland Garden." In *Light & Dark* (St. John's: Harry Cuff Publications, 1980): 15. Reprinted by permission of the author.

Keeble, Midge Ellis. "It Grows Beautiful Weeds." In *Tottering in My Garden: a gardener's memoir with notes for the novice* (Camden East, Ontario: Camden House Publishing, 1989): 85–90. Reprinted by permission of Camden House Publishing.

Burton, Claudette. "From Russia With Love: Doukhobor traditions in Canadian gardens." *Harrowsmith*, 14 (September 1990): 74–79.

LAYING OUT THE GROUNDS

Claus, William. Garden Book for 1806-1810. National Archives of Canada, Claus Papers, MG 19, F 1, Vol. 21, Pt. 2, Item 14.

O'Brien, Mary S. Papers (1828–1838). Archives of Ontario, F 592, MS 199, Journals 2, 3, 14, 23, and 39; and Miller, A.S., ed. *The Journals of Mary O'Brien, 1828–1838* (Toronto: Macmillan of Canada, 1968).

Parker, Asa. "Fencing." In *The Canadian Gardener; Containing Practical Directions for the Kitchen and Fruit Garden; and also a Brief Treatise on Field Culture; Adapted to the Climate and Soil of Canada* (Aylmer, Quebec: Thomas Watson, Printer, 1851): 11. Collection of the Metropolitan Toronto Reference Library.

Woolverton, Linus. "A Few Hints on Landscape Gardening." *The Canadian Horticulturist*, 12 (May 1889): 119–121.

Macoun, W. T. "Lady Grey and the Gardens at Rideau Hall." *The Canadian Horticulturist*, 35 (January 1912): 5–6.

Todd, Frederick G. "Where Nature Is Abetted." *Canadian Homes and Gardens*, 6 (April 1929): 26–27, 54.

Lugrin, N. de Bertrand. "Canada's Most Famous Garden." *Canadian Homes and Gardens*, 8 (March 1931): 17–21, 66, 68.

King, William Lyon Mackenzie. Diaries. National Archives of Canada, MG 26, J 13, Vol. 1931.

Dunington-Grubb, Lorrie A. "The Artist in the Rock Garden." *Canadian Homes and Gardens*, 15 (March 1938): 14–15, 47–48.

Banks, Kerry. "The Most Honourable Gardeners." *Harrowsmith*, 4 (January 1980): 48–59. Reprinted by permission of the author.

Pollock-Ellwand, Nancy. "A Homestead Restored." In *The Prairie Garden, 1987* (Winnipeg: The Prairie Garden Committee of the Winnipeg Horticultural Society, 1987): 15–19. Reprinted by permission of the author and the Prairie Garden Editorial Committee, Winnipeg Horticultural Society.

Kennedy, Des. "Planning." In *Crazy about Gardening* (Vancouver: Whitecap Books, 1994): 144–147. "Planning" in *Crazy about Gardening* by Des Kennedy is reprinted by permission of Whitecap Books.

GARDENING IN PUBLIC

[Editor.] "The Improvement of Halifax." *The [Colonial] Pearl*, 3 (8 November 1839): 358.

[Editor.] "Railway Gardens." *The Canada Farmer*, 15 June 1868: 185–186.

Engelhardt, H. A. "Graveyards and Cemeteries." In *The Beauties of Nature Combined with Art* (Montreal: John Lovell, 1872): 28–30.

[Agnes Scott.] "Notes by the Marchioness." *Ottawa Daily Free Press*, 23 May 1900: 2.

Penhallow, Prof. D. P. "Shade Trees for Our Cities." *The Canadian Horticulturist*, 30 (April 1907): 86–87.

Woolverton, C. Ernest. "The Value of Parks." In "Welland's Possibilities and Its Opportunities in the Building of a Great and Model Industrial Centre." *The Welland Telegraph*, 28 December 1909: 1. Reprinted by permission of *The Tribune*, Welland, Ontario.

Simpson, Cecil M. "A Prince Edward Island Garden." In "The Beaver Circle." *The Farmer's Advocate*, 50 (2 December 1915): 1892–1893. Reprinted by permission of the *Winnipeg Free Press*.

Wood, Henrietta. "My Garden–1917: A Dream." *Agricultural Gazette of Canada*, 4 (January 1918): 86.

Perkins, Dorothy. "The Kitchen Garden and Production." In *The Canadian Garden Book* (Toronto: Thomas Allen, Publisher, 1918): 103–116.

Sara, F. Leslie. "Rockery Holds Peace and Charm." *The Calgary Daily Herald*, 9 June 1934: 25. Reprinted by permission of *The Calgary Herald*.

Stevenson, Collier. "Flowers for Morale, Vegetables for Victory: Here's the Logical Slogan for 1943!" *Saturday Night*, 58 (20 March 1943): 4–5. Reprinted by permission of *Saturday Night* Magazine.

Dale, H. Fred. "Apartment Gardeners Find A Way." *The New York Times*, 10 September 1972: D43. Reprinted by permission of the author.

Giangrande, Carole. "Political Gardens." *Harrowsmith*, 11 (January/February 1987): 15–18.

NAMING FRIENDS AND FOES

Russell, Elizabeth. Diaries, 1805–08. Metropolitan Toronto Reference Library, Elizabeth Russell Papers, L 21, entry for Thursday, May 31, 1806; and Firth, Edith G. *The Town of York, 1793–1815* (Toronto: The Champlain Society, 1962): 262–263.

Farmer, A Canadian. "Does It Pay to Hire a Gardener." *The Canadian Agriculturist*, 11 (May 1859): 115.

Smith, A. M. "Prize Essay on Impositions of Dishonest Tree Pedlars: 'By Their Fruits Shall Ye Know Them'." In *Annual Report of the Fruit Growers' Association of Ontario, 1873* (Toronto: 1874): 38–39.

Jack, Annie L. "Doorweed for Dry Places." *The Canadian Horticulturist*, 34 (October 1911): 236.

Thompson, Geo. "The Private Gardener." *The Canadian Florist*, 14 (22 August 1919): 250–251. Reprinted by permission of Horticulture Publications Limited.

Harcourt, Miss Ella M. "Garden Visitors." In *The Rose Society of Ontario Year Book 1930* (Toronto: The Rose Society of Ontario, 1930): 31. Reprinted with kind permission of The Canadian Rose Society, formerly The Rose Society of Ontario.

Morgan, F. Cleveland. "Rock-Gardening in the Province of Quebec." In *Rock Gardens and Rock Plants: Report of the Conference Held by the Royal Horticultural Society and the Alpine Garden Society* (London: The Royal Horticultural Society, 1936): 20–29. Reprinted by permission of The Royal Horticultural Society.

Rosalinda, Sister Mary. "Lace." In *From a Garden Enclosed: A collection of Community Verse in tribute to Reverend Mother Mary Leopoldine, Superior General, on the occasion of her Golden Jubilee* (Victoria, British Columbia: The Sisters of Saint Ann, 1944): 37. Reprinted by permission of The Sisters of Saint Ann, Victoria, British Columbia.

Hamilton, G. H. "Ornamental Accessories." In *A Gardener's Source Book* (Toronto and Vancouver: J. M. Dent & Sons (Canada) Limited, 1953): 16. Reprinted by permission of J. M. Dent & Sons Canada Limited.

Leslie, W. R. "Let Snow Be Help To Your Garden." *Winnipeg Free Press*, 24 November 1956: 44. Reprinted by permission of the *Winnipeg Free Press*.

Jackson, Bernard S. "How to Start a Butterfly Garden." *Nature Canada*, 6 (April/June 1977): 10–14. Reprinted by permission of the author.

Pridie, Marjorie. "The Horticultural Security Blanket: Six-week-wonder compost in the Far North." *Harrowsmith*, 5 (September 1980): 76–78. Reprinted by permission of the author.

Fawcett, Brian. "Some Advantages of Cramped Quarters." In *The Compact Garden: Discovering the Pleasures of Planting in a Small Space* (Camden East, Ontario: Camden House Publishing, 1992): 18–20. Reprinted by permission of Camden House Publishing.

National Capital Freenet "Invisible bug problem." In the "Gardening" Special Interest Group of the National Capital FreeNet, 28–30 July 1994. Reprinted by permission of Alfred K. Neilson, Sandra P. Hoffman, and John Foulds.

Harris, Marjorie. "How to Garden Defensively." *The Globe and Mail* (Toronto), 27 August 1994: D4. Reprinted by permission of the author.

PRAISING FAVOURITE PLANTS

Traill, Catharine Parr. "Letter IX." In *Backwoods of Canada: Being Letters from the Wife of an Emigrant Officer, Illustrative of the Domestic Economy of British America* (London: Charles Knight, 1836): 141–150.

Ewing, Juliana Horatia. "Letter 76." In Blom, Margaret Howard, and Thomas E. Blom, eds. *Canada Home: Juliana Horatia Ewing's Fredericton Letters, 1867–1869* (Vancouver: UBC Press, 1983): 265–269. This excerpt is reprinted with permission of the publisher of *Canada Home: Juliana Horatia Ewing's Fredericton Letters, 1867–1869*, edited by Margaret Howard Blom and Thomas E. Blom. All rights reserved by the publisher.

Hood, A. "Tomatoes." *The Canadian Horticulturist*, 2 (September 1879): 154–156.

Symmes, Mrs. "Flower Culture." In *Report of the Montreal Horticultural Society and Fruit Growers' Association for the year of 1879* (Montreal: Witness Printing House, 1880): 73–77.

Peterson, Velma. "Our Garden: A horticultural achievement in Alberta's driest corner." *The Country Guide*, 58 (September 1939): 25, 54. Reprinted by permission of *The Country Guide*.

Reford, Mrs. R. Wilson. "Gentiana Macaulayi, variety Wellsii, at Estevan Lodge, Grand Metis, P.Q. Canada." Eight-page typescript, n.d. [1944]. Printed with the permission of Alexander Reford.

Wright, Percy H. Letter to Isabella Preston, March 17, 1950. Centre for Canadian Historical Horticultural Studies, Isabella Preston Papers. Printed with the permission of the Centre for Canadian Historical Horticultural Studies, Royal Botanical Gardens Library, Hamilton, Ontario, Canada.

Preston, Isabella. "Note sent to Mr. Charles H. Curtis for the R.H.S. [Royal Horticultural Society] Lily YearBook, 1956." Centre for Canadian Historical Horticultural Studies, Isabella Preston Papers. Printed with the permission of the Centre for Canadian Historical Horticultural Studies, Royal Botanical Gardens Library, Hamilton, Ontario, Canada.

Tobe, John H. "Tobe's Folly." In *Romance in the Garden* (Toronto: George J. McLeod, Limited, 1958): 349–352. Reprinted by permission of Allan D. Tobe.

Wilson, Lois. "Winter Beauty in Your Garden." In *Chatelaine's Gardening Book: The Complete All-Canada Guide to Garden Success* (Maclean-Hunter Limited and Doubleday, Canada Limited, 1970): 2–3. Reprinted from *Chatelaine's Gardening Book: The Complete All-Canada Guide to Garden Success*, copyright © 1970 by Lois Wilson, by permission of Doubleday Canada Limited, and courtesy of *Chatelaine's Gardening Book* © Maclean Hunter Ltd.

Skinner, Helen. "Heirloom Gardens: Where are the plants that grandmother grew?" *CenturyHome*, 2 (September–October 1984): 12–14. Reprinted by permission of the author and *CenturyHome: Canada's Magazine for Today's Traditional Home*.

Gardner, Jo Ann. "Black Currants." In *The Old-Fashioned Fruit Garden: The Best Way to Grow, Preserve and Bake with Small Fruit* (Halifax: Nimbus Publishing Limited, 1989): 70–73. Reprinted by permission of the author and Nimbus Publishing Limited.

Bradbury, Elspeth. "Little gods of the garden." In *Saturday Review* insert, *The Vancouver Sun*, 30 April 1994: D12. Reprinted by permission of the author.

LOOKING BACK

[Scherck, Michael Gonder.] "The Old-Time Garden." In *Pen Pictures of Early Pioneer Life in Upper Canada, by a "Canuck" (of the Fifth Generation)* (Toronto: William Briggs, 1905); and facs. repr. (Toronto: Coles Publishing Company, 1972): 105–108.

Montgomery, L. M. "A Garden of Old Delights." *The Canadian Magazine,* 35 (June 1910): 154–160. "A Garden of Old Delights," by L. M. Montgomery, was published in *The Canadian Magazine* in June, 1910, and is reprinted here with the authorization of Ruth Macdonald and David Macdonald, who are the heirs of L. M. Montgomery.

Potts, Ada. L. "Early Canadian Gardens." *The Chatelaine,* 2 (July 1929): 19, 42. Courtesy *Chatelaine* magazine © Maclean Hunter Publishing Ltd.

Harper, J. Russell. "Loyalist Gardens." *The Maritime Advocate and Busy East,* 45 (February 1955): 5–10. Reprinted by permission of Jennifer Harper, from *The Maritime Advocate* and *Busy East.*

Douglas, William. "Winnipeg Parks." In *Transactions of the Historical and Scientific Society of Manitoba,* Series III, No. 14 (Winnipeg: Historical and Scientific Society of Manitoba, 1959): 61–65. Reprinted by permission of the Manitoba Historical Society.

Broadfoot, Barry. "His Garden Was a Marvel." In *Years of Sorrow, Years of Shame: The Story of Japanese Canadians in World War II* (Toronto: Doubleday Canada, 1977): 211. The above, copyright © by Barry Broadfoot, reprinted by permission of Doubleday Canada Limited.

O'Neill, Anne. "Discipline and Beauty: The orderly gardens of 18th century Louisbourg." *Canadian Collector,* 20 (March/April 1985): 43–44. Reprinted by permission of the author.

Moodie, D. Wayne. "Historical Indian Gardens." In *The Prairie Garden, 1987* (Winnipeg: The Prairie Garden Editorial Committee, The Winnipeg Horticultural Society, 1987): 122–125. Reprinted by permission of the Prairie Garden Editorial Committee, Winnipeg Horticultural Society.

Ball, Tim. "Fur Trade Gardens." In *The Prairie Garden, 1987* (Winnipeg: The Prairie Garden Editorial Committee, The Winnipeg Horticultural Society, 1987): 117–119. Reprinted by permission of the Prairie Garden Editorial Committee, Winnipeg Horticultural Society.

Hennessey, Catherine, and Edward MacDonald. "Arthur Newbery and the Greening of Queen Square." *The Island Magazine,* No. 28 (Fall–Winter 1990): 25–29. Reprinted by permission of the authors, from *The Island Magazine,* published by the Prince Edward Island Museum & Heritage Foundation, Charlottetown, Prince Edward Island.

Saunders, Charles R. (with the help of many others). "A Visit to Africville." In The Africville Genealogical Society, selectors and editors. *The Spirit of Africville* (Halifax: Formac Publishing Company Limited, 1992): 21. Reprinted by permission of James Lorimer and Company Limited.

Antoft, Mrs. H. O. "Afterthoughts." In *Thoughts from my Gardens: A Handbook of Hints for garden-lovers in Atlantic Canada* (Kentville, Nova Scotia: Mrs. H. O. Antoft, 1972; rev. 1974): 57. Reprinted by permission of Kell Antoft.

ILLUSTRATIONS

Staples, Owen. Eight original pen-and-ink drawings for *The Evening Telegram* (Toronto). n.d. [1920s–1930s]. Used by permission of Rod Staples.

Owen Staples (1866–1949) was a lifelong Toronto resident and a prodigious artist who chronicled the Canadian scene in pencil, pen and ink, etching, pastel, watercolour, and oil. As staff artist at *The Evening Telegram* for many years, he provided historical sketches for John Ross Robertson's "Landmarks of Toronto" series as well as lively depictions of current events.

Also a talented gardener, Staples created around his home east of the Don Valley the landscape which appeared frequently in his art: a soft, freeflowing space heightened by old-fashioned flowers, a magnificent cutleaf European birch, and a summerhouse overlooking the city skyline. And he was a keen observer of nature. During the 1920s and 1930s his own garden, his visits to other gardens, and his rambles in and around the valley inspired the dozens of illustrated articles on gardens and natural history that he produced for *The Evening Telegram*, where the eight pen-and-ink drawings that enhance this book were originally published.

INDEX

—∿—

Acadia Nurseries, 316
Africville, Halifax, N.S.,
    314-315
Alberta, 45-48, 156-159,
    235-237
Alix, Alta., 45
allotment gardens (commu-
    nity gardens), 150-151,
    152-155, 163-166, 169-
    170
Antoft, Asta, 316-317
ants, 214
apiary, 107
Apple, Heather, 256
Arbor Day, 310-311, 312
arbour, 176, 272
archery, 106
Arnold, Benedict, 287
Assiniboine Park,
    Winnipeg, 100, 291
Austin, Adele, H., 152
Aylmer, Louisa A., 37-38
Aylmer, Quebec, 232
Bailey, Liberty Hyde, 183
Ball, Tim, 306-308
balustrade, 109-112
bandstand, 313
Banff, Alta., 13
Banks, Kerry, 118-121
Barrie, Ont., 229
Beadle, D.W., 5, 8-9, 92,
    179, 229
Bealby, J.T., 43-44
bees, 84
Belleville Cemetery, Ont.,
    139
Belleville, Ont., 139

Ben-My-Chree, B.C., 58
Berton, Laura, 58-59
Berton, Pierre, 56
bird bath, 110
Bond, William, 3-4
Bonnington Falls, B.C., 43
botanical gardens, xv, 19,
    259
botany, 143
Boucher, Thelma 17, 18
Bowring Park, St. John's,
    Nfld., 30
Bradbury, Elspeth, 265-267
Brampton, Ont., 137
British Columbia, 10, 15,
    29, 41-42, 43-44, 48,
    53-55, 56-57, 58, 76-
    79, 103-108, 118-121,
    127-129, 193, 265,
    296-297
Broadfoot, Barry, 296-297
Brown, George, 5
Buckley, Alwyn, 238
Bullock-Webster, Julia, 41-
    42
Burton, Claudette, 76-79
Butchart Gardens
    (Benvenuto), B.C., 103-
    108
Butchart, Jennie, 103
butterfly gardening, 200-
    204; butterflies, 202-
    203, 236
Byng, Lady, 14, 247
Calgary, Alta., 156-159
Calgary Daily Herald, The,
    156

Castlegar, B.C., 78
Cambridge, Ont., 170
Canada Farmer, The, 5, 7, 8
Canadian Agriculturist, The,
    90, 177
Canadian Commentator, 20
Canadian Gardening, 163
Canadian Geographic
    Journal, 13, 103, 118,
    200
Canadian Home Journal,
    160
Canadian Homes and
    Gardens, 17, 56, 103
Canadian Horticulturist,
    The, 8, 10, 92, 160,
    179, 280
Canadian Magazine, The,
    103
Canadian Organic
    Growers, 256, 258
Canadian Pacific Railway,
    135
Canadian Society of
    Landscape Architects
    and Town Planners, 49,
    56, 113
Cape Breton Island, N.S.,
    260, 300
Carver, Humphrey, 56
Casa Loma, Toronto, 185
caterpillars, 43, 315
cemeteries, 139-140, 157,
    185, 251, 291
Central Park, Winnipeg,
    293
CenturyHome, 256

Champlain, 280-281
Charlottetown Arbor
    Society, 313
Charlottetown, Prince
    Edward Island, 309-313
Chatelaine, The, 103, 118,
    280
Chinese-Canadians, 118-
    121, 210-211
Chipman, Ward, 286, 287,
    289, 290
Christofaro, Raffaele, 63-67
City & Country Home, 58
city beautiful movement,
    xiv, 50, 113, 133-138,
    143-145, 148, 150, 274,
    291, 309-313
City Farmer, 168, 169
city gardening, xiii, 114,
    167-171, 210-212, 265-
    267
city square, 133-134
Clarke, W.F., 135
Claus, William, 83-86
cold frame, 77, 119, 247
Colonial Pearl, The, 133-134
compost, 24, 38, 77, 171,
    205-209
container gardening, 54,
    57, 120, 164, 203, 225-
    226, 232
country homes, xiii, 10, 37-
    38, 71-75, 93, 100-102,
    109-112, 186, 191-192,
    227, 238, 282, 284,
    286, 311
Cox, Holland, 53-55
crop rotation, 120-121
croquet, 106, 160
Crow, J.W., 238, 246, 247
Cullen, Mary, 390
cultural landscapes, xiv,
    122, 301-305
Dale, H. Fred, 163-166
Dalton, Thomas, 260
Davies, Louis H., 311
Dawson City, Yukon, 56
de Puisaye, Count, 282

DeGannes, Michel, 299
Dempsey, Lotte, 164
dogs, 66, 210, 217
Dominion Atlantic
    Railways, 25
Dougall, James, 90
Douglas, William, 291-295
Doukhobor, 76-79
Dr. Sun Yat-Sen Classical
    Chinese Garden,
    Vancouver, 118
drives, 93-94, 101, 105,
    106, 140, 201
Dropmore Hardy Plant
    Nursery, Man. 60
Dunington-Grubb, H.B.,
    49-52, 113
Dunington-Grubb, Lorrie
    A., 49, 113-117, 189
e-mail, xvi, 213
earwigs, 214
Eaton, Nicole, xv
Englehardt, H.A., 139-140
Erichsen-Brown, Charlotte,
    301
Ewing, Juliana Horatia,
    224-228
Experimental Farm System;
    19, 96, 263; Central,
    18, 96, 98, 246; Indian
    Head, 125; Morden,
    197, 199
Family Herald and Weekly
    Star, The, 195
Fawcett, Brian, 210-212
Federal Plant Gene
    Research Centre, 259
fences, 4, 89-91, 94, 101,
    107, 140, 272-273,
    283, 285, 310, 313
Ferguson, Donald, 311
fertilizing, soil improvement,
    24, 38, 64-65, 75, 104-
    105, 120, 149, 158, 190,
    192, 208, 240-241, 292
Fillmore, Roscoe A., 25-27,
    316
Finaly, Mr., 289

Fisher, Beatrice, 164-165
Fletcher, George, 312
flower arranging, cut flow-
    ers, 98, 149, 253, 256
flower garden, 46-47, 53,
    286, 297, 306, 313
Fort Douglas, Man., 293
Fort Rouge Park, Winnipeg,
    293
Fortress of Louisbourg,
    N.S., 298-300
Foulds, John, 213, 214
foundation planting, 102
fountains, 106, 107, 137,
    218, 309
Fredericton, New Brunswick,
    224-228, 289, 290
French-Canadian garden-
    ing, xv-xvi, 35, 232
frost, permafrost, 39-40, 54,
    64, 89, 119, 192, 206,
    208-209, 225, 292, 301,
    305
Fruit Growers' Association
    of Upper Canada, 8
Fruit Growers' Association
    of Ontario, 92
fruit growers, 8, 92, 179-182
fur traders, 302-303, 306-308
Gage Park, Hamilton, Ont.,
    49
garden archeology, xv, 124,
    299-300
garden broadcasters, 17,
    28, 156, 167, 253
Garden Club of Toronto,
    253, 256
Garden Club of Ontario,
    The, 19
Garden Clubs of Ontario, 256
garden competitions, 96, 97
garden design, xiv, 5, 6, 26,
    43, 45-47, 49-52, 54-55,
    71-75, 87-88, 92-95, 97,
    103-117, 124, 127-129,
    136-138, 167-168, 253-
    255, 263, 265-267, 271-
    279, 283, 298-300

garden furniture, 57, 110, 253
garden help, 177-178; professional, 186-188
garden history, xiv, xv, 256, 271-285, 296-305
garden ornaments, 106, 110, 154, 180, 195-196; bridges, 159, 106
garden party, 24, 141-142, 156, 160
garden paths and walks, 6, 38, 43-44, 46, 93-94, 101-102, 106, 107-108, 115, 117, 120, 128, 159, 272, 274, 276, 297
garden pests, xiv, 79, 120-121, 175, 180, 190, 216-218
garden pools, 1, 57, 65, 75, 106-107, 124, 158
garden writing, xv; journalists, 8, 18, 20-21, 30, 56, 160, 163-164, 183, 195, 197, 216, 249, 253, 280
Gardeners' and Florists' Society, 185
gardeners, professional, 177-178, 185-188, 287-289; education, 187
gardening and the environment, 171
gardening for health, 5-6, 25-27, 161
gardening, duty of, 6, 20-24
gardening, love of, xiii, xiv, 6-12, 17, 19, 26-27, 47, 54, 97-98, 316-317
gardening, political, 25-27, 167-171
Gardner, Jo Ann, 260-264
Giangrande, Carole, 167-171
Globe and Mail, The, 195, 216
Grand Banks, Nfld., 29
Grand Falls, Nfld., 30
Grand Trunk Railway, 136-138

Great Western Railway, The, 137
greenhouse and conservatory, 30, 38, 44, 70, 77, 98, 119, 185, 192, 202, 232-233, 247, 282, 288
Grenfell, Wilfred, 39
Grey, Lady, 14, 96-99
Grimsby, Ont. 146
Guy, Ray, 28-31, 39
Halifax Public Gardens, 291, 312
Halifax, 133-134
Hamilton, George H., 195-196
Hamilton, Ontario, 49, 137, 280
Harcourt, Ella M., 189-190
Harper, J. Russell, 286-290
Harris, Marjorie, xv, 216-218
Harris, Robert, 311
Harrowsmith, 118, 127, 265
Hay River, NWT, 205
Hébert, Louis, 281, 282
hedges, 17, 30, 90-91, 99, 115, 283
Hedrick, U.P., 263
Hennessey, Catherine, 309-313
Herbert, H.F., 20-24, 25
heritage plants, old-fashioned plants, 125-126, 202, 256-263, 274
Heritage Seed Program, 256, 258
heritage seeds, 256-259
Hoffman, Sandra P., 213, 214
homesteading, xiv, 36, 44, 53-54, 70-71, 87-88, 222
Hood, A., 229-231
horticultural exhibitions, 7, 41-42, 191, 247
horticultural societies, 50, 96, 148, 213
Horticulture Research Institute of Ontario, 259, 263

houseplants, 6, 232-234, 228
Hudson's Bay Company, 40, 304, 306-308
Hudson's Bay, 306-308
Indians, as gardeners, xiii, 259, 280-281, 301-305
insects, 23, 51, 120, 121, 198, 213-215, 246, 248, 266, 315
Island Magazine, The, 309
Italian garden, 107
Jack, Annie, 152, 183-184
Jackson, Bernard S., 200-204
Jacobs, Ferdinand, 308
James, Edward, 284
Jameson, Anna, 283-284
Janes, Percy, 68-69
Japanese garden, 106
Japanese-Canadian gardens, 296-297; internment, 296-297
Keeble, Midge Ellis, 70-75
Keith, Bob, 17
Kennedy, Des, 127-129
Kent, Dutchess of, 284
Keremeos, B.C., 41
King, W.L. Mackenzie, 109-112, 296
Kingsmere, Que., 109-112
Kingston, Ont., 35, 137
kitchen garden, 4, 15, 38, 89, 90, 175
Klondike, 58-59
Lake of the Woods, Ont., 304
Laking, Leslie, 19
landscape architecture, 49-52, 56, 92, 100, 113, 122, 139-140, 146
landscape history, 122-126, 314-315
landscape restoration and preservation, xiv, xv, 122-126, 298-300
lattice, 106, 273
Laurier, Sir Wilfrid, 142; Lady Zoe, 142

lawn, 6, 38, 54, 87-88, 94, 99, 101-102, 106, 109-110, 136, 183-184, 191, 195-196, 273

Leonard, George, 286

Les Jardin de Métis, 238

Leslie, W.R., 156, 197-198

Levenston, Michael, 169

Lily Yearbook of the North American Lily Society, The, 238

Lloyd, F.E.J., 39-40

Logan, Robert, 287

Lugrin, N. de Bertrand, 103-108

MacDonald, Edward, 309-313

Macoun, W.T., 96-99, 150, 246, 247

Manitoba Agricultural College, 197

Manitoba, 60-62, 163, 197, 291, 292, 301, 303, 305

Manning, Warren H., 146

Marchioness, The, 141-142

Mawson, Thomas, 49

Maxwell, Edward and W.S., 101

McClung, Nellie 45

McKinley, Jean, 17-19

McVittie, Thomas, 185

Meredith, Lady, 101-102

Merritt, W.H., 284

Minto, Lady, 97, 142

mission, convent, seminary gardens, 35, 39, 193, 205

Montgomery, L.M., 274-279

Montreal, 63-67, 100, 145, 191, 283, 289

Montreal Daily Witness, The, 183

monuments, 313

Moodie, D. Wayne, 301-305

Morgan, F. Cleveland, 156, 191-192

Motherwell, William Richard, 122-126

Mount Pleasant Cemetery, Toronto, 139

Murray, John, 290

museums, national historic sites, 122-126, 259, 298-300

National Capital FreeNet, 213

Nature Canada, 200

Neilson, Alfred K., 213, 215

Nelson Daily News, 10

Nelson, B.C., 10, 43, 77

New Brunswick, 224-228, 286-290

Newbery, Arthur, 311-313

Newfoundland and Labrador, 28-31, 39-40, 68-69, 200-204

Niagara Peninsula, 71, 92, 179, 271

Niagara, 83, 284

Niagara-on-the-Lake, Ont., 249

noise pollution, 216-218

Northwest Territories, 205-209

Nova Scotia, 25, 260, 298-300, 314, 316

nurseries and nurserymen, 3, 19, 25, 60, 179, 180-182, 195, 243, 249-252, 260, 284, 287, 316

nursery stock, 249-252

O'Brien, Mary Gapper, 87-89

O'Neill, Anne, 298-300

Odell, Mary, 290

Oliver, R.W., 18, 19

Ontario Agriculture College, 146, 148, 246, 247

Ontario Gardeners' Chronicle, The, 185

Ontario Horticultural Society, 113

Ontario, 3, 5, 8, 13, 17, 20, 35-36, 49, 70-75, 83-86, 87-89, 92-95, 96-99, 113, 123, 135-138, 139-140, 141-142, 146, 152-155, 160, 163, 175, 177, 182, 185, 189, 195, 221-223, 229, 249, 253, 256, 271-273, 280, 282-285, 302, 303

Orangeville, Ont., 70

orchards, xiv, 4, 30, 35, 51, 71, 78, 94, 101, 177, 179-182, 285, 287

Ottawa, 21, 48, 97, 109, 141, 213

Ottawa Daily Free Press, 141

Ottawa Horticultural Society, 13

Ottawa Improvement Commission, 96, 100

Oxen Pond Botanic Park, Nfld., 200

Palmer, Beatrice, 238

Parade square (military), 133-134

Parker, Asa, 90-91

Parks Canada, 122-126, 298-300

parks, 93, 100, 133, 146-147, 291-295; design, 157, 291, 312-313; history, 291-295, 309-313; legislation, 292-293

Parlby, Mary Irene, 45-48

Parmentier, Andre, 283

Partridge, Kate and Otto, 58

Patmore Nurseries, 126

Patterson, Nancy-Lou, 271

Pellat, Sir Henry, 185

Penhallow, D.P., 143-145

Pennsylvania Dutch (Mennonite) gardens, 271-273

perennial border, 11, 15, 70, 98, 105, 191, 202

pergola, 98, 107

Perkins, Dorothy, 150, 152-155

Perron, W.H., 65

pesticides, 23, 65, 190, 192, 201, 214-215

Peterson, Velma, 235-237
Picturesque landscape style, 35, 87, 133-134
plants, breeding, 15-16, 60-62, 191, 197, 243-246, 257-258, 263; collecting, 116; gene bank, 257-259; hardiness, 17, 23, 29-31, 39-40, 47-48, 54, 61-62, 126, 266-267; laws and regulations, 47-48, 60, 182, 261-163
poetry, 68-69, 151, 193-194
Pollock-Ellwand, Nancy, 122-126
Port Hope, Ont., 139
Port Royal, N.S., 281
Potts, Ada L., 280-285
Prairie gardening, 60-62, 124, 198
Preston, Isabella, 15, 238, 243-245, 246-248
Pridie, Marjorie, 205-209
Prince Edward Island, 148-149, 274-279, 309
Prince Rupert News, 54
Prospect Cemetery, Toronto, 185
Quayle, Moura, 169
Quebec, 37-38, 63-67, 90, 100-102, 109-112, 183-184, 191, 232, 238, 281-283, 289, 299
Queen Square Gardens, Prince Edward Island, 309-313
raccoons, 66
railway gardening, 25, 135-138
Rainbow Bridge Garden, Niagara, Ont., 49
raised beds, 120, 299
Reader Rock Garden, Calgary, 156-159
Reader, William, 156, 157, 159

Reford, Elsie, 238-242
Rideau Hall (Government House), 14, 96-99, 141-142
rock gardens, 14, 104-105, 113-117, 156-159, 191-192, 201, 239-242; plants, 114-115, 116, 157-159
roof gardening, balcony gardening, 56-57, 205
root cellar, 77, 288
Rose Society of Ontario, 152
Rose Society of Ontario, The, 189
Roseberry Camp, B.C., 296-297
Ross, Alexander, 293
Royal Botanical Gardens, Hamilton, Ont., xv, 19, 259
Royal Horticultural Society, 14
rural gardens, xiii, 123-126, 274-279, 285
Russell, Elizabeth, 175-176
Rutherford, Edith Stevenson, 10-12
Sanders, Frances Steinhoff, 56-57
Sara, F. Leslie, 156-159
Saskatchewan, 122-126, 243
Saskatoon Star Phoenix, 243
Saturday Night, 28, 160
Saunders, Charles R., 314-315
Scherck, Michael Gonder, 271-273
school gardening, 148-149
Scott, Agnes, 141-142
Scott, Norman, 17
seeds, 15, 42, 59, 65, 75, 84-86, 153, 222, 223, 226, 236, 257-259, 272, 281, 287, 289, 290, 292, 299-300, 307; catalogues, 257

shelterbelt, 123-124, 125, 157, 183, 198, 202, 254
Sheridan Nurseries, Toronto, 49
Sherk, M.G., 271-273
Simcoe, Elizabeth, 35-36, 53, 87, 282
Simpson, Cecil M., 148-149
Sister Mary Rosalinda, 193-194
Skelton, Isabel, 285
Skinner, Frank Leith, 60-62, 156
Skinner, Helen, 256-259
slugs, 215, 266
Smith, A.M., 8, 179-182
snow, 23, 50, 54, 198-199, 205, 225, 227
Soeur Marie de l'Incarnation, 193
soil, 38, 64-65, 70, 71-72, 73, 115, 120, 140, 153, 205-206
Sorel, Que., 37
Sproule, George, 290
squirrels, 66
St. Catherines, Ont., 8, 284
St. John's Park, Winnipeg, 293
St. John's, Nfld., 200
Stairs, Carol, 63-67
Stamford Park, Ont., 284
Steele Briggs Seed Company, 126
Stevenson, Collier, 160-162
Stewart, John, 124
stone wall, 91, 107, 275, 279
street tree planting, 143-145
suburban gardens, xiii, 21-24, 26
Sullivan, W.W., 311
summer house, 106
sundial, 154, 190, 299
Sutherland, Saskatchewan, 244-245
Symmes, Mrs., 232-234
Talbot, Colonel, 284, 285
Tanner, John, 304

Tarrant, David, xv
tennis, 124, 142,160, 191
Thompson, George, 185-188
Thompson, Thomas W., 185
Thornhill, Ont., 87
Tobe's Treery, Ont. 249-252
Tobe, John H., 249-252
Todd, Frederick G., 100-102, 146, 291
tools, 23, 74-75, 94, 149, 153, 162, 184, 191, 207, 209, 298
Toronto Horticultural Society, 185
Toronto, 5, 49, 145, 152-155, 163-164, 169-170, 175, 185, 189, 216, 253, 260, 280, 284
Toronto Star, The, 163, 164
Traill, Catharine Parr, 87, 221-223, 283
tree peddlars, 180-182
trellis, 106, 123, 272
Turo, N.S., 200
United Empire Loyalists, 271, 282, 288, 289
United Farm Women of Alberta, 45
Upper Canada Gazette, 3
Upper Canada Village, Ont., 17
Ursuline convent, 35, 193

vacant lot gardens, 148, 150-151, 163
Valley Nurseries, N.S., 25
van der Meulen, Emil, 164
Vancouver, 56, 57, 118, 120, 210, 265-267
Vancouver Sun, The, 265
vegetable gardens, 39, 42, 53, 64-67, 70, 74, 77-79, 83-86, 119-120, 125, 149-155, 161-162, 173-176, 178, 206, 210-212, 214, 178, 229-231, 236, 258, 276, 286, 297, 299-300, 302, 307-308
verandah, 37, 41, 110, 221-222, 227, 283, 292
Verrier, Etienne, 299
Victoria Park, Winnipeg, 293
Victoria, B.C., 13, 20, 29, 193
Victory gardens, 160-162, 164
von Baeyer, Edwinna, xv
W.T.G., 5-7
war gardening, 150, 152-155, 160-162
wasps, 217
water features, 105, 106, 108, 116, 158,
watering, 65, 84, 85, 86, 98, 124, 165
well, 107, 278

Welland, Ontario, 146
Weston, Hilary, xv
white-pine blister rust, 261-263
Wilde, Oscar, 310
Willingdon, Lady, 14
Wilson, Henrietta Tuzo, 13-16
Wilson, Lois, 19, 253-255
wind, 202
window gardening, 224-227, 232-234
Winnipeg Free Press, 197
Winnipeg, 122, 291-295
Winslow, Edward, 286, 287, 288, 289, 290
winter, 54, 61-62, 198-199, 225, 227, 253-255; gardens, 253-255
women as gardeners, 13-16, 152-155, 235
Wood, Henrietta, 150-151
woodland, 101, 102, 103
Woolverton, C. Ernest, 146-147, 179
Woolverton, Linus, 92-95, 179
World War I, 10, 143, 150, 185, 247
World War II, 160, 164, 238
Wright, Percy H., 243-245
xeriscaping, 183-184
York (Toronto), 3, 4, 175
Yukon, 58-59

Plant Index

—⚹—

acacia, 285; aconite, 225; ageratum, 202; alyssum, 108, 154, 202; amaranthus, 272; American elm, 125; anemone, 89, 108, 192, 225; angelica, 300; annuals, 45-46, 59, 75, 108, 149, 154, 202-203; anthemis, 154, 158; apples, 4, 42, 61, 71, 84, 85, 86, 96, 101, 180, 222, 259, 281, 287, 301, old varieties, 259; arabis, 202; Arbutus menziesii, 267; asparagus, 84, 85, 86, 277, 287; asters, 58, 149, 203; aubretia, 108; azalea, 266; bachelor buttons, 154, 272, 285; balm, 175, 288; balsam, 38, 149; basil, 65; beans, 15, 64, 66, 85, 86, 119, 120, 149, 175, 205, 211, 214, 257, 272, 281, 287, 299, 302, 304; beets, 66, 149, 153, 154, 165, 205, 208, 272, 290, 296; biennials, 108, 203; birch trees, 101, 276; blackberry, 222; bleeding heart, 277; bluebells, 107; bok choy, 119, 211, 212; Bouncing Bet, 277; box, 107; bulbocodiums, 192; bulbs, 11-12, 14, 98-99, 101, 106, 192, 222, 225-227, 233, 272; cabbage, 6, 39, 40, 42, 59, 66, 77, 78, 85, 120, 154, 205, 272, 285, 290, 299, 308; butter-and-eggs, 277; calla, 233, C. ethiopica, 225; campanula, 108; candytuft, 108, 149; canna, 154; cantaloupe, 165; Canterbury bells, 59; caragana, 125; caraway, 273, 277, 300; carnation, 84, 272; carrot, 42, 66, 85, 149, 153, 154, 165, 205, 208, 214, 302; catnip, 273; cauliflower, 59, 84, 205, 290; Cedar of Lebanon, 250; cedar, 37, 57, 250, 265; celery, 84, 85, 205, 208; chee koo, 120; cherry, 4, 11, 35, 43, 44, 48, 222, 265; chicory, 300; chives, 300; chokecherry, 125; chrysanthemum, 58, 149; chung ho, 121; columbine, 12, 158, 277; comfrey, 175; convolvulus, 227, 266; corn, 66, 86, 153, 154, 165, 211, 281, 302, 303, 304; cosmos, 108, 154, 202; cotoneaster, 251; crabapple, 37, 243, 246, 248; cranberry, 222; cress, 153, 154; crocus, 225, 226, 272; cucumber, 77, 149, 165, 205, 208, 272, 287; currants, 4, 83, 89, 222, 260-264, 273, 283; cyclamen, 226; daffodil, 272, 273, 277; dahlia, 38, 149, 272; daisy, 12, 128, 202, 203, 272, 277; daphne, 283; daylily, 243; delphinium, 59, 74, 75, 108, 127, 128, 158; dianthus, 108; dill, 73; dogwood, 48, 254; doorweed, 183-184; echium, 202; eggplant, 165; egg plum tree, 175; elecampane, 300; Erythronium grandiflora, 14, 104; evergreens, 37, 93-94, 116, 254, 265, 276, 277; fallugia, 198; fennel, 273; ferns, 102, 104, 107, 157, 227, 278; feverfew, 128; firethorn, 254; fireweed, 203; flowers, 6, 19, 38, 42, 46-47, 53, 57, 94, 98, 105, 126, 136, 149, 165, 180, 183, 272, 286, 292, 297, 306, 313; foestiera, 198; forget-me-not, 106, 108, 128, 158; four o'clocks, 272; foxglove, 12, 108, 128; fritillaria, 14; fruit, 4, 41, 42, 43, 61, 71, 78, 90, 222, 260, preserving, 78-79; fuchsia, 228, 233; gai choy, 119; gai lan, 119; gaillardia, 149; gentians, 108, 238-242, G. macaulayi, 239; G. wellsii, 239, 241-242; geranium, 6, 38, 154, 226, 233; golden glow, 12; goldenrod, 203; gooseberry, 4, 88, 178, 222, 262, 273, 283; grapes, 64, 65, 84, 85, 91, 181, 212, 272, 283, 301; hawthorn, 105; heather, 30; heliotrope, 6, 233; hellebores, 192; hemlock, 102; hepatica, 102; herbs, 73, 288, 290, 272-273,

300; high bush cranberry, 222, 254; holly, 30, 251; hollyhocks, 6, 30, 59, 108, 273, 277; honeysuckle, 104, 243, 283, vine, 273, 278; hop vine, 41, 222, 272, 285; hyacinth, 225, 226, 272; hyssop, 73; iberis, 202; iris, 12, 46, 47, 107, 191, *I. reticulata*, 192, Siberian, 246, 248; ivy, 254, 292; Japanese barberry, 115; Jacob's ladder, 202; Jerusalem artichokes, 119, Joe-Pye-weed, 203; juniper, 254; kale, 85; *Kantranthus rubra*, 202; knapweed, 203; knotweed, 183-184; kochia, 154; kohlrabi, 119; kuk oo, 119; lachenalia, 226; lady slipper, 104; larkspur, 128; lavender, 30, 277; leather-wood, 283; lettuce, 40, 84, 153,165, 208, 272, 287, 308; lilac, 61, 176, 246, 248, 273, 285; lilies, 14, 15, 238, 243, 244, 246, 247-248, 277; lily-of-the-valley, 107, 278, 285; live-forever, 272; lotus, 31; loveage, 273; lychnis, 158; madrona, 267; mahonia, 254; maple, 10, 17, 99, 101, 106, 125, *Acer ginnala*, 250; *A. negundo*, 125, Japanese dwarf, 150; marguerites, 12, 57; marigold, 202, 272; melon, 35, 178, 211; *Metasequoia glyptostroboides*, 250; mignonette, 47, 272, 285, 292; mint, 175, 275; mock orange, 71, 74; monkshood, 127; morning glory, 222, 283; muskmelon, 85; muskmallow, 128; narcissus, 12, 98-99, 107, 225, 226, 276; nasturtium, 86, 149, 154; native plants, 14, 15, 48, 61, 87, 88, 205, 208, 222; nicotiana, 46; oak, 101; oleander, 233; onion, 42, 84, 119, 153, 272, 290, 302, 304; pansy, 58, 149, 154, 272; parsley, 66, 85, 153, 287; parsnip, 153, 214, 290; peach, 4, 35, 85, 180; pear, 61, 64; peas, 42, 59, 86, 120, 153, 165, 205, 227, 287, 308; pennyroyal, 273; peony, 256, 272, 273, 277; peppers, 66, 84, 208; perennials, 11, 59, 98, 101, 108, 272; petunia, 57; phlox, 74, 149, 149, 202, 272; *Picea glauca*, 125; *Pieris japonica*, 251; pinks, 47, 272, 276, 285; plum, 4, 12, 35, 43, 88, 89, 222, 243, 265, ornamental, 108; *Polygonum aviculare*, 183-184; poplars, 125, 278; poppy, 12, 46, 108, 129, 149, 158, 277; potato, 6, 39, 42, 78, 85, 96, 165, 205, 208, 290, 299, 303, 304, 305; primrose, 106, 107, 227, 272; pumpkin, 35, 166, 281, 299, 301, 302, 304; pyrethrum, 46; radichetta, 66; radish, 40, 84, 85, 86, 149, 153, 214, 308; raspberry, 78, 89, 198, 222, 301; rhododendron, 30, 254, 266, 267; ribbon grass, 277; rose, 37, 66, 106, 107, 128, 189-190, 225, 243, 244-245, 246, 248, 256, 272, 273, 276, 281, 283, 284, 285, 292; rouquette, 66; rucchetta, 66; rudbeckia, 202; rue, 273; sage, 73, 273, 288; saggetalis, 108; salsify, 85, 290; saskatoon berry, 48; savory, 85, 273, 288; saxifrages, 46, 159; scabiosa, 202; scarlet creeper vine, 222, 283; schizanthus, 149; scilla, 226; sedums, 202; shallots, 175; Shasta daisy, 202; shrubs, 38, 51, 87, 90, 91, 93, 94, 102, 116, 134, 159, 284; Siberian wallflower, 203; snapdragon, 154; snowball bush, 175, 273, 275; snowdrops, 11, 101, 192, 225; *Solidago graminifolia*, 203; southernwood, 285; spinach, 59; spirea, 283; spruce, 48, 125, 158, 198, 250, 251; squash, 15, 166, 211, 302; stephanandra, 23; stocks, 47, 149, 285; strawberry, 78, 88, 89, 166, 178, 222, 301; sunflowers, 149, 214, 215, 273, 281; sweet clover, 277; sweet marjoram, 288; sweet peas, 149, 272, 292; sweet rocket, 158, 203; sweet William, 202, 227, 236, 272, 277, 285; Swiss chard, 66; tamarack, 17; thyme, 73, 273; tobacco, 30, 281, 302; tomato, 42, 65-66, 73, 77, 118, 149, 165, 205, 212, 214-215, 229-231, 272, 299; tulip, 12, 99, 108, 226, 272, 277; turnip, 40, 84, 86, 149, 205, 208, 287, 290, 299, 302, 307, 308; vegetables, xiii, 39-40, 41-42, 59, 73, 77-78, 90, 118-121, 126, 149, 151, Chinese, 119-121, 211-212; verbena, 202, 232-234; vines, 37, 41-42, 59, 222, 281, 283; viola, 108; Virginia creeper, 37, 275; watermelon, 29, 85-86, 215; waxberry bush, 276; weeds, 73, 203, 266, 285; wild flowers, 14, 15, 73, 87, 98, 104, 200-204, 227, 292; wild parsnip, 300; willows, 38, 108, 125; wintercreeper, 254; wormwood, 273; yarrow, 203; yew, 254, zucchini, 65, 66